Stopping by Woods

Robert Frost as
New England Naturalist

Owen D. V. Sholes

McFarland & Company, Inc., Publishers
Jefferson, North Carolina

ISBN (print) 978-0-7864-978-1-4766-7318-9 ∞
ISBN (ebook) 978-1-4766-3519-4

LIBRARY OF CONGRESS CATALOGUING DATA ARE AVAILABLE

BRITISH LIBRARY CATALOGUING DATA ARE AVAILABLE

Front cover: Robert Frost, 1959 (Library of Congress);
background photograph by Grisha Bruev (iStock)

Printed in the United States of America

*McFarland & Company, Inc., Publishers
Box 611, Jefferson, North Carolina 28640
www.mcfarlandpub.com*

For Claire and Colin,
all of my farm family

Contents

Acknowledgments ix

Preface: Why Would an Ecologist Write About
Robert Frost? 1

Prologue: "Country things" 7

Introduction: "Like a pistil after the petals go" 13

Subduing the Land: "Teams that came by the
stony road" 23

Farming: "The place's name" 48

Seasons: "Brush the mow with the summer
load" 68

Agrarian Diaspora: "From too much dwelling
on what has been" 95

Ecological Succession: "They rejoiced in the
nest they kept" 102

Life Cycles in a Resurgent Nature: "For them
there was really nothing sad" 113

Conclusion: "Versed in country things" 138

Chapter Notes 147

Further Reading and Sources 163

Index 173

Acknowledgments

This book started off as an unimaginable project but soon became a consuming quest. My wife Claire was an English major in college before she became an elementary school teacher, and her love of literature has permeated our lives together. When her brother David pursued creative writing and teaching, it was one more reason for me to contemplate the intersection of science and literature. Thus, my family was the core influence on my exploration of Robert Frost, for which I am unendingly grateful.

This book would have been impossible without the compilations of Frost's poetry, prose, notebooks and letters produced by Henry Atmore, Robert Faggen, Robert Bernard Hass, Edward Latham, Richard Poirier, Mark Richardson, Donald Sheehy and Lawrance Thompson. Their considerable efforts have made access to Frost the writer and Frost the person immeasurably easier. Thanks also to Jonathan Barron and *The Robert Frost Review* for permission to include "Bleeding Trees" in this volume.

Teaching at a small college has allowed me to interact with colleagues from many disciplines. I got advice on writing from Jim Lang, Chris Beyers and Paul Ady, all of which made this project go more smoothly. I was warmly welcomed into the enjoyment and exploration of poetry through many conversations with Lucia Knoles, Ann Murphy and David Thoreen, and they helped me find my voice regarding Robert Frost. Deborah Kisatsky, Jeana Edmonds and Kim Schandel encouraged me throughout the process and I can't thank them enough for their support and friendship. Two other generous friends, John Rawlins and Susan Beatty, helped fill in the gaps where my own experience and memory fell short.

Assumption College provided financial support through the Faculty Development Fund, and approved a timely sabbatical that gave me the opportunity to write. I also thank the staff of the Emmanuel D'Alzon

Acknowledgments

Library for compiling an annotated list of digital sources for as many of Robert Frost's collections and individual poems as they could find.

Gary Mitchem at McFarland and Company guided the editorial and review process, from big picture to detail, in ways that have improved every aspect of my book. I thank him and his staff, and the anonymous readers for their thoughtful, honest and supportive suggestions.

Obviously, this book is the result of friendship and collective effort, reminiscent of "The Tuft of Flowers" (paraphrased here to encompass all involved): "'People work together,' I told them from the heart, 'Whether they work together or apart.'"

Preface

Why Would an Ecologist Write About Robert Frost?

My immersion in the work of Robert Frost is not as strange as it might seem. It began in the 1960s and followed the trajectory of a typical reader and admirer for many years. Only gradually did poetry and science converge into the project that resulted in this book. It has become a joyful obsession that I hope will go on for quite some time. I'm sharing my story for anyone who might want to join in the fun.

I was ten years old when John Fitzgerald Kennedy was inaugurated as president of the United States on a cold, sunny day in January 1961. As part of the ceremony, Robert Frost was supposed to read his new poem in celebration of the new president. I had heard of Robert Frost, but I knew nothing about him. As I watched the small screen of our black-and-white television, I saw that he was an old man, and that he appeared to be struggling with the cold as he tried to read on the steps of the Capitol. The news announcers thought that something below the podium might have caught fire, but if that were true, it apparently wasn't serious. Far more serious was the glare. Frost could not see the page well enough to read his new poem, so he recited one of his poems from memory ("The Gift Outright").[1] I didn't pay that much attention or realize the significance as I watched the torch being passed from his generation to that of JFK, but this event was the only time I would see Robert Frost recite his work in public. He lived for only two more years.

When I eventually read some of Frost's work in school, the poems I remember reading were the same ones assigned to nearly every student who endured American public education: "The Road Not Taken," "Stopping

1

by Woods on a Snowy Evening" and "Mending Wall." These are all wonderful poems (though the first is often misunderstood),[2] and they might have remained my only introduction to Frost if some other things hadn't happened.

A friend in college showed me a poem one evening that he had been assigned to read in his English course (I took different English courses and still graduated—imagine that). He was supposed to comment on this sonnet, but he said that the only word that came mind was "perfect." The poem was "Design." When I read it myself, standing there next to him, I had to agree.

I didn't think very much about "Design" again until I was wallowing in my dissertation research several years later. My project focused on the response of insects and other invertebrates to the development of flowers, from bud through blooming into fruit. Most of the plants I studied were goldenrods, and the flowers attracted a fair number of spiders, especially jumping spiders and crab spiders. On the yellow blossoms of goldenrods, the largest crab spiders were also yellow, though they had the ability to change color between yellow and white.[3] If they caught moths at night, they nearly always finished eating them by the time I arrived the following morning. I usually found the spiders either waiting to catch something or feeding on flies, bees or the occasional beetle, their typical daytime prey. I also didn't study the insects on heal-all (the flower in "Design") though it was common in the fields among the goldenrods.[4] But despite the differences in the plant, prey, and color, here was the spider from "Design," dimpled and fat, holding up insects in its jaws (I found a dimpled spider, fat and yellow, on a yellow goldenrod, holding up a fly). Frost's poem became the literary sidekick for my research.

After I finished that project, my wife and I purchased a home in rural Massachusetts in 1978. Our ten acres has a broad margin of mature trees around an area that had been cleared by the previous owner. Some of the white pine trees from that clearing were cut for lumber (perhaps on site with a portable saw, perhaps elsewhere), and some of that wood was used to build a small barn behind the house (we presume that the rest of the lumber was sold). The barn housed at least one cow that grazed in the cleared space (the cows departed before we moved in, leaving behind some piles of dried dung). We used the barn for a horse, our four-legged lawnmower, for nearly twenty-five years. In our first summer, we picked low-bush blueberries in the clearing, but these were overgrown in just a few years by tree saplings, some of which have now grown large enough to be cut for firewood. We keep trees from growing on the land right behind the barn so that we can grow a vegetable garden. We never farmed for a living as Frost and his family did in the early 1900s, but our neighbor is a farmer, and we bought feed for our horse from another farmer in town. While walking the land, growing food, chasing the horse when she got through the fence (the farmer was a good neighbor even though our fences were bad), we got to know what life was like in the country.

There was a ramshackle room on the back of our house that was far easier to tear down than to repair. I uncovered a large salamander while pulling the stones up from the too-shallow, frost-heaved foundation, a reminder that old human dwellings often become dwellings for others. As we restored the rest of the house, we noticed other decaying structures on neighboring properties, a continuation of the decline Frost had witnessed when he arrived in New England nearly a century earlier.

As the decades have passed, a few more properties have begun to decline in our part of town. One of these was a house and shed that had been occupied when we first moved in. The occupants changed over time, but at some point that I didn't immediately notice, there were no more occupants. The house was dark and still, day and night. With nobody to maintain it, the roof of the shed began to sag, seeming to make fun of the pair of crossed skis on the front wall, and warning of impending collapse, just in case anyone ignored the No Trespassing sign at the foot of the driveway. After years of decline, all of the structures were suddenly gone, torn down and hauled away. Now the weeds and shrubs and trees are slowly taking over. If someone decides to use the property for a new home, many of the growing plants will be killed and cleared away. The cycle will repeat.

When I think about the inexorable change in the landscape around our house, I wonder whether the rural lowlands of New England in 1830 looked something like parts of rural Ireland today. Seen from the air, the Irish countryside has irregular polygons of borders (hedgerows, fences and/or stone walls) filled edge to edge with managed farmland. Houses, barns and other structures are clustered here and there among the fields. Trees are in small patches near the buildings, or along the borders of fields.

Much of New England once had this density of working farms, and there are still remnants of this landscape here and there in New England. But mostly, it is a memory, a memory revisited in Frost's poetry.

3

I also wonder whether the sides of the mountains of New England looked like the sides of hillsides in Connemara, with farms climbing up the steepening slope until it seems impossible for sheep to graze or hay to be cut. In Ireland today, the hilltops have few or no trees. In colonial New England, trees would have been high on the slopes except on the very tops of the tallest peaks that were above treeline. Europeans have been in New England for only several hundred years, bending the landscape to their will. In Europe, the landscape has been exploited for thousands of years, at least ten times longer than New England. There, the trees are mostly gone. Here, the forest survived settlement and now thrives where agriculture and villages have been abandoned. Here, unlike the British Isles, nature still commands the high ground.

The project that led to this book began in earnest in 2007 when I read Robert Faggen's transcriptions of Robert Frost's notebooks. I was first attracted to the notebooks when, in a radio interview, Faggen quoted Frost's phrase "Life is that which can mix oil and water."[5] Of course it is, I thought: an oily membrane surrounds the water-based cytoplasm of every cell. I immediately wanted to see what other biological imagery Frost had used. I discovered that, even though Frost wrote infrequently about cells, his writing was replete with descriptions of the flora, fauna and ever-changing landscape of New England.

Frost's focus on natural history fit perfectly with my own interests and expertise. I teach biology and environmental science at a local college, and I lead students into the woods whenever possible, mostly to show them some of what goes on there, but sometimes to get them to explore their own research questions, such as the growth of vines on trees (the setting in the poem "Wild Grapes") or the influence of shade on the plants below the canopy (anticipated in the poem "Spring Pools"). My research focuses mainly on insects that feed on plants, and those plants are often trees. The rings of tree growth are fascinating because they tell far more than the age of a tree.[6] For instance, the outbreak of gypsy moths in central Massachusetts in 1981 is evident as a distinctly narrow ring among all the others. After a severe ice storm in 2008 (which knocked out our electricity, including our water pump, for a week), trees that lost a significant portion of their crowns had much narrower growth rings than before the storm and much narrower rings than their undamaged neighbors, some of whom benefited from the extra light let in by the damaged trees.

Why Would an Ecologist Write About Robert Frost?

When I began this project, I was confident that my familiarity with the ecology of New England would allow me to say something useful for readers and writers who want to explore and understand Frost's poetry. Because much of Frost's poetry had its birth in the countryside, usually with a focus on specific features and places,[7] I hoped that an examination of the subjects and images he drew from that countryside would reveal something significant about the landscape of New England.

To achieve my goal, I had to explore Frost's own texts in detail. I used other sources (dictionaries, floras, biographies, critical monographs, peer-reviewed articles, websites, etc.) when needed for clarification of vocabulary, wording, content and context, but Frost's own words were always my main focus. I used two main sources for Frost's poetry: *The Poetry of Robert Frost* (edited by Edward Latham), and *Collected Poems, Prose & Plays* (edited by Richard Poirier and Mark Richardson). I also used Frost's letters, prose and notebooks (cited in the list of sources) to gain insight into his thinking, writing and speaking. Though I have included many quotations, I rarely transcribed entire poems or pieces of writing. Readers will find it useful to have the poems and other documents close at hand.

I also used the primary and secondary literature of biological, ecological and environmental research. In some cases, I have chosen sources published early in the twentieth century during Frost's tenure on farms in New England. Frost did not read this literature (though he did read *Scientific American*),[8] but his work as a farmer and his frequent walks through the countryside made him a skilled naturalist. In the end, I found that his descriptions are nearly always consistent with those reported in the research literature. Best of all, I found that Frost's writing contained a compelling narrative about a dynamic landscape.

In his notebooks, Frost asked, "What can you do with a poem besides read it?" He followed his question with a list of nearly forty suggestions.[9] I have focused on just one of them: "impart information through it." This objective is intentionally narrow because it matches my expertise. While I hope I have clarified some of Frost's content and themes for other readers, there is a risk that I may have violated Frost's admonition at the end of his list of things to do with a poem: "Do nothing to a poem that it never was written to have done to it." I have tried to stick to things that I know, adding brief speculations that seem to be logical extensions of that knowledge. I hope that I have "done" something useful.

Preface

Robert Frost wrote hundreds of poems, perhaps two thousand letters, dozens of prose pieces and a handful of plays. He also jotted down wide-ranging notes in at least forty-eight notebooks. He published his first writing when Benjamin Harrison was president, and his last a year after the inauguration of John Kennedy. His descriptions, metaphors, accounts and imagery from seven decades of writing connect with every facet of the environmental history of New England. We learn most about the events during his lifetime, but he revisits earlier times, explicitly or by inference. He also imagines the future because he is aware of process and transformation and understands the context of change. Among his elegant and copious writing, we find an account of a changing people and a changing landscape in which some things disappear, other things stay the same (or try to), and still other things arrive or reappear. It is a complex history of a complex environment, and it is an altogether gripping tale.

Prologue

"Country things"

When Robert Frost arrived in New England in 1885, at age eleven, he was surrounded by a landscape in transition from farm to forest. Some of the farms were more than two centuries old, but farming was in decline as people moved to cities or farther west. Farm families had begun to abandon their land in the mid 1800s, and as more people left, Frost watched the process of ecological succession "bring back nature in people's place" ("The Times Table"). Empty farms were "no more a farm" ("Directive"), just stone walls and cellar holes, vanishing year by year among the weeds, shrubs and trees that inevitably took over once farming ceased. Of course, some families stayed on their farms, plowing fields, grazing livestock on pastures and mowing meadows within the rhythm of the seasons. Their constant toil kept ecological succession at bay.

Stunned by the departure of people, but enchanted by the resurgence of nature, Frost understood the broad sweep of environmental change. He knew how farms had been carved out of the forest, how they were sustained by farm families year after year, and how trees and other wild plants would inevitably take over after farms were abandoned. In Frost's poetry, we see these dynamic processes playing out in the New England countryside more than a century ago.

Change is not always obvious, though, as in the last line of "The Wood-Pile": "The slow smokeless burning of decay." At first glance, nothing seems to be happening; the pile has been sitting in the same place for several years, the wood turning gray, the bark warping, the pile "somewhat sunken." Today, it appears static and inert. But Frost's narrator knows better. Whether it is decay, seasonal change or ecological succession, the landscape is always changing, often at a pace so slow that it is perceptible only to those who are patient, perceptive or experienced enough to notice. Those people include farmers, or naturalists, or poets. Robert Frost was all three.

"The Need of Being Versed in Country Things," published in 1920, uses one farm to encapsulate the transition of New England from farmland to forest at the turn of the last century:

> The house had gone to bring again
> To the midnight sky a sunset glow.
> Now the chimney was all of the house that stood,
> Like a pistil after the petals go.
>
> The barn opposed across the way,
> That would have joined the house in flame
> Had it been the will of the wind, was left
> To bear forsaken the place's name.
>
> No more it opened with all one end
> For teams that came by the stony road
> To drum on the floor with scurrying hoofs
> And brush the mow with the summer load.
>
> The birds that came to it through the air
> At broken windows flew out and in,
> Their murmur more like the sigh we sigh
> From too much dwelling on what has been.
>
> Yet for them the lilac renewed its leaf,
> And the aged elm, though touched with fire;
> And the dry pump flung up an awkward arm;
> And the fence post carried a strand of wire.
>
> For them there was really nothing sad.
> But though they rejoiced in the nest they kept,
> One had to be versed in country things
> Not to believe the phoebes wept.

The Story in the Poem

This farm once included a house, a barn, fences, a well, a meadow for hay, and a pasture for the livestock that grazed during the growing season and pulled the hay wagon. There were trees nearby that had been cut, split and dried for fuel to burn in the hearth at the base of the chimney. There was likely an orchard and a brook nearby because farms nearly always had those things ("In the Home Stretch").

This farm and others like it were cut from the forest as Native Americans were being killed or displaced. Farms in New England eventually covered 50–90 percent of the land, depending on the town, the topography, the latitude, and the available transportation on rivers, roads, rails or sea.

But things changed over two centuries, and sometime not too long ago, this farm was no longer sustainable, at least in the eyes of the people who lived there. Cities burgeoned and the West beckoned, both promising a better life. The family left its farm, and because there were more farms than farmers, nobody would buy it ("The Star-Splitter"). People took what possessions they could and left the rest behind. The agrarian diaspora was underway.

In a countryside in decline, dotted with abandoned farms, who is there to stop a fire, especially at midnight? The flames produced a glow in the night as the house burned to the ground, leaving only the brickwork that was once the warm heart of the dwelling, the hearth inside of which fire had burned safely. A hearth is broad at the base, the ovary of the flower, with the chimney rising above, narrow as a flower's style. But its opening at the top is cold and dark, not nearly as inviting as a floral stigma. The masonry suggests a pistil, the female parts of a flower, a source of renewal for a plant, but it is only "like" a pistil. It is, in fact, barren, with not even a petal, a clapboard of color, to suggest any hope of procreation. The flower analogy ends with the shape. The pistil has function and gives us hope. The chimney has none, not anymore.

The pump handle and strand of wire are equally useless to humans. There is no one to seek water, and no livestock can be confined by a fence with only one strand. The stony road might serve others, but not this family. Their lives are lived elsewhere, or not at all—maybe the farm was abandoned because too many members of the family had died.

The barn windows are broken, and there will be no hay stored here where rain might reach it and ruin it, no wagons with a drooping load of hay that brushes the mown stubble, and no horses thumping their shod hooves on the wooden floor. The vital things of summer, the cutting, drying, hauling and storing of hay, made it possible for livestock to survive the winter when their pastures were covered in snow. The livestock are gone. Though the barn might "bear forsaken the place's name," it is now a farm in name only.

But the broken windows, halfway through the poem, permit the transition from human to wild. Glass panes keep birds out ("Questioning

Faces"), but broken glass is a gateway through which birds can reach shelter under the roof, and can reach beams that provide support for their nests. The things so vital for a farm are not vital for the phoebes, or the elm, or the lilac. These species can maintain themselves through the seasons, migrating south or dropping their leaves to endure winter. It is their land now.

In "The Times Table," a sigh is enough to drive people from the land and to allow nature to return. "Sigh" reappears in "The Need of Being Versed in Country Things" when the song of the phoebe reminds us of a human sigh of regret because people are gone. Together, these sighs foretell departure and mourn the loss. How are we to endure the disappearance of humanity when the numbers "shrink to none at all" ("The Census-Taker")?

In "Directive," we are to weep over a ruined house that has nothing but lilacs to watch the cellar hole fill slowly, inexorably, with dead plants and soil. In "The Need of Being Versed in Country Things," we are to imagine that the phoebes wept for the burned house, the empty barn and the absence of a farm family.

But if you are versed in country things, you know that phoebes neither sigh nor weep. Your "Directive" is to drink from the persistent stream by "a farm that is no more a farm" and you will "be whole again beyond confusion." You will understand that "country things" include more than you, more than a house, more than a farm. Country things include the resurgence of nature. The house and farm are gone, but nature is back. Your losses are their gains. Avoid "too much dwelling on what has been," and notice that your old barn is the birds' new dwelling. Notice that the lilac you planted years ago "renewed its leaf" each spring for the phoebes, while the pump handle, the bare branches where the elm was singed, and the strand of fence wire all serve as elevated places for phoebes to perch while they search for prey. The brief golden hues of emergent life ("Nothing Gold Can Stay") surround the birds as they rejoice over their nest with its own emergent life. The phoebes are taking advantage of country things, the old barn that is their new home, the old farm where they can forage for food. They are not confused. And if you are properly versed in country things, neither should you be.

Environmental History in Robert Frost's Poetry

If you live long enough in rural New England, you realize that it isn't as static as calendar photos would have you believe. Things change in more ways than the seasonal cycle that we all anticipate. Things grow. Organisms die and get replaced. Species rise and fall. Trees get tall (if you let them). If you pay attention—and Robert Frost paid lots of attention—you watch the landscape go through transformations that are slow and subtle, but inexorable. It's not a snapshot, and not even a time-lapse video. It is the process of life.

Frost focused on specific things in each poem, stanza, line or phrase about the New England landscape, but he managed to leave us an environmental narrative because he was so prolific. The story comes to us in multiple voices with multiple moods and in no particular order, but we can trust the tale because the author—the poet—is authentically in and of the countryside. His coverage is uneven and disproportionate (we hear more about orchids than ferns, though the latter are far more abundant), but it is not the quantity that matters. Frost, the poet of New England, is giving us far more than snapshots of the region he knows so well. He is showing us how the region changes, how the components of the landscape transform over time, sometimes quickly, often imperceptibly, always in relation to one another. Transformation is a consistent thread throughout the poetry of Robert Frost. When we follow that thread, the dynamics of the landscape come alive through the deceptively simple words of the region's most celebrated poet.

Among the excellent accounts of environmental history in New England, none is as vivid and elegant as Robert Frost. But few people know the fullness of Frost's narrative because it is fragmented in hundreds of poems. In contrast to the systematic development of a story by a scholar, pieces of environmental history accumulated in Frost's work "like burrs where [poets] walk in the fields."[1] In the chapters on his narrative, I will piece together the tale of New England ecology that resides in the poetry of Robert Frost. As the story unfolds, it will also become clear how environmental history was the basis for much of Frost's art.

Introduction

"Like a pistil after the petals go"

Robert Frost's botanical metaphor was no accident. He lived among the flora and fauna of New England and became a skilled amateur naturalist who understood the life cycles and habitats of organisms and the dynamics of the landscape. He also owned several farms during his lifetime, raising cows, poultry and fruit when he had a family to support or when he had enough time away from other tasks. Farming also taught him much about rural people and rural ways.

But Frost was raised in California, not on a farm in New England. How did he become a farmer and naturalist? The key events are recounted in several biographies and chronologies[1]: Born in 1874, he lived in San Francisco until his father died of tuberculosis in 1885. Robert, his sister Jeanie and mother Isabelle moved to Lawrence, Massachusetts, to live briefly with his father's parents, but they soon moved to smaller communities in southern New Hampshire. San Francisco and New Hampshire differed radically in climate, culture and economic development in the 1880s. Even an eleven-year-old boy had to notice the contrast.

Eighteen eighty-nine was a formative year for the fifteen-year-old Frost. He spent time working on the farm of Loren Bailey learning how to build stone walls and how to make hay using the scythe, pitchfork and grindstone.[2] His experience with farming was sufficiently positive that, eleven years later, he moved to a farm in Derry, New Hampshire. As he learned about farming, he also came to know the farmers, farm hands and farm families of rural New England.

Also in 1889, Frost met Carl Burell, roughly ten years his senior, who introduced him not only to various works of literature but also to botany and astronomy, which became life-long passions. Whenever possible, he went on walks "botanizing" in the countryside, no matter where he was living or visiting at the time.[3]

After he was married in 1896, Frost and his wife Elinor spent much of the summer in a cottage where Carl Burell visited to discuss literature and natural history. When Frost was botanizing, he often had a copy of *How to Know the Wild Flowers* by Mrs. William Starr Dana, a guide laced with quotations from literature.[4] In 1900, after the death of their first child at age three, Robert and Elinor moved to the farm in Derry. The Frost family lived longer on that farm than anywhere else.[5]

For someone who was to write poetry about rural life and nature in New England, his early experience on farms and in the woods prepared him to be a keen observer of the countryside and its people. It would seem that Louis Pasteur's assertion applies to poets as much as it does to scientists: "in the fields of observation, chance favors only the prepared mind."[6]

Observation: Originality Depends on the Faculty of Noticing[7]

In his wedding year of 1896, Frost came across Thoreau's claim that "a true account of the actual is the purest poetry."[8] As a budding naturalist, he seems to have taken Thoreau's assertion seriously. In his poetry, the descriptions of the landscape are elegantly precise, an almost certain indication that Frost observed these things himself. Looking back in 1931, he said, "The best part of observation we do before we are old enough to know we are doing it."[9] He considered observation and experience to be essential starting points: "We have to begin there with things observations preferences [sic] that are our own"; "About all we can do is write about things that have happened to us...." Though he refused to be characterized as an expert ("Don't put me down for a botanist"), he was dismissive when poets "invented" tales (e.g., Wilfrid Gibson) or were flat out wrong. Of W.H. Davies, Frost concluded, "He doesn't really know nature at all."[10] Regarding observation, Frost concluded, "It is never safe to write down anything that has not come to you definitely as an experience previous to this time of writing."[11]

The influence of observation is obvious in Frost's poetry. In poem after poem, his descriptions of the countryside ring true to anyone familiar with the ecology and environmental history of New England. The spider in "Design" really was dimpled, fat and white. The moth really was in the woods in the middle of winter ("To a Moth Seen in Winter"). In "Pod of the Milkweed," the scales on the wings of butterflies really did get rubbed off and turned to dust, the many milkweed flowers did produce just one or a few pods, and milkweed sap really is bitter (and toxic[12]), in contrast to the sweet nectar. Young paper birch trees ("Birches") do have black branches and snow white bark on their trunks. Fallen maple leaves ("Maple") do show two colors, scarlet on the top and pink on the bottom.

The frequent encounters of people and bears near Sugar Hill, New Hampshire, inspired "The Bear," including its opening description of a bear foraging on small cherry trees (Frost had found the remnants of cherries and blueberries in the droppings of bears). "Two Look at Two" is based on Robert and Elinor Frost's own observation of two deer near their farm in Franconia, New Hampshire. Their daughter Lesley described the encounter in a letter to Delphis Gardner in Ireland: "when mama and papa went up in the woods a few minutes after a buck and doe stood within a few feet of them and looked quietly at them and then softly trotted off among the firs." The poem includes a precise description of the buck's behavior in the presence of people: "He viewed them quizzically with jerks of head, / As if to ask, 'Why don't you make some motion?'" Anyone who has remained motionless as a deer approached knows that this is accurate. A deer will bob its head to get a fix on an object of interest. Its eyes are on the sides of its head (better to see oncoming predators) and its stereoscopic forward vision is imprecise. A deer can improve its depth perception by moving its head (which may also improve its perception of odor). If a person stays still, the deer stands and looks for a while, then resumes other activities. As soon as the person moves, the deer will run away.[13]

Frost's understanding of natural history was coupled with his experience as a farmer and gardener. He knew about mowing hay, raising apples, keeping hens, milking cows and putting in the seed. His familiarity with farming and gardening, and with the farmers that did both, provided a diverse array of images, stories and metaphors. For example, as a landowner, he came to understand boundaries.[14] In "Beech," we find a description of the formal, legal method of marking property boundaries ("imaginary line") and especially the corners. Where the boundary reaches a corner ("square" in many cases, but often not), there has to be a marker. In one case, the corner is marked by "an iron spine / And a pile of real rocks." At another corner, the surrounding vegetation is "wild" and there is a tree in the right place, a beech (if the title comes from this tree) that is "deeply wounded" and thus marked as a "Witness Tree."

This is how surveyors marked boundaries in New England for centuries. For comparison, here are the boundaries for one piece of property from the *New Book of the Proprietors of New and Undivided Land for Shrewsbury* [Massachusetts]: "March 13, 1730. Laid out for Daniel Ran fourteen acres and one hundred and fifty four rods ... begins at a red ash, at sd brook and runs southerly sixteen rods to a pine marked for sd way, then runs easterly by sd way, forty five rods to a heap of stones, then runs north 3 degs, easterly five rods to a stake & stones, then runs angling by sd meadow to where it began."[15] The pine (and probably the red ash) was "marked" ("deeply wounded") and the last marker was a "stake & stones" ("an iron spine" in the midst of a "pile of real rocks"). The lines are "imaginary" but corners have either a witness tree or something put in place by humans: a stake, some stones, or both. These corners, living or dead, will last a long time.

Some authors have misconstrued or challenged Frost's descriptions of the natural world, but in nearly every case, Frost was right. Robert Faggen claimed that "no such creature as a *white-tailed* hornet exists," despite the fact that "white-tailed hornet" is a widely used common name for *Dolichovespula maculata*.[16] Even though the thrush is safely perched for the night in "Come In," Joseph Brodsky claimed that it was "doomed."[17] The poem "Design" has been a source of much confusion. Jeffrey Meyers referred to the "normally black spider" when these spiders are actually white or yellow, but never black.[18] George Monteiro's lengthy discussion of web-spinning spiders is irrelevant because crab spiders do not use webs to catch prey.[19] Paul Muldoon is almost certainly wrong when he suggests that the white "heal-all" is *Prunella laciniata* instead of *Prunella vulgaris*.[20] Though Frost might have made the occasional mistake (was the "purple-fringed" flower an orchid or a gentian?), readers should trust his observations because they came from decades of experience in the countryside.

Thomas Bailey recognized the significance of observation in Frost's poetry: "But in our need to understand Frost as a thinker and craftsman, we often forget that he was a man who spent time outdoors, carefully observing natural phenomena and recording them as accurately as he could. The insights that arise from some of his most celebrated poems, we sometimes neglect to remember, came to him as a result of his having observed the world of nature with care and caution."[21] In his notebooks, Frost acknowledged (if somewhat dismissively) the importance of observation: "I'll thank the environment for giving me now and then something I couldn't make up."[22] When he described farming, forests or fauna, his descriptions originated from all that he had seen and heard. He observed the countryside more carefully, more thoroughly and more thoughtfully than most people, and recognized how the countryside was being transformed in space and over time. What he described was real.

New England

Frost lived in the New England landscape for decades, took time to look and listen, and made use of all that he learned. He was so thoroughly immersed in New England that his original title for "The Need of Being Versed in Country Things" was "The Importance of Being Versed in New England Ways."[23]

By 1950, Frost had concluded, "The only source of sane originality is in the subject matter of the ground around you." The first ground around Frost was San Francisco, California. His father took Robert to newspaper offices and introduced him to writers (e.g., Henry George) and politicians (e.g., Christopher "Blind Boss" Buckley), all of which made a lasting impression on the young Robert.[24] Frost's childhood memories were the basis for several poems set in California. Examples include "Once by the Pacific" (published in 1926), "At Woodward's Gardens" (1936), and "Auspex" (1960). In "Auspex," a short poem set in the Sierra Nevada, the narrator remembers being nearly captured and swept away by an eagle "when I was small" (almost certainly Frost's reference to his own childhood). Judging from the dates of publication, Frost's California experiences never left him. When events from his youth connected with a new idea, image or metaphor, he would write about them, even decades later.

But after his father died, leaving an estate of eight dollars, Robert, his sister and mother had to leave California and live in New Hampshire. To an eleven-year-old boy, rural New England must have seemed worlds apart from pre-earthquake San Francisco. Thirty years after the transition, Frost said of his early poetry, "I am supposed to have caught in my book the last moments of a dying race." He had seen abandoned farms being overtaken by nature, with a few "rustics" hanging on as best they could, some of them capable of behaving in the "worst New England manner." He blamed the region's climate for his son's mysterious illness and for bad health in general.[25] It would have been understandable for Frost to paint his new "ground" as inhospitable and depressing.

But for the most part (perhaps because he had no alternative), Frost came to appreciate New England, even the climate: "the region has a shrewdly beautiful climate and a scenery of beauty subdued to poetry and not grand or grandiose enough for rhetoric." Poetry was indeed what the region inspired: "All of my [early] poems come from a little circle about 14 miles in diameter." Frost characterized the "beauty" in some of those poems as "the unforced expression of a life I was forced to live."[26] By 1937, after publishing his sixth collection of poems, Frost still felt a meaningful attachment: "I don't give up New England too easily.... And the thing New England gave most to America was the thing I am talking about: a stubborn clinging to meaning."[27]

Long aware of the mountains of New England, Frost was struck anew by the White Mountains when he spent several weeks in Bethlehem, New Hampshire in 1907. There he found a respite from his hay fever within sight of "the blue black Lafayette." After returning from England in 1915 and spending more than a year closing the deal, he bought a farm "facing all the Franconia range" in Franconia, New Hampshire. Though he sometimes seemed apologetic for having "buried myself in mountains," he invited many friends and colleagues to join him and experience the beauty all around his new farm. When he was working at Amherst College, he encouraged people to "have me early in the season while I am still fresh from the mountains."[28] Years later (1944), he approved of "the wall of mountains around us" at the Bread Loaf School of English in Vermont, a setting that "makes the place cloistral enough to ensure an easy intellectual concentration."[29] He had buried himself in the mountains of New England once again.

Yet Frost refused to be branded as merely a New England poet.[30] As he repeatedly pointed out, regionalism did not mean that he had nothing to say about the world outside his region. Though his poems came from his farm: "that's where they come from but not where they go to." Though his poems were written in New England, "they have proved of interest to more than New England."[31] New England just happened to be his region, but any region could be a source of poetry, and Frost said that writing *must* be rooted geographically: "All writing ... must be ... colloquial....

One half of individuality is locality; ... the other half was colloquiality." Or locality could be even more significant: "nine-tenths of personality is locality." It was in this locality that the poet had to observe in all ways possible: "We value the seeing eye already. Time we said something about the hearing ear."[32] Both senses were essential to grasp the region's locality and colloquiality. Only then could the poet weave them into art.

Frost's art focused on the whole of the New England countryside, including the people. Though he did admit that in his youth, "I thought I greatly preferred stocks and stones to people," by 1933, he said, "the country and nature of New England have been [my] background, but the poems are almost without exception portraits of people." In 1915, he wrote, "Country people are not so peculiar..." and he elaborated the point in 1934[33]: "Another reason for being versed in country things is for the understanding of people. I don't think any one understands people unless he has learned from country life that lots of people are smarter than they look. I learned that from farmers. They are more important than they look. And city people are not aware of it."

In letters and prose, he went further. "Inspiration" Frost claimed, "lies in the clean and wholesome life of an ordinary man," as long as he was willing to "like them for their bitter as well as their sweet." Though he confessed that his career had involved "brushing a good many people aside" and that success "cut me off from meeting ordinary people," he still felt an obligation to the people that read his poetry: "The most humane thing you can do is to let people know what you are talking about. Let them in." For both the crafting and the consumption of his poetry, Frost knew that people were essential,[34] and people are an inextricable part of the environmental history of New England.

Metaphor

According to Frost, "fresh metaphor is everything in poetry." Only through metaphors can poetry grow and mature: "Poetry begins in trivial metaphors, petty metaphors, 'grace' metaphors, and goes on to the profoundest thinking that we have."[35] Metaphors arise with sentences doing "double duty," providing "extra meaning," or they arise with words that produce a double effect: "'double meaning' or 'ambiguity' or 'double-entendre' or 'metaphor.'" The poet is "saying one thing and meaning another,

19

saying one thing in terms of another."[36] Some of the best metaphors connect "the thing in front of you" with "its strange analogue, its surprising analogue," some of which "are as surprising to you as they are to the reader."[37] And Frost intended his metaphors to be recognizable: "How can anyone fail to see / Where perfectly in form and tint / The metaphor, the symbol lies!" ("A Missive Missile").

The mixing of things appears explicitly in his poem "The Door in the Dark," in which the narrator hits his head on a door and has "my native simile jarred" (in an earlier version of the poem, "Speaking of Metaphor," the wording is "my basic metaphor jarred"). Addled by the impact, the narrator observes that pairs of "people and things" are separated and paired differently (in the earlier draft, the new and old pairings are both metaphors).[38] Frost obviously didn't depend on concussions to generate new metaphors, but he does seem to be telling readers that originality does not always come easily.

But some pairings are easier than others. Many words in English lend themselves to metaphor and double entendre because they have multiple definitions. Regarding the poem "Lodged," for example, George Bagby inferred that the flowers that "lay lodged" were "domiciled" in the mud, forced to reside there by the rain and wind. "To lodge" also means "to beat down crops," and I suspect that Frost was using it in that sense (at least initially) because of his experience as a farmer.[39] But the last line, "I know how the flowers felt," suggests that Frost was using both meanings, as he did in other poems with other words: "versed," "quarry," "dwelling," "appall," "waste" and more.

Frost's poetry was metaphorical, but his metaphors were firmly rooted in the rise of realism in the late nineteenth and early twentieth century.[40] Frost's own words show how metaphors often arise from the reality of everyday life: "There are two types of realists: the one who offers a good deal of dirt with his potato to show that it is a real one, and the one who is satisfied with the potato brushed clean. I'm inclined to be the second kind. To me, the thing that art does for life is to clean it, to strip it to form."[41] Continuing on the garden theme, first with carrots: "A man who makes really good literature is like a fellow who goes into the fields to pull carrots. He keeps pulling them patiently enough until he finds a carrot that suggests something else to him. It is not shaped like the other carrots." Then there is cultivation: "It is that particular kind of imagination that I cultivate rather than the kind that merely sees things, the hearing imagination rather than the seeing imagination though I should not want to be without the latter." Ultimately, "real art" involves "believing the thing into existence, saying as you go more than you even hoped you were going to be able to say, and coming with surprise to an end that you foreknew only with some sort of emotion." "Real art," initiated by observation, locality and colloquiality, breaks free from these points of origin and takes on a life of its own: "I know where the poetry must come from if it comes."[42]

In Frost's poetry, there is an essential connection between observation and metaphor in which the "fresh noticing of the details"[43] of reality is the point of departure for imagination. Irving Howe said, "Frost writes as a modern poet ... through a disciplined observation of the natural world and a related sequel of reflection."[44] Nina Baym points out how these reflections connect the modern poet with his antecedents: "In these poems [nature lyrics], Frost shares with Emerson nothing more than the assumption that nature can be used to uncover and illustrate the underlying laws of the universe, because it operates by such laws."[45]

Jay Parini connects Frost with Coleridge in the reworking of observation and reality[46]: "It is intriguing to consider how many of Frost's best poems reflect on the act of creation, the process of breaking down the forms of reality given by the world and remaking them, restoring them to freshness.... But Frost gives clear signals that he wants us to read beyond the natural phenomenon, to search for its symbolic implications. ... The poet's imagination takes the beautiful world and scrambles it, remakes it."

Frost created his metaphors in a sequence of steps: the "disciplined observation" of a rural New Englander, the "prepared mind" of a skilled naturalist, and the "reflection" of a modern poet. Jay Parini summed up the process succinctly with regard to "Nothing Gold Can Stay": "A poem like this is a product of close natural observation, a passionate sympathy for the processes of nature, and a finely tuned awareness of nature's metaphorical potential."[47] The process is evident throughout Frost's writing. His descriptions are precise and evocative, elegant in their simplicity, and intrinsically compelling. The metaphors arising from these descriptions become revelations of something greater, new, surprising or sublime. The two are inseparable: description fuels metaphor, and metaphor crystallizes description.

Thus we see in "The Need of Being Versed in Country Things" that a chimney stands alone "like a pistil after the petals go." Frost's delicate metaphor showers the reader with new connections: flower and farm, past and future, promise and failure. It is stunning in its simplicity, vivid in its reality, and surprising in its contradictions. Yes, the house and petals are gone, but though the house has no future, though the pistil-chimney cannot actually produce any seeds, there is still the potential for renewal. Humans are done here, but nature is preparing the next generation. With the floral metaphor in hand, we are ready to explore the stony road, the summer load, the abandoned barn and the rejoicing birds. Flowers were only the beginning.

Subduing the Land
"Teams that came by the stony road"

Europeans began their continuous occupation of what is now known as New England with the founding of the Plymouth Colony in 1620.[1] At the time the *Mayflower* landed, most of New England was covered in old-growth forest. In some places near the coast and along major rivers, the land was open or park-like, with widely spaced trees where Native Americans had collected firewood, opened up small areas for crops, burned out the underbrush, or harvested timber to trade with ship-borne Europeans. Early settlers gravitated toward these open sites, but as the population grew, settlement moved into the forest for commercial and agricultural exploitation of the land. By the mid 1800s, 50–75 percent of the land (90 percent in some towns) had been cleared.[2]

Colonists in New England replicated their European pattern of agriculture with crop fields, pastures, orchards, woodlots and meadows (hay from the meadows was hauled to barns by "teams that came by the stony road"). To establish their farms, they had to displace the native people (those who hadn't already succumbed to disease) and clear the trees, a transformation characterized by William Cronon as "Taking the Forest" and by Gordon Whitney as an "Assault on the Forest."[3]

In the 1890s, Robert Frost read Richard Anthony Proctor's book *Our Place Among the Infinities*, the second chapter of which was titled "Of Seeming Wastes in Nature."[4] Thus began a life-long interest in wasteful human behavior, ranging from thoughtless destruction to justifiable extravagance. Frost was well aware that a wasteful transformation of the landscape had begun in earnest with European settlement. His poem "Genealogical" recounts the process of establishing agriculture in Maine:

Stopping by Woods

"To wipe out the whole of an Indian tribe to order, / As in those extravagant days they wasted the woods / With fire to clear the land for tillage." The setting in Maine and accounts in "Genealogical" reflected Frost's own ancestry. Nicholas Frost, the first member of the Frost family in New England, established a farm near present-day Eliot, Maine, in 1636. In 1650, "his wife and daughter [Bertha and Anna] were captured by Indians," and during an unsuccessful attempt to rescue them, Nicholas's son Charles killed two Native Americans. The next day, Bertha and Anna were found dead. Undeterred, the Frost lineage continued to participate in the settlement and subjugation of New England.[5] Among Frost's poems, a mill owner's antipathy toward Native Americans leads to murder in "The Vanishing Red," with the mill owner clearly depicted in a negative light. More often, Frost's poems include expressions of admiration for Native Americans, as in "A Cliff Dwelling," "The Vindictives" and "America Is Hard to See."[6]

In "The Birthplace," Frost describes the founding of a mountain farm by the narrator's father, who after taking possession of a spring, "Strung chains of wall round everything, / Subdued the growth of earth to grass."[7] Settlement required a radical transformation of the forest into farmland by logging, uprooting and burning of trees, followed by plowing, mowing and grazing to keep the land open.

Though trees declined precipitously as farming spread, ragweed (*Ambrosia artemisiifolia*), an indigenous herbaceous weed, increased dramatically on soil laid bare by the plow. Frost suffered horribly from ragweed-induced hay fever, so it is not at all surprising that, in a parody of Thomas Hood's poem "November," ragweed was at the top of Frost's list of things he found to be absent in England.[8] By retreating with his family to his British motherland, Frost, a child of colonists, had temporarily freed himself from colonially-enhanced ragweed.

Carving land out of the forest was just the beginning of the subjugation of the New England landscape. Frost saw first-hand how waste continued in the nineteenth and twentieth centuries. People maintaining their homesteads worked "to push the woods back from around the house" ("A Cabin in the Clearing"). Frost encouraged his daughter Lesley to complete her poem about a "cut-over hillside. You were just going to name some of the slain trees when you stopped." In Frost's prose piece *Dalkins' Little Indulgence*, a man is "snaking out logs in a grove recently laid waste."[9] Dalkins' grove was merely cut for timber, not burned for conversion to farmland, but the same cannot be said of "Patterson's pasture" in "Blueberries": "But get the pine out of the way, you may burn / The pasture all over until not a fern / Or grass-blade is left, not to mention a stick." The farmer harvested pine timber from the land and then set fire to the remnants, hoping to leave nothing alive but grass. He got blueberry bushes instead. Fire did not generate a pasture, but at least it did produce a crop of tasty fruit.

Despite its unpredictable nature and effects, rural folk continued to set fires to accomplish tasks, or for no particular reason at all. A pile of brush was most easily disposed of by setting it alight, despite the risk of having the fire get out of control. It does just that in "The Bonfire" when a gust of wind "put the flame tip down and dabbed the grass." The narrator is forced to fight the fire with all his strength, a fight that he just barely wins. While on his farm in Franconia, New Hampshire, Frost complained about the lack of summer rain: "we don't get enough [rain] to put out the forest fires and clear the air of smoke." We don't learn who set the fires or why, just that the entire town had to endure the haze. But only a year earlier, Frost promised a potential visitor, "the ground will be wet, so that we can have a bonfire of spruce boughs to talk around." One year before that, he published "The Bonfire" where a group of boys will "have our fire and laugh and be afraid." With so many people willing to set fires, it is understandable why Frost worried about his house in Pelham, Massachusetts that was "so close to the woods that if the woods burn our house must go too."[10]

Farming could generate unintended waste and destruction even without a conflagration. In "The Exposed Nest," the mechanical mowing of hay endangers a nest of birds. In "Fish-Leap Fall," after a small stream has been dammed to make a farm pond, the altered flow forces some of the fish swimming upstream to leap the dam and land on the grass. These are not calamitous events, but they are still injurious, still wasteful. Frost was sufficiently observant to see these costs of manipulating the landscape for farming, even when it was only on a small scale.

Frost was also willing to celebrate small victories where waste was avoided. In "The Tuft of Flowers," a mower left a small patch of blooming flowers among the cut hay, an example of what Robert Faggen called "survival of beauty in waste."[11] In "A Young Birch," the narrator imagines how someone, in "cutting brush," had "spared" a small tree from "the number of the slain" and left it "to live its life out as an ornament." Was this tree a survivor of the destruction described in "Pea Brush"?

In contrast to the birch that was spared, the American chestnut suffered a two-pronged assault. For centuries, trees were logged for lumber, especially for woodwork that ornamented the interiors of houses. Starting in 1904, chestnuts suffered one of most calamitous unintended consequences ever to befall the forests of North America: the importation of chestnut blight. Robert Faggen noted that Frost would have seen the effects of the blight first hand on his farms.[12] Chestnut blight appears in two poems, and is the main subject of "Ten Mills IV. Evil Tendencies Cancel." In that poem, Frost's description of the disease in lines three and four is exactly right. The blight kills chestnut trees above ground before they can produce more than a few nuts, but the roots survive and keep "sending up new shoots." I use the present tense here because the farmer's logical prediction that the blight would not "end the chestnut" has turned out to be wrong. The blight is still very much with us, and American chestnut trees have not recovered.[13]

As early as 1939, the blight had killed enough mature trees that Frost wrote about the demise of chestnut as a useable wood ("The Old Barn at the Bottom of the Fogs"). The wooden door locks on the barn are "specimens / In chestnut now become a precious wood / As relic of a vanished race of trees." More than seventy years later, American chestnuts are still "a vanished race of trees" because the blight killed nearly every mature tree in North America (a handful of large, healthy chestnuts have been found along the fringes of the species' former range).[14] Other species of trees have taken the place of the dead chestnuts in the forest canopy, but the absence of the annual crop of nuts and the absence of these fast-growing trees have significantly altered the ecology and timber management of the forests of eastern North America.

Bleeding Trees

When Frost wrote about the trees in New England, he often paid particular attention to the wounds that trees suffered, ranging from minor to lethal. In several of his poems, he mentions the sap, resin or other fluids that sometimes bleed from these wounds. The oozing liquids are the result of some kind of injury, and in most of Frost's poems about bleeding trees, the source of injury is identified as human, and the injury is deliberate. What are we to make of these injured and bleeding trees?

Trees were not scarce in New England at the start of the twentieth century. The landscape was dotted with abandoned farms that left plenty of space for trees to move in: "The mountain pushed us off her knees. / And now her lap is full of trees" ("The Birthplace"). Trees, and sometimes their exudates, were important resources for Frost and his neighbors. He understood and participated in the utilitarian exploitation of trees, an exploitation that was a metaphor for survival and success. But exploitation could leave destruction and desolation in its wake, and Frost could question or even mourn the loss of trees. His empathy and personification of trees helped give voice to moderation, conservation and common sense. And the voice could become indignant or angry when the trees were injured by outsiders. What did intruders know about the value of our trees?

Frost tells the tales of bleeding trees through the everyday lives of farm families, woodsmen, children and naturalists. Trees were nearly as ubiquitous as the air people breathed, and injuries to trees did not go unnoticed. But how were trees injured and why did they bleed? The reasons varied widely, and for Frost, it was the reason that mattered.

A useful type of bleeding occurs in "The Gum-Gatherer": "What this man brought in a cotton sack / Was gum, the gum of the mountain spruce. / He showed me lumps of the scented stuff / Like uncut jewels, dull and rough." Spruce gum can be used as a sealant or caulk or even as something to chew. Frost seemed to be amused that "The Gum-Gatherer" "is the only poem I know of that has found a way to speak poetically of chewing gum."[15] Gum can be gathered from the bark around wounds: "I told him this is a pleasant life / To set your breast to the bark of trees / That all your days are dim beneath, / And reaching up with a little knife, / To loose the resin and take it down / And bring it to market when you please."

The gathering of gum might be "a pleasant life" for the gum gatherer (at least from the perspective of someone else), but what about the life of the spruce trees? Michael McDowell[16] presumes that the gatherer is "exemplifying a moderation in the use of nature" because the gatherer lives "a pleasant life" (line 34), but that is the assessment of the narrator, not the gatherer. If "loose the resin" means that the gum gatherer used his "little knife" to pry off the resin, then no additional harm is done to the tree. But if "loose the resin" refers to slicing the bark deeply enough for the tree to bleed, the tree is suffering new damage. Did the gum gatherer, like rubber tappers in the tropics, spread his cuts among many trees so that each spruce was only lightly injured? Both he and the trees would benefit if he did.

The gum gatherer is profiting from the defense mechanisms of "the mountain spruce." Exudation of gum and resin is one of the ways that trees heal wounds and block the invasion of insects and fungi.[17] It is to the gum gatherer's advantage to let the trees heal completely before harvesting the gum. They retain their health and he collects the scabs from their sealed wounds.

In the poem "To a Young Wretch," a different spruce is not just injured but killed. "You nick my spruce until its fiber cracks," the speaker observes; the tree "goes down swishing." Resins from this spruce cannot possibly heal a felled tree, but its resins still have a role to play. The spruce, stolen from the narrator's property, is going to be the wretch's Christmas tree, and the narrator says: "I could have bought you just as good a tree / To frizzle resin in a candle flame." In the early twentieth century, the candles used to illuminate a cut Christmas tree could heat the resin in the twigs and needles to the point of boiling and (if care was not taken) ignition. The purloined tree might be dead, but its resin lingers on. In the spirit of the season, "with Christmas feeling," the owner of the tree wishes only that the resin will "frizzle," not ignite. That sizzling warning, through sound and scent, will suffice as a lesson during the holidays.

Flammable resin also appears in "The Bonfire," but in this case, ignition is the goal. The first speaker wants his group of youngsters to "scare ourselves" that night "by setting fire to all the brush we piled/ With pitchy hands to wait for rain or snow." The piles of "pitchy" brush are the remains of trees cut earlier for firewood or lumber, essentials of rural life. The trees bled in a vain attempt to heal their boles and branches. Like the stolen tree in "To a Young Wretch," the brush will never heal. Instead, the doomed brush has been set aside to dry so it could be burned later when rain or snow would contain the flames. But now, the boys will burn it without that protection, giving the "pitchy" wood free rein to light the night sky. When they set it alight, the pitch will serve as an accelerant for the flames, a "scary" aid for these young arsonists. Will the pitch make the fire spread out of control? A raging fire is a "scary" prospect indeed, but with war looming, "The Bonfire" might not be the most terrifying thing these boys will face.

The tree in "'Out, Out—'" is definitely being cut for firewood. In this poem, the wood is "sweet-scented stuff when the breeze drew across it." The "scent" is from the sap seeping from the "stove-length sticks of wood." If people are to stay warm and cook food, they have to cut wood for their stoves, killing the trees and releasing the sap in the process. But in line twenty, the boy holds up his hand that has had "the meeting" with the saw "as if to keep / The life from spilling." The words "blood" and "sap" do not appear in the poem, yet both are obvious. Life-giving liquids are spilled first from the tree and then from the boy, both by the same saw. Both victims die, the tree in service to the sawyer, the sawyer in service to his family, his blood relatives. The poem gets its title from lines in *Macbeth* about a candle being blown out by the wind: "Out, out, brief candle, /Life's but a walking shadow." In Frost's poem, two lives are snuffed out when the saw delivers its blows and the blood flows from their bodies.

Death has touched another family in the poem "Maple." The father tells his daughter Maple how she got her unusual name: "Well, you were named after a maple tree. / Your mother named you. You and she just saw / Each other in passing in the room upstairs, / One coming this way into life, and one / Going the other out of life—you know?" Maple's mother, as she was going "out of life," made certain of Maple's name, even if it was never certain how Maple was to "be like a maple tree." Still, as Maple and her husband searched for the namesake maple tree (assuming there was one), one thing was certain: "They kept their thoughts away from when the maples / Stood uniform in buckets, and the steam / Of sap and snow rolled off the sugarhouse." They did not think of life draining away,[18] whether it was sap from trees that shared their name with Maple, or something worse. Had Maple's mother bled to death after giving birth to Maple? It didn't bear thinking about.

As in "'Out, Out—,'" scent permeates the site of cut trees in "Pea Brush." Coming just after the poem "Birches" in the collection *Mountain Interval*, "Pea Brush" also describes birch trees, but these have been cut down for unspecified reasons by someone named John. The narrator goes to the site where the birches have been cut, expecting to find branches to support the pea plants in his garden. The brush is there, but the scene is startling in two ways. First, the scent of death is palpable:

> The sun in the new-cut narrow gap
>   Was hot enough for the first of May,
> And stifling hot with the odor of sap
>   From stumps still bleeding their life away.

Trees have two kinds of aqueous sap: one is water conducted from the roots by the xylem tissue, and the other contains sugars, amino acids and other essential molecules transported by phloem tissue from places of abundance to places of need. Stems that are merely injured (such as those in "The Gum-Gatherer") can grow new vascular tissue to replace the conducting cells that were lost.[19] In "Pea Brush," however, the stems have been completely severed and both kinds of life-giving sap are bleeding hopelessly from the vascular tissues of the birch stumps. The trees appear to be doomed.

Second, not only are the cut trees "bleeding their life away" but there are "birch boughs enough piled everywhere" on "the wildflowers' backs":

> Small good to anything growing wild,
> They were crooking many a trillium
> That had budded before the boughs were piled
> And since it was coming up had to come.

The narrator is pleased to be able to use some of the cut boughs to help pea plants grow straight, but is concerned that the wild trillium plants "were crooking" under the excessive piles of brush in a wasteland of bleeding stumps in the former woods. Spring wildflowers have enough problems growing up through the dead leaves of last autumn (see "In Hardwood Groves") and getting sufficient sunlight before the tree leaves cover them in shade (see "Spring Pools"). The added obstacle of heaps of dead branches may make it impossible for trillium flowers to bloom, attract pollinators or produce seeds. Thus in "Pea Brush," a trivial task has been marred by a confrontation with death.

By the end of the poem, however, there is a tone of resignation. Though the trees are gone, and it will take "a cart and pair" to remove all the brush, perhaps all is not lost. The malleable trilliums might find a way through the maze while avoiding the footfalls of large animals, including people. The birch stumps will send up sprouts and might repopulate this spot with small trees that are worthy of admiration ("A Young Birch"), though the "narrow gap" where the trees were cut might be too shady for the sun-loving young birch.[20] Thus, this amount of destruction seems to be an acceptable, if unpleasant, part of everyday rural life.

Other trees have been cut down and allowed to bleed in "The Census-Taker": "The time was autumn, but how anyone / Could tell the time of year when every tree / That could have dropped a leaf was down itself / And nothing but the stump of it was left / Now bringing out its rings in sugar of pitch." "Pitch" in this case is the accumulated sap that has bled from stumps left longer than those in "Pea Brush." The moisture has darkened and swollen the wood, making the rings more distinct than one would see in either freshly-cut or dry stumps. The conspicuous rings accentuate the many years of growth of these trees "in a waste cut over / A hundred square miles." Though the ages of the trees are evident, traces of the fall season have been erased, prompting the narrator to repeat the word "waste" in lines four and nine. Unlike "The Gum-Gatherer," people have wasted all the trees and left nothing useful behind. The poem ends: "The melancholy of having to count souls / Where they grow fewer and fewer every year / Is extreme where they shrink to none at all. / It must be I want life to go on living." The "melancholy" is not just for the absence of people but also for the absence of any kind of life, whether it is life that serve the needs of humans or life for its own sake.[21] The trees have bled away more than their own life in this thoughtless wasteland.[22]

Bleeding can be inferred in two poems in *Mountain Interval* about the intrusion of electricity and telecommunication into rural New England, things that many people would consider beneficial. Both poems focus on dead trees, trees whose bleeding is in the past, but the poems differ in the intensity of the reaction. In "An Encounter," the wandering narrator, taking a break from the search for orchids, has the enjoyment of the blue sky interrupted by a utility pole: "Stood over me a resurrected tree, / A tree that had been down and raised again— / A barkless specter. He had halted too." This pole, a tree raised from the dead, is an unwelcome sight. At the end of the poem, however, the narrator is able to dismiss the dead "resurrected tree" and the news it might be transmitting through its wires. One need only turn away and resume the search for orchids. A single pole in a diverse landscape can be ignored.

But later in *Mountain Interval*, the narrator in "The Line-Gang," is furious: "They throw a forest down less cut than broken. / They plant dead trees for living." Not only is the utility line intrusive, its intrusion is destructive, laying waste to broad swaths of forest[23] merely to connect "towns that set the wild at naught." The workers kill trees, breaking them wastefully to make way for the wires, and the utility company kills other trees to make the poles, a doubly destructive process. To Frost (who was perfectly happy to write letters all his life) there has to be a less wasteful way for people to communicate.[24] Trees don't deserve to bleed for mere wires.

Stopping by Woods

Of all the poems about bleeding trees, only "Traces" mentions "rosin" that has been released without obvious injury caused by humans: "Yet the conifers sigh to the warblers," their bark shedding "tears everlasting / Of silvery rosin drops." It is likely that these resin-beaded conifers had experienced some form of trauma, perhaps storms that broke branches or bark-hungry porcupines, or an invasion of bark beetles that had subsequently drowned in the resin.[25] The "tears" of the tree are the "traces" of the harm that has been done. However they are formed, beads of resin do seem to be "everlasting" on the bark of conifers. They become less "silvery" as they oxidize over time, though, and more translucent "like uncut jewels, dull and rough" ("The Gum-Gatherer").

In each poem about bleeding trees, there is a unique term or combination of terms for the fluid: gum, resin, pitch, sap, rosin or stuff. "Resin" appears both in "The Gum-Gatherer" and in "To a Young Wretch," but each poem also has something additional and different. "Pitch" ("The Census-Taker") and "pitchy" ("The Bonfire") share the same origin, but as noun or adjective. Frost might have been avoiding repetition, or simply applying the term with the proper nuance, emphasis, part of speech, number of syllables or rhyme.

But one sensation connects multiple poems. In both "'Out, Out—'" and "The Gum-Gatherer," Frost refers to the resin as "scented stuff," in "Pea Brush" he notes the "odor" of the sap, and in "To a Young Wretch" the cut tree is "smelling green." We can smell the damage, even when we can't see it. Olfaction, that primal perception, grabs and engulfs our attention. The surviving family members at the end of "'Out, Out—'" may have "turned to their affairs," but they will not fully escape the scent of death.

In his poetry, Frost gives us many ways to respond when trees bleed, and in all cases, motives matter. We can be incensed when people damage or destroy trees for a reason we consider unimportant, or worse, for no reason at all. We can wish that the sizzling resin of a stolen tree will serve to chastise the thief. We can admire the silvery brightness of "rosin drops" that occur naturally, or someone who seeks out the resin for practical purposes.

Frost's most common response is pragmatic. We can accept the inevitability of "scented stuff" when the motive is necessity. We understand when land has to be cleared for farming, when timber has to be sawn for buildings, and when firewood has to be gathered for cooking and warmth. Pragmatism trumped idealism when survival was on the line. Regarding one of the characters in "New Hampshire," "He knew too well for any earthly use / The line where man leaves off and nature starts," and his knowledge made him unwilling to cut down a tree. The narrator explains, "I wouldn't be a prude afraid of nature" and scoffs at the man's "Matthew Arnoldism" and "dendrophobia." He made the same point in a commencement address: "I had a city friend who bought a place in the Adirondacks. He had lots of trees, trees to burn. He wouldn't cut down any of the trees because he felt all trees must be spared. This attitude is mere sentimentality."[26] People had to take care of their needs, and as long as those needs were not excessively intrusive and destructive, any wastefulness one could attach to them was still acceptable.

Orchids

Though much smaller than trees, several types of orchids appear in Frost's poetry. Despite the elaborate flowers on every type of orchid, he does not treat all species equally, which raises the question: which orchids are prized and which can be sacrificed?

There are more species in the orchid family (most of them tropical) than in any other family of flowering plants, but many of them are rare, even endangered, for a variety of reasons. Some species of orchid are pollinated by only one or a few species of pollinators, so if anything happens to the pollinator, the orchid suffers as well. Some species have spectacular flowers that are prized by collectors and thereby reduced in abundance in the wild. Many temperate species prefer wetland habitats, which are among the first habitats to be filled or drained when land is developed for human use.[27]

All those problems would be bad enough, but orchids have an unusual and vulnerable process of seed germination. Their seeds are tiny, often like dust, with no nutrients stored inside for the embryo to use when the seed germinates. A newly-germinated orchid is incapable of photosynthesis because it has insufficient materials to form new leaves. Instead, the seedling must quickly form an association with one or more species of fungi. When orchid and fungus meet, the fungus grows inside the orchid and provides the seedling with organic nutrients. An orchid seedling can produce new leaves only after it has accumulated sufficient energy, which may take months.[28] It is not surprising, therefore, that nearly all orchid seeds fail somewhere along the way to adulthood.

Despite all these problems, some seeds of orchids do manage to succeed and produce the remarkable shapes and colors that Frost sought in the countryside.[29] In "Rose Pogonias," Frost hopes that a small meadow with "a thousand orchises" will be spared from mowing:

> We raised a simple prayer
>   Before we left the spot,
> That in the general mowing
>   That place might be forgot;
> Or if not all so favored,
>   Obtain such grace of hours
> That none should mow the grass there
>   While so confused with flowers.

As the common name implies, the flowers of these orchids are large, showy and rose-colored. A field full of these orchids would indeed be worth preserving (though only while they are in bloom; after the flowers fade and the stems wither, after the "grace of hours," the hay can be cut without destroying their beauty or their subsequent resprouting).

As impressive as rose pogonia may be, the "orchid Calypso" (*Calypso bulbosa*) in "An Encounter" is even more colorful and complex. Frost's narrator has found his way to a cedar swamp, a habitat that often favors orchids,[30] but the thicket of branches and uneven ground has brought him to a momentary halt. When he looks up and sees a utility pole, a "barkless specter," he pretends not to care: "'Me? I'm not off for anywhere at all. / Sometimes I wander out of beaten ways / Half looking for the orchid Calypso.'" He is ready to claim that his indeterminate search for a showy orchid had a value equal to any information that might be transmitted by wires. Flamboyant orchid flowers found by accident are at least as special as any deliberate message transmitted "from men to men."

An even rarer flower is worthy of a more deliberate search in "The Quest of the Purple-Fringed." Though each flower of the purple-fringed orchid (*Platanthera grandiflora*) is smaller than the single blossoms of rose pogonia or calypso orchids, all three species of flowers have similar levels of structural complexity. The purple-fringed orchid is especially stunning because of its "purple spires" with dozens of flowers open all at once. The "chill of the meadow underfoot" suggests that the searcher waited until late in the blooming period (August) to make the search, or it might reflect the preference of the orchids for wetter soil, the type of wetland soil one can find "'Neath the alder tree."[31]

In contrast to his protective, even covetous approach to these vivid orchids, Frost did not object to cutting down "pale orchises" in "Mowing." The "pale" flowers were light green, hardly different from the stem, and apparently not sufficiently attractive (despite the intricate shape of the flowers) for Frost to spare them from his scythe. Down they went, even though they were probably unpalatable to the livestock that were fed hay from that meadow.

Color seems to have elevated another orchid only slightly higher on Frost's scale of protection. A single reddish flower of the leafless coralroot (*Corallorhiza*) could be removed without rebuke in "On Going Unnoticed." Simpler in structure than a pale orchis, but more colorful, the sacrifice of one flower (but not the whole plant?) could be overlooked. Perhaps the red color of the stem that matched the flower, plus the fact that the blossoms "hang meanly down," allowed the loss of one flower to go "unnoticed." With no chlorophyll, this orchid is incapable of photosynthesis even when mature and continues to depend on its associated fungi for nutrition.[32] Frost observed that it had no leaves. Did he suspect that this leafless plant was dependent on other organisms for its survival? Did the absence of leaves enter into his evaluation of this species?

Among orchids, as among all flowers, Frost thought that some should never be picked but that others could be cut down with impunity. The dividing line was imprecise, probably a reflection of Frost's willingness to approach his world from multiple points of view. Flowers provided so many starting points for exploring other ideas that it would have been startling if Frost had remained consistent. Flowers, especially orchids, were richly suggestive.

According to the Oxford English Dictionary, the word "orchid" is a nineteenth century variation on the sixteenth century word "orchis," which itself was derived from the Greek word for "testicles" (noted by Katherine Kearns with regard to "Mowing"[33]). In somebody's mind, the bulbs of certain orchids suggested human testicles, and to this day, orchidectomy (and similar variants) means male castration.[34] Frost did not use the term orchidectomy, but it is possible that he implied it in "The Self-Seeker." The poem had its origin in actual events. Frost's good friend Carl Burell was seriously injured while working in a factory, and was left physically unable to complete his scholarly monograph on the orchids of New Hampshire.[35]

In "The Self-Seeker," a man ("the Broken One") who collects and raises orchids has had his feet and legs mangled in a mill accident. At the start of the poem, the Broken One speaks to his friend Willis who objects to the whole of the deal the Broken One has struck regarding compensation for his accident. The small sum of money is bad enough: "'But your flowers, man you're selling out your flowers.'" His flowers, as we learn throughout the poem, are extraordinary. The Broken One tells Willis: "I had a letter from Burroughs—did I tell you?— / About my *Cyprepedium reginæ*; / He says it's not reported so far north." Other people in the poem are quite familiar with the Broken One's expertise. He has trained a girl named Anne to collect orchids for him, and she appears mid-poem holding something behind her back. The Broken One wants to know what she has: "'Come, hold it out. Don't change.—A Ram's Horn orchid!'" Later Anne explains her decision not to bring him a yellow lady's slipper, and further that "'I didn't bring a Purple Lady's Slipper. / To *You*—to you I mean—they're both too common.'"

At this point in the poem, four species of orchids have come into the conversation and it is clear that the Broken One is not a novice but an expert on orchids found in the region where he lives. While this information unfolds, the lawyer arrives with the offer of compensation and brings it to the bedside. Eventually, the Broken One signs it and the lawyer departs as the Broken One ends the poem: "'Good-by.' He flung his arms around his face."

Robert Faggen has elaborated on the complexity of the characters and situations in "The Self-Seeker."[36] The characters respect, tolerate, distrust or exploit one another to various degrees, mostly in a civil manner despite the calamity that has befallen the Broken One. Asymmetrical relationships abound: industry and individuals, expert and novice, victim and friends, victim and benefactor, orchids and humans. The orchids provide not only intricate beauty for the collectors but also broader connections with Charles Darwin (author of an entire volume on orchid pollination) and evolution. "The Self-Seeker" is a remarkable and multilayered poem.

But this poem is also a tale of orchidectomy in at least two ways. First, the Broken One is losing his literal orchids because his injury leaves him unable to tend flowers at home or search for them in the wild. Second, he has lost the physical ability to complete his monograph on orchids, a task at the very center of his being. This is a figurative orchidectomy. In the last line, he tries to hide from the crushing weight of his loss because, compensation notwithstanding, he will never be the same person without his pursuit of flowers. Were he to be literally castrated, could it be any worse for him than what actually happened?[37]

Though the poem did not address it, the Broken One was not alone in experiencing orchidectomy. New England began to lose its orchids while Frost was still alive, and orchid species continue to disappear from their native habitats—wetlands in particular—more rapidly than most other groups of flowering plants.[38] The Broken One in "The Self-Seeker" had planned to publish a list of the "forty orchids" from New Hampshire (line 13). Botanists found nearly the same number (37) in Worcester County, Massachusetts, in the 1800s and 1900s. By 2012, nine could no longer be found there. Of the four species in "The Self-Seeker," two are now among the missing in Worcester County: *Cypripedium reginae* (showy lady's slipper) and the ram's horn orchid (*Cypripedium arientinum*). The other two species occur today at levels of abundance similar to those described in lines 137–144 of the poem: the yellow lady's slipper (*Cypripedium parviflorum*) is "rare" and the purple lady's slipper (*Cypripedium acaule*) is "common." The "pale orchises" (*Platanthera flava* var. *herbiola*) that were so conspicuous in "Mowing" are now rare throughout the county. The occurrence of rose pogonia (*Pogonia ophioglossoides;* "Rose Pogonias") is "sporadic" in Worcester County, and it has entirely disappeared from the city of Worcester where it had previously been found. Overall, the city lost more than half of its orchid species by 2002, a clear indication that an urban setting is even worse for orchids than the countryside.[39] Frost, I expect, would have mourned the decline of these floral jewels, even though he was willing to mow those that dared to be pale.

Erosion

Farming, logging, digging up orchids, or any other severe disturbance of the soil is likely to lead to erosion, especially during times of flooding. In "The Mountain," Frost describes the results of the spring flood of a river, a flood that was probably enhanced by the open fields of surrounding farms: "But the signs showed what it had done in spring: / Good grassland gullied out, and in the grass / Ridges of sand, and driftwood stripped of bark." Not only was "good" land gone, but deposition of sediment, the flip side of erosion, had made a mess of the remaining grass. Erosion and deposition were inevitable along the river, and the small community of people at the base of the mountain simply had to cope, apparently unaware that their presence on the land had made it worse.

In 1936, Frost put erosion in a deeper geological context ("In Time of Cloudburst")[40]: "When my garden has gone down ditch," the narrator would merely have to wait for the eroded soil to settle in the ocean, followed by uplifting of the ocean floor to a height above sea level: "The bottom of seas raised dry." Of course, no single person could possibly live that long, but could humankind find any solace in the inevitability of deep geological time? Was this "hope" a form of wishful thinking, an appeal for time to heal the wounds of farmers exploiting the land? Or was it merely the product of artistic imagination?

In "Build Soil," Frost was clear that the widespread agricultural erosion in the early twentieth century, whether by wind or water, had to be faced immediately, no matter what the cause, whether individual farmer or government policy: "For what is more accursed / Than an impoverished soil, pale and metallic?" The farmer had to find a way to fix the land and the economic viability of a "run-out mountain farm" in New England. Business as usual was not going to suffice, and there was no place nearby to go and exploit new land. There was no easy way to "build soil" where it had been widely and severely abused.[41]

Erosion becomes a political metaphor in "On Taking from the Top to Broaden the Base." Published in 1939, Frost decries the redistribution of material from the top to the bottom on a thoroughly eroded mountain that has nothing left to erode: "Your last good avalanche / Was long since slid." Faced with an actual policy of redistribution of income (his perception of The New Deal), the metaphor of erosion was Frost's choice for expressing his opposition to the policy.

Frost said of himself, "in me sea and land meet ... I am a son of sailors ... and farmers."[42] Thus it is not surprising that he wrote several poems featuring erosion and deposition along the coastline. In "Sand Dunes," the shifting sands, "the sea made land," seem to seek human destruction by burying "The men she could not drown." But despite ships sunk by the sea and sinking buildings swallowed by sand, humans still manage to retain free will.

Frost admired the power of the shore to endure the persistent waves ("Devotion"): "Holding the curve of one position, / Counting an endless repetition." The poem seems to say that the shore will not erode but will instead remain in "one position" forever, permanently successful in its Sisyphean role. This expectation of permanence has an almost derisive tone directed toward the waves in "Does No One at All Ever Feel This Way in the Least?": "Grind shells, O futile sea, grind empty shells." The "futile sea" is not going to do anything but erode shells down to sand, while the coastline itself will endure.

But when Frost acknowledges the incessant nature of ocean waves, admiration for the shore gives way to a prediction of inevitable and destructive coastal erosion. The power of a sea could beat back any shore ("Once by the Pacific"), even one "backed by cliff" that was itself "backed by continent." There is no relief from the pounding, and it only gets worse in a storm: "Someone had better be prepared for rage." No matter how humans might prepare to fight the waves, the ceaseless, tireless erosion of the sea would change the face of any continent: "What now is inland shall be ocean isle" ("I Could Give All to Time"). Though willing to accept the indifference of time writ large, the narrator is not willing to dispense with his own experience. Erosion can bring mountains low and drive the sea inland, but this human being, like the humans in "Sand Dunes," wants to resist any erosion of his self, his individuality, his life. When waste becomes personal and individual, it is to be resisted.

Self Destruction

Frost ended his poem "November" with the line "The waste of nations warring." How had Frost come to this view of war by the time he published this poem in 1938? And how did Frost's experience with war fit into the broader context of war in New England?

As soon as citizens of colonial powers set foot on North American soil, they coveted the tall white pines of New England to provide masts for their ships. Many of those ships were warships. To sustain this supply of giant timber, the largest trees were reserved for the Royal Navy, protected by decree against harvest by mere civilians (a decree that was often ignored). Meanwhile, military needs on land involved the harvest of smaller trees for stockades and forts placed strategically within the landscape. These demands for military materials helped jumpstart the deforestation of New England.[43]

Pre-colonial conflicts among Native Americans are not well documented but almost certainly turned violent on occasion. After Europeans settled the region, they engaged in King Phillip's War, the Seven Years War, the American Revolution and Shay's Rebellion. There has not been anything like a full-blown war on New England territory since the War of 1812 ended in 1814, but soldiers from New England have been sent to other wars, medical personnel from New England have treated battlefield casualties, industries in New England have supplied the military, and New England residents have borne the costs and burdens of war.

Robert's father, William Prescott Frost, Jr., tried to become one of those soldiers from New England. He left his home in Massachusetts as a young adolescent in at attempt to join the Confederate Army, but he was intercepted in Philadelphia before reaching his goal. His Southern sympathies persisted, however, and he named his son Robert Lee Frost in honor of the Confederate general under whose command he had hoped to serve.[44]

Robert Frost's first published poem, "La Noche Triste," appeared in his high school newspaper in 1890. In a style reminiscent of Tennyson, the poem glorifies battle between the Spanish and the Aztecs. At the end, the combatants retreat in opposite directions, both sides having behaved with nobility and courage.

In 1897, as the likelihood of war with Spain was increasing, Frost wrote another poem about wars of the past ("Greece"). Despite their reluctance to fight ("'Let there be no more war!'"), the ancient Greeks answer the "call to arms" and fight the irrepressible Persians. The narrator calls on Greece to show "once again" how "a few may countless hosts o'erthrow." The rising sentiment for war at the time he wrote the poem seems consistent with Frost's enthusiasm for noble combat.

After living for over a decade in southern New Hampshire, Frost travelled with his family to England in August 1912. They were still there when their host country went to war two years later. They sailed back to the United States in February 1915, ships being the only means of transoceanic travel at the time. Frost wrote in a letter to Ernest Silver that he was able to depart from Liverpool with some trepidation, "Kaiser permitting."[45] It is in this and many other letters where we learn the most about Frost's views on war. Of the 560 known letters from 1912 to 1920, at least 83 of them (approximately 15 percent) include references to World War I or war in general.

In these letters, Frost often expressed support for the war ("I hate the

Germans but I must say I dont [sic] hate the war. Am I a jingo?"), and agreed with the opinion that a terrible war was "better than no war at all." Once Frost was back home from England, he criticized "peace talk" and "quasi pacifism," and seemed to support the entrance of the United States into the war. As late as 1918, he wrote, "Glorious war, isn't it?" and "The war has helped, I'm sure."[46]

Yet at the same time he was criticizing "peace talk," he wrote "The Bonfire" with its mixture of innocence, caution, fear, exuberance, and rebellion. The end has a bit of everything: "*War is for everyone, for children too. / I wasn't going to tell you and I mustn't. / The best way is to come uphill with me / And have our fire and laugh and be afraid.*" Even a far-away battle can extend its reach, take the lives of hometown soldiers and touch the lives of those left behind. The young narrator who is leading the construction of the bonfire will likely be drafted into battle if his country decides to go to war. And if the conflict rages long enough, these children around the fire, who are only just beginning to lose their innocence, will feel the effects themselves.

The ambivalence of "The Bonfire" fits with Frost's misgivings about war that we find in other letters. From a personal (and somewhat selfish) perspective, he wrote, "This war mars all" and "The war has been a terrible detriment to pleasant thinking" (he was unable to write poetry at times because "pleasant thinking" was impossible). But he was also well aware that the suffering was widespread: "it does so much worse for a million others." By the end of October 1918, he was fed up: "Too much war!" His distaste for war continued after the war ended. Within a year of the armistice, Frost predicted, "The wars of the future are to be fought with gasses" that leave corpses "lying beautiful in death."[47]

It is somewhat of a surprise that Frost wrote one of his most poignant descriptions of World War I while still in England in August of 1914: "They have to speed the enlisting to keep ahead of the wastage at the front.... A cartload of [recruits] swept out this hamlet tonight.... The place seems lonelier. The moon looks to me as if it tried to look the same as usual to hide something it knows (actually sees in France), but it looks as if it doesn't quite succeed." Even though the carnage had been underway for less than a month, Frost seemed to anticipate that it was going to get much, much worse.[48]

The war became intensely personal for Frost because some of his friends and fellow writers served in the armed forces of the Allied powers.

Wilfrid Gibson and Lascelles Abercrombie both enlisted but were not sent to the front. Frost despaired of Jack Gallishaw, who had fought in the Canadian, English and American armies: "As to their drafting Jack: I'm damned if I can believe it of them. A man who has been through what he has been through has seen and done enough." He was deeply relieved that his American friend Sidney Cox survived the war, telling Cox in a letter in December of 1918, "Thanks be that the war has spared you to me."[49]

Frost had become close friends with the writer Edward Thomas while in England, and he wrote to Thomas often during the war from the safety of North America. In June of 1915, Frost said, "As for the war, damn it! You are surely getting the worst of it. You are not through the Dardanelles and we know that you are not. Nothing will save you but Lloyd George and a good deal of him. You must quit slacking." Frost obviously used "you" in the plural form, but perhaps Thomas took it as singular (especially the last line) because he enlisted in the army the very next month. In September 1915, Frost wrote to Lascelles Abercrombie, "I forgot to mention the war in this letter. And I ought to mention it, if only to remark that I think it has made some sort of new man and a poet out of Edward Thomas." Two months later, in a letter to Thomas, Frost conveyed a personal and heartfelt message: "I don't want you to die."[50]

Frost said of the poem "Range Finding," "I wrote it in a time of profound peace (circa 1902?)." Having read the poem and seen the battlefields of Europe, Thomas told Frost that the poem was "so good a description of No Man's Land."[51] In the poem, a single bullet has cut a flower stalk (thereby displacing a feeding butterfly) and fooled a spider into examining its web for captured prey. Immediately after this brief, violent intrusion, all of the plants and animals display resilience: the blossom still provides nectar for the butterfly, a nearby bird "revisited her young," and the spider "finding nothing, sullenly withdrew." But the reader knows that if the bullet has found its range (and if it comes from a soldier and not a lone hunter), all of these pastoral lives will soon be obliterated in battle.

Thomas wrote to Frost about returning home on leave for Christmas 1916, an account that inspired "Not to Keep," a wrenching poem about a brief interlude of peace that ends all too soon when the soldier must return to the front. The fear in this one family is nearly unbearable—he is whole now, but for how long?—and it is multiplied across all the families of all the soldiers who have no idea when or how the fear will end.[52]

Then on April 27, 1917, Frost wrote to his English friend Jack Haines:

"Thomas was killed at Arras on Easter morning [April 9]." It had taken time for the news to reach Frost and more time for him to be able to write of it, but then he poured out the news in a series of letters: "He was the bravest and best and dearest man"; "He went to death because he didn't like going"; "Edward Thomas was the only brother I ever had.... His poetry is so very brave—so unconsciously brave. He didn't think of it for a moment as war poetry, though that is what it was"; "Everything has gone to pieces with the coming of the war."[53]

By August 17, 1917, Frost still found himself incapable of composing verse about Thomas's death because "I care too much." In 1920, he published the memorial poem "To E.T." that he admitted was a struggle and that some of his friends did not like.[54] His 1927 poem, "A Soldier," imagines how the weapons of war that killed the soldier "shot the spirit on" beyond the target. The soldier's spirit went far beyond this weapon that had caused this death on this battlefield. Whether this poem had anything to do with Edward Thomas is unknown.

Nearly twenty years after Thomas's death, Frost wrote a recollection of a "misty evening" when a rainbow miraculously encircled two dear "elected friends" as they were trying to find their way home. This "Iris by Night," this rainbow descending from the moon, embraced them "in a ring" where they stood, "And I alone of us have lived to tell."

Frost returned to England in 1957: "The last stop was Oldfields, where Edward Thomas had lived. Frost started toward the house, but was overcome with emotion. 'There is no need to go inside,' he said, turning instead to the nearby orchard, where he and Thomas had been sitting together when the news broke that the Great War had started."[55] In this orchard, the "Iris" had confirmed their deep friendship and foretold that, of the two friends who had become brothers, only one would survive to recount the story of their bond. Frost was finally able to honor his departed friend in exquisite verse.

Having suffered deep personal loss in World War I and having seen the despair and disruption experienced by so many people in England and America, Frost's view of war had hardened. He published "November" in 1938,[56] a time when many people saw the rising tide of war. Hitler had taken the Sudetenland, Japan had invaded Manchuria and Italy had subdued Ethiopia, yet nobody seemed able to do anything about it. In the fifteen short, three-beat lines of "November," Frost makes a rapid transition from everyday experience to "the waste of nations warring," and his last two lines in particular are meant to shock the reader. Frost had already lived through one war, seen "the wastage at the front," and suffered the death of Edward Thomas, his dearest friend.[57] In the poem, it is autumn and we're worrying about the waste of leaves. The horrendous "waste" of war is coming as surely as the arrival of winter, yet we're doing nothing to prevent it or prepare. Wake up!

People did not wake up. Eight years later, even after the slaughter of tens of millions of soldiers and civilians, Frost was compelled to write that humanity could still "be wiped out" by nuclear weapons ("Why Wait for Science"). The rising stockpiles of atomic weapons, coupled with the graphic evidence of devastation at Hiroshima and Nagasaki, fed post-war fears of "a new Holocaust" ("U.S. 1946 King's X"). Science (actually technology; Frost often conflated the two) had made it easy to obliterate thousands or even millions of people with weapons as bright as the sun. How could treaties (the "King's X") hope to prevent annihilation in the face of such force? It could well have been these fears that contributed to his notebook entry: "Can you think of any purpose in the universe more important than to keep the human race going on this planet. It makes all other interests seem insignificant."[58] To the extent that anything was necessary for this "purpose," Frost accepted and even encouraged some types of waste and some degree of the subjugation of Nature. Beyond that, however, waste should not be tolerated, especially waste as cataclysmic as nuclear war.

Essential or Excessive?

Frost considered some waste essential and some waste tolerable, but some waste was egregious, with no purpose of any kind. What distinguished one form of waste from another? A farmer committing arson for the insurance ("The Star-Splitter") could be forgiven for performing a "sacrifice," especially when he used the proceeds to buy a telescope, "to satisfy a lifelong curiosity/ About our place in the infinities."[59] The carpet of red apples under the tree in "Unharvested" is an opportunity to celebrate waste. Music pouring forth from the "old, old house renewed with paint" ("The Investment") is an "extravagance" to be enjoyed, even savored. In "The Ax-Helve," the craftsman Baptiste "brushed the shavings from his knees," the inevitable by-product of carving an ax handle, but the shavings would fuel the fire and thus not go completely to waste. As for wasting time and effort, "Baptiste knew how to make a short job long / For love of it, and yet not waste time either," and Baptiste's lengthy explanation of the design of the handle was "not being wasted" on the narrator, the person who would benefit from revitalization of his ax.

In other cases, excess comes into question. In "The Housekeeper," extravagance is a mixture of guilt and pride: "Our hens and cows and pigs are always better / Than folks like us have any business with." In a draft of an unpublished poem, Frost wondered, "If it was fanciful to have in mind / A fairer field for mowing than was needed."[60] Regarding his own actions, Frost characterized his "gadding" among fellow poets in England as "extravagance," while admitting that he had already planned "one or two more indulgences."[61] Frost knew that different people could view waste differently, even when the same thing was being wasted. The smoke in "A Cabin in the Clearing" is mystical and therefore tolerable, but in "The Cocoon," it is obviously excessive. Rural electrification allowed people to waste light whenever they wanted, compared to lamp oil that had to be conserved for the lantern ("On the Heart's Beginning to Cloud the Mind").[62] But the farmer views it differently in "The Literate Farmer and the Planet Venus." The invention that provides people with light also threatens to deprive them of sleep. Edison's invention may be flourishing, but Frost said elsewhere, "to flourish is to become dangerous."[63] It might be no bargain to trade one type of waste for another.

On a global scale, what is "our place in the infinities"? Humans are near the top of the food chain, vulnerable only to large predators (as well as tiny disease organisms). Incapable of photosynthesis, we must consume some amount of plants, animals, fungi or bacteria to gain sufficient energy to survive. For us to stay alive, other living things must die.

In addition to food, we exploit the landscape to satisfy other needs, desires and follies. We cut trees to build and heat our homes, pick orchids to decorate our tables, seek new land if we are foolish enough to exhaust the land we have, and celebrate the ends of wars that we ourselves began.

As a species, how do human actions balance out? Frost points out in "Our Hold on the Planet" that "there is much in nature against us," whether it be nature that surrounds us or our own "human nature." In a poem published in the aftermath of World War II, Frost addresses the broad characterization of human civilization as a disease that was infecting Earth ("The Lesson for Today"): "Space ails us moderns: we are sick with space.

/ Its contemplation makes us out as small / As a brief epidemic of microbes / That in a good glass may be seen to crawl / The patina of this the least of globes." Frost emphatically rejects this characterization, and in response, blames "science," in its process of scientific "contemplation," for having produced this metaphor of humans as a fleeting infection on an insignificant Earth.

If there is a disease, it is not humans as a species. Instead, Frost repeatedly makes the point that strict, narrow adherence to one theory or ideology is in itself a disease. In his notebooks, Frost hints that something protected a person's mind from "infection" by ideology. He worries that the flawed ideas (from his perspective) of Darwin, Marx, Freud and Einstein are too self-reinforcing. If you adhere too tightly and too narrowly to a single theory, if you only "mind your own business" of ideology, you will perish from "obedience as it were a disease." These flaws in thinking (and action) need to be exposed for "purification" by other ideas, perhaps as a "septic tank that purifies itself against being shut in on its diseases."[64]

Having shown how science had become too arrogant, Frost goes on to yoke religion together with science because both "belittle" humanity[65]: "The cloister and the observatory saint / Take comfort in about the same complaint / So science and religion really meet." He then dismisses scientists and theologians as mere "philosophers" who are "unoriginal as any rabbit." He doesn't want "science" or "religion" to decide what meaning we should take from the small size of the Earth in the cosmos or the actions of the human "patina" upon it. Finding meaning was his job, the job of the artist.[66]

In his assessment of humanity ("Our Hold on the Planet"), Frost notes that human numbers and human civilization "have so increased." The simple fact of increase is, to Frost, clear evidence that nature, as a whole, "must be a little more in favor of man." Despite waste in nature and waste by humans, the net result is positive. He acknowledged ("The Bad Island— Easter") that things could sometimes go wrong: "Until overtaxed / In nerve and resource / They started to wane." In sum, though, humans seemed to be successful even in the face of their failings and their wasteful ways.

Where did a New England farmer fit into this scale of wastefulness and exploitation of the landscape? Frost was well aware that farms existed at the expense of the forest, but his judgment of farms was, in the end, both personal and pragmatic. After all, he was a part-time farmer himself, first out of necessity and later out of satisfaction. He took pride in raising poultry, planting apple trees and selling vegetables. In the end, no matter how wasteful farming might be, it replaced one form of productivity with another. Agricultural productivity sustained the farmer, farm families, and all of human society. It was not merely tolerable; it was essential. For Frost, farming became essential both for food and for poetry, as we will see in the next chapter.

Farming
"The place's name"

The Forest Primeval doesn't stand a chance against determined farmers. Indigenous trees have to go (some are replaced by orchards), fields are either plowed or (in contemporary agriculture) doused in herbicide to set back the weeds and give the crops a head start. Meadows are mowed for hay, pastures are grazed by livestock that originated outside of North America, and streams are diverted, dammed and used as watering holes.

Even though New England had lost most of its farmers by the late 1800s, some families stayed on their farms, keeping ecological succession at bay, and continued to make their living from the land. Their lives could be hard. The soil was acidic and full of stones, the seasons were too wet, too cold, too long or too short, and the economy was merciless. But life on a farm could also be fascinating, and farming certainly fascinated Robert Frost.

What was a farm to Frost? As a couple moves into an old farm in "In the Home Stretch," the husband sums it up: "'The first thing in the morning, out we go / To go the round of apple, cherry, peach, / Pine, alder, pasture, mowing, well and brook. / All of a farm it is.'"

In 1933, Frost wrote about his experience as a farmer in a third-person autobiographical sketch: "Between 1900 and 1907 he kept a one man farm in Derry, New Hampshire.... Since then, he has always had an interest in the land, and has owned small farms in either New Hampshire or Vermont." At other times, he counted the years on his farm in Derry as "eight," "nine," or "nearly ten years," depending on whether he was promoting himself as a farmer or as something else. Frost further claimed, "His life has been spent in farming, teaching and writing poetry" and that he was "one-half teacher, one-half poet and one-half farmer." His attitude toward farming varied depending on which of his vocations he was *not* doing. While living in England, he wrote, "I had much rather farm than write for money," and while teaching at Amherst College, "I wish I was far far from here a-farming," but then, "two weeks' farming has made me think better of teaching." But then, after being back at teaching for a few years, he resigned in 1920: "I have decided to leave teaching and go back to farming and writing."[1] Thus did Frost repeatedly seek change and rejuvenation that often (but not always) included farming.

Frost lived among farmers for decades and noticed how people "become more attuned to the rhythms of nature and take great satisfaction in wresting order from chaos as they cultivate the soil."[2] From his own farming experience, Frost was familiar with fields, meadows, pastures, orchards and woodlots, as well as the houses, barns and other structures built by farmers. His farms were part of the patchwork and culture of rural New England, all of it a rich source of subject matter for his writing. There is no question that much of Frost's poetry was a "farm product." Regarding his farm in Derry: "There he wrote a large share of his first two books," so much so that he could tear the pages out of those books and "could lay the poems pretty much nearly to cover the little thirty-acre farm. I could find places where every single one of the poems took its rise."[3] So along with fruit, eggs, hay and milk, Frost's farms produced poems, many of which helped illuminate the significance of farming in society by painting a "realistic portrait of country life."[4]

Among the components of a farm listed in "In the Home Stretch," the three that most often received Frost's attention were apples, brooks and haying. First, though, we will consider two other aspects of farms: plowing (because of Frost's ambivalence toward it) and poultry (for its surprising rarity in his poetry).

At the Plow

When Frost included plowing in his poems, it was usually as a cautionary tale, or in a disparaging tone. Sometimes, the word "plow" was not in reference to actual plowing of the soil. The "plowed ground" in "The Investment" is being "plowed" by "a digger / Among unearthed potatoes," not an animal-drawn plow. On roads, each vehicle with "metal shoes and tires ... still plows in season"[5] through the mud, or (in "Plowmen")[6] through the snow where "they cannot mean to plant ... having cultivated rock." Robert Faggen wrote that one of the men in "The Mountain" is "laboring behind a plow,"[7] but the man's "white-faced oxen" are actually pulling "a heavy cart" (line 17), not a plow. And "A Girl's Garden" was so small that "it was not enough of a garden, / Her father said, to plow."

Though Frost referred to plowing as "artifice" in "America Is Hard to See," he knew that plowing was hard work, not to be taken on lightly. In "The Bonfire," the narrator says that fighting a spreading brush fire is as physically exhausting as plowing: "By leaning back myself, as if the reins / Were round my neck and I was at the plow." In "The Nose Ring," a poem Frost wrote for Louis Untermeyer, figurative plowing is painful: "It makes me wince when I use my nose for a plow."[8]

Boulders and bedrock (all too common in New England) frustrate both plow and farmer in Frost's notebooks ("plowing rocky land"; "There had been twenty boulders to the acre"[9]) and again in "The Star-Splitter" ("There where he moved the rocks to plow the ground / And plowed between the rocks he couldn't move"). Rocks (and more) eventually drove Brad McGlaughlin to give up on farming. There is not even a mention of plowing on the boulder-strewn farm in "Of the Stones of the Place" because any sensible farmer would know that "no plow among these rocks would pay" ("Something for Hope"). The poem "In Time of Cloudburst" depicts plowing in a positive light only because of the happy accident of finding an ancient tool that had been "turned up by the plow."

Even where successful, plowing cannot guarantee an entirely positive result. As the garden plots are plowed in spring in "The Strong Are Saying Nothing," there is too much uncertainty about the eventual harvest for anyone to be optimistic. "The Hill Wife" followed her husband "where he furrowed field," but later, she impulsively left him. As for the food grown in fields in "Build Soil," there is the political admonition to "Eat it or plow it under where it stands, / To build the soil." What plowing begins, plowing might have to bury.

In at least two poems, the absence of plowing is hailed. Once a meadow is no longer mowed for hay ("The Last Mowing"), there will be glorious proliferation of all the flowering plants "That can't stand mowers and plowers.") This hands-off approach to the land appeals because "'It's a nice way to live, / Just taking what Nature is willing to give, / Not forcing her hand with harrow and plow'" ("Blueberries"). When we forgo the plow, we reap colorful flowers or tasty fruit.

With so many references to it in his poetry, it is obvious that Frost both understood and avoided plowing. So in 1925, when he playfully threatened that he would "go back like Cincinattus [sic] to my plough,"[10] we know he didn't really mean it.

Poultry

In contrast to his avoidance and denigration of plowing, Frost took some pride in his ability to raise poultry and produce eggs, letting the birds run free on the farm. He was involved in breeding hens as a child in San Francisco, and among his earliest prose were several articles about poultry, articles "a little out of the usual line" for the poultry journals of his time.[11] In his letters, including several to his daughter Lesley while she was away at college, Frost frequently mentioned the chickens he was tending, including their success in laying. He also invented images based on his poultry. In 1916, "though in bed with the temperature of a sitting hen," Frost refused to die just to please other poets of his day. Three years later, he teasingly proposed to write a book "on the Barred Plymouth Rock by the Plymouth Rock Bard."[12] But even though poultry provided Frost with food, satisfaction and amusement in his life as a farmer, we read about hens, chickens and eggs in just a handful of his poems ("The Egg and the Machine," "Blue Ribbon at Amesbury," "New Hampshire" and "The Housekeeper"). Poultry did not inspire the poet as much as they inspired the farmer.

Apples in the Orchard

> Essence of winter sleep is on the night,
> The scent of apples: I am drowsing off.
> "After Apple-Picking"

Among the trees that Frost mentions by name, apple tops the list. From the orchard in "Ghost House" (*A Boy's Will*, 1913) to humankind falling from the apple tree in "Kitty Hawk" (*In the Clearing*, 1962), we hear about apples again and again. Through most of his life, Frost grew, picked, savored, fermented, observed, admired, defended and wondered about apples. From blossoms in spring to windfalls in autumn, apples were often on his mind.

In Frost's life and poems, a farm isn't a farm at all without apple trees. On his Derry farm, he "earns more money" from one apple tree than from writing or teaching.[13] The new occupants of an old farm ("In the Home Stretch") fully expect to find apple and other fruit trees that they can continue to tend, and there are apple trees growing on the narrator's side of a stone wall in "Mending Wall." Everywhere in "New Hampshire" (lines 159–162), one can find unsprayed apple trees (like those that grew up from "A Girl's Garden") whose fruit is perfect for cider. Apple blossom petals that inevitably fall into a garden from the nearby orchard become free fertilizer ("Putting in the Seed"). When the young boy who is "Not of School Age" wants a snack, he eats an apple. "The Man in the Tree" looked down from an apple tree.[14] When John, the incompetent farmer in "The House-keeper," heaved his hoe into the air in frustration, where did it land? In an apple tree.[15]

A farmer has many reasons to worry about apples. Will the trees survive the winter with its intense cold, unseasonable warmth or gnawing animals ("Good-by and Keep Cold," "A Winter Eden")? Will the blossoms be killed by frost, ruining the harvest before it can even set fruit ("Peril of Hope")? Will the fruit fall prey to insects or disease ("The Gold Hesperidee") or midnight raids by porcupines? The risks taken on with the planting of an orchard hang over farmers for as long as they are farming, yet they keep hoping for apples. About his farm in Franconia, New Hampshire, Frost wrote, "Apples are not a success where the winter temperature sometimes drops to 40 below," yet he still tried: "Irma and I and Carol captured about forty young wild apple trees ... and are setting out an orchard."[16]

Concerning apples, one might expect repeated references to the forbidden fruit, but Frost used apples explicitly in that image only twice in his poems. The first required just two lines in "Unharvested": "For there had been an apple fall / As complete as the apple had given man." The second, in "Kitty Hawk," is flippant in its language and brevity: "Pulpiteers will censure / Our instinctive venture / Into what they call / The material / When we took that fall / From the apple tree." In his notebooks, Frost imagines that Eve's apple was a "rotten" city apple, the kind eaten by people who hadn't "lived in the country and seen apples as they should be."[17] Original sin was much less important than the quality of a good apple.

But as Frost describes country apples in detail, he shows us that raising apples is far from easy and that the farm orchard is far from Eden. A young apple tree ("The Gold Hesperidee"): "Began to blossom at the age of five; / And after having entertained the bee, / And cast its flowers and all the stems but three, / It set itself to keep those three alive." As in "Pod of the Milkweed," many blossoms yielded few fruit (only three apples on an entire tree, only one milkweed pod from dozens of flowers), an apparent waste of effort that is briefly noted for the apples but explored in detail for milkweed pods. But then it gets worse: the three apples disappear just when young "Square Hale" expects them to be ready to eat. Whether aborted or stolen, this injustice leads Frost into biblical analogies and lessons, but ultimately acceptance of the inevitable, as at the end of "Good-by and Keep Cold": "But something has to be left to God." Farmers have to be ready to deal with loss.

They also have to deal with bounty. The farmer in "After Apple-Picking" is exhausted: "For I have had too much / Of apple-picking: I am overtired / Of the great harvest I myself desired. / There were ten thousand thousand fruit to touch, / Cherish in hand, lift down and not let fall." He is also feeling some guilt from having stopped picking before every last apple was off the tree, without every barrel full, and with so many apples in the "cider-apple heap" where they don't require careful transport to the cellar. After a spring and summer of worrying about apples but not having any, the fruit ripens with a sudden rush and demands to be picked all at once. The harvests of all crops work this way, and we inevitably alternate between "seasons of want and plenty."[18] Store the apples, get the hay into the barn, gather the nuts, harvest the corn, can the vegetables—there seems to be no end to it when only a little while earlier there was no certainty of a beginning. Just as a failed harvest seems unfair, so does a bumper crop.

The farmer is ready for sleep after apple picking ("The scent of apples: I am drowsing off"), so tired that he is unsure whether to hibernate like a woodchuck or sleep through winter like a farmer: "This sleep of mine, whatever sleep it is. / Were he not gone, / The woodchuck could say whether it's like his / Long sleep, as I describe its coming on, / Or just some human sleep." As the poem wonders about sleep, it has gone well past apple picking into the wider world of human endeavor and endurance. Thus does a seemingly simple fruit lead to explorations of being human.

It should come as no surprise that Frost considered apple picking from more than one point of view. He goes from being the responsible "ant" that cossets all its apples to being the wastrel "grasshopper" that celebrates an entire apple crop on the ground in "Unharvested." Here is an apple tree that has dropped its entire "summer load" of fruit. Frost was in a mood to celebrate the fallen apples that had been "forgotten and left" and enjoy the pleasant but trivial scent: "smelling their sweetness would be no theft."

Perhaps it was this kind of sweet scent that made "The Cow in Apple Time" so defiant of walls and dismissive of pastures. And once she tastes apples, "she'll simply go apple crazy."[19] Here, though, there is a price for defiance. No matter how much "she bellows on a knoll against the sky. / Her udder shrivels and the milk goes dry." The windfalls are tasty, but they cannot sustain her, especially if she wastes energy rambling all over the farm. The poem describes these events, real or imagined, and allows the reader to derive any number of possible lessons from this errant cow.[20]

Apples can also induce bizarre behavior in people, especially when cider is involved. Though he extolls the virtue of cider apples in "New Hampshire," a cellar full of cider leads to utter irrationality in Frost's five-scene play *The Guardeen*. At the end of the last scene, the players tie up and drag Prof. Titcombe across the ground to extinguish a fire. In "The Bonfire," dragging a coat on the ground to stop a fire is noble (even if desperate). But dragging a trussed human being along the ground to stop a fire shows how people have gone even more "apple crazy" than the cow, with a craziness born of cider, cider born of apples. Craziness, worry, disappointment, depression, discord[21]—the forbidden fruit keeps causing problems beyond the fall, yet farmers can't seem to live without them. Just be careful what you wish for with your orchard.

Apple trees do not live forever, and old apple trees come to represent decline, a common theme in Frost's observations of the decline of agriculture in New England. In "The Grindstone," the overused grindstone is outside in the winter, unlike all the other equipment. At first, its location is stated simply: "It stands beside the same old apple tree." A few lines later, though, it is "under a ruinous live apple tree," in keeping with the chain of ruin inflicted on the grindstone by men, and by the grindstone on blades. The abuse that had been done to the wheel "had gradually worn it an oblate / Spheroid that kicked and struggled in its gait, / Appearing to return me hate for hate." So the man punishes the grindstone by leaving it in the snow with no protection under the old, leafless apple tree. The tree is in decline, and so is the grindstone. Neither may be put to use again, at least not as originally intended.

What uses can be made of a dead apple tree? On an abandoned farm in an urban setting, "the apple trees [are] sent to hearthstone flame" ("A Brook in the City"). No longer tended for fruit, these apple trees die when humans cut them down for fuel. But some apple trees simply die from old age, disease, or the shade of other trees. Then the dead apple wood, either single branches or whole trees, joins a different part of the food chain. In "Ghost House," "The orchard tree has grown one copse / Of new wood and old where the woodpecker chops," and in "Directive," tall trees have shaded out an old orchard, leaving the apple trees with dead limbs (lines 26–28). Though useless for fruit production, the decaying wood feeds insects, themselves food for woodpeckers.

For Frost, apples exemplified change and contradiction: blossom to harvest, germination to death, deficit to excess, and innocence to calamity. The beauty of apples could enchant, but their bounty could bring people low. Both a mainstay and a curse, apples were a prime source for metaphors of the countryside, "saying one thing and meaning another, saying one thing in terms of another."[22]

Brooks and Streams

> Each laid on other a staying hand
> To listen ere we dared to look,
> And in the hush we joined to make
> We heard, we knew we heard the brook.
> "Going for Water"

Jay Parini pointed out that "the stream is a central metaphor in many of Frost's poems."[23] Whether as description or metaphor, when Frost wrote about farms, he often included a brook or a spring, even if only in the background. A farm simply had to have running water to be a real farm ("In the Home Stretch," line 197) and when Frost dedicated *Mountain Interval* to his wife Elinor, he wrote "that the first interval was the old farm, our brook interval."[24] A brook beside a meadow is mentioned twice in "The Tuft of Flowers," the flowers being "beside a reedy brook the scythe had bared." The farm in "The Housekeeper" is "with the brook going by below the yard." A brook can be useful in most seasons should the well run dry ("Going for Water"), but in winter, it turns to ice and is best used for recreation ("Down the Brook ... and Back"). One of Frost's best-known references to flowing water is in "The Pasture": "I'm going out to clean the pasture spring." Here, the spring is useful as a source of drinking water for livestock.

But if a farm is overtaken by a city, the result is nothing short of tragic ("A Brook in the City"). Not only is there no land remaining to farm, the brook has been driven underground: "Deep in a sewer dungeon under stone / In fetid darkness still to live and run— / And all for nothing it had ever done." The loss of the brook doesn't bother the city in the least, but it dismays the narrator who knew the brook when it was an essential water source for a farm. To farmers, the mindless encroachment of the city, the waste of a clean, useful stream, is a reason to grieve.

The sound of running water is often part of the country setting. Of the Gale River in Franconia, New Hampshire, Frost wrote, "It runs clear and broad and shallow on cobble stones with a noise more like talking than writing."[25] In "Going for Water," the pair in search of the brook is quiet enough that they can hear it flowing "in the hush we joined to make." The sounds from the flowing water, "a note" and "tinkling," induce their imaginations to envision "pearls" and "a silver blade" in the moonlight of late autumn. The gentle sounds of flowing water become jewelry.

The sounds of a brook can also overwhelm. Members of the Stark family in "The Generations of Men" do not go beyond the bend in the road: "No one went home that way. The only house / Beyond where they were was a shattered seed pod. / And below roared a brook hidden in trees, / The sound of which was silence for the place." The white noise of the monotonous roar quickly faded from notice, yet it muffled the sound of everything else, making all seem silent. But the newly-acquainted Stark cousins, man and woman, urge each other to listen as they describe what they claim to see of their relatives who once dwelt in the house that once stood above this cellar hole: "'We have seen visions—now consult the voices.'" Then they strive to decipher the loud noise of the brook. The man says:

> "I wanted to try something with the noise
> That the brook raises in the empty valley."
> ...
> "I've never listened in among the sounds
> That a brook makes in such a wild descent."

56

He has heard voices speaking from the noise of a train, and now claims to hear voices from the brook: "'I'll tell you what the voices really say.'" The woman is doubtful, but agrees to hear him out:

"I'm waiting."
        "Don't! The voices seem to say:
Call her Nausicaä, the unafraid
Of an acquaintance made adventurously."

He wants her not to fear him, and though she is unsure at first, she chooses to focus on what he claims to have heard. They quibble gently over which Stark family member's voice was speaking from the noise of the brook. Eventually they agree that they sometimes "make too much/ Of the old stock."[26] Among the accents of New England, the pronunciations of "stock" and "Stark" are often indistinguishable.[27] Thus, the sound of the family name sinks back into the white noise of the roaring brook, and their argument fades away. As differences are erased by sound, the man and woman agree to meet again. If they choose to pursue a romantic relationship and risk inbreeding (acknowledged among the Stark family earlier in the poem), the noise of the brook surrounding the ancestral cellar hole will drown out any objection.

When brooks originate in the mountains and cascade down steep slopes toward the farms below, they make a lot of noise. We can almost hear the roar when "melted mountain water led by flume" pours downhill ("The Wind and the Rain"). These mountain streams ("The Gum-Gatherer") can be so loud that "we talked like barking above the din / Of water we walked along beside."

In contrast to these roaring brooks, the stream in "Class Hymn" really is silent. Some stream channels are indeed so smooth that even fast water is not disturbed. Then it is up to someone or something else to bring sounds to the brook. The "runnel's silent rush" sets the stage for a "dreamer" to drop stones in the water so that "the stream makes music." The speed of the "runnel" quickly smooths the surface and the music can repeat whenever it receives the next stone.

Streams often alternate between flood and trickle. In "The Onset," the spring thaw brings on many changes, including small-scale floods: "And I shall see the snow all go downhill / In water of a slender April rill / That flashes tail through last year's withered brake / And dead weeds, like a disappearing snake." (A stream was also a snake in "A Serious Step

Lightly Taken.") In "Paul's Wife," Frost includes an aside about "willow whistles" being made "in April by subsiding meadow brooks." It isn't clear whether the water is subsiding after the snow has finished melting, or the ground of the meadow is subsiding under the force of spring floods. Depending on the snowpack and spring weather in any particular year, it could be either one. In spring, "Hyla brook" has sufficient water to serve as a firebreak ("The Bonfire"), but come summer, the brook shrinks and sometimes stops flowing ("Hyla Brook").

Summer decline is predictable for a brook, as is high flow in spring, but floods from storms could occur any time. A major flood can erode "whole capes caked off in slices" ("One Step Backward Taken") and hang debris on barbed wire and thorny trees or plants ("Directive"). People knew well that torrential rains could be a time "when my garden has gone down ditch" ("In Time of Cloudburst"). Sometimes one has to be resigned to the loss of soil in a flood.

In other places, though, water doesn't run off fast enough and just sits there, waterlogging the soil. If standing water can be drained off, the land will dry out more quickly and allow meadows or fields to begin growth earlier in the season. Thus Warren says of Silas, "'He said he'd come to ditch the meadow for me'" ("The Death of the Hired Man"). In this case, Warren wants the water to go "down ditch" (not with the soil, though, he hopes). Once the meadow is dry, he can produce more hay. But Silas never got the chance to do that job.

Back up on the mountain, streams start out small, running through cracks between "blocks split off the mountain mass" ("The Gum-Gatherer"), split off by something other than the liquid of the tiny stream, perhaps something that happened long ago. Here, the springs are quiet. In "The Mountain," "there's the spring, / Right on the summit, almost like a fountain." Because water flows from springs at a nearly constant rate, springs are not prone to flooding. This constancy applies to the stream in "Directive," which is really a spring, high up on the slope. The "lofty" stream, high in the hills, dependent on ground water, not precipitation, could not "rage" (flood) over its banks, a reassuring and reliable feature for any water source.

In "The Times Table," a farmer and his mare also encounter a "spring with a broken drinking glass." When his horse sighs, the farmer worries about a cascade of words that could ultimately "close a road, abandon a farm." Just such an abandoned farm and closed road are in "Directive":

"There is a house that is no more a house / Upon a farm that is no more a farm / And in a town that is no more a town." The narrator in "Directive" instructs the reader to find the drinking glass hidden under a root and partake of the cold flow of water in the stream, a source of clarity: "Drink and be whole again beyond confusion."

Mark Richardson noted how the "broken drinking glass" and "broken drinking goblet" are a link between "The Times Table" that threatens to drive people from the land and "Directive" where people have done just that, abandoning a farm.[28] There is further clear evidence of this link in Frost's notebooks. A draft of "The Times Table" includes the line: "a lilac clump by a cellar hole,"[29] wording that is strikingly similar to line 46 in "Directive": "But only a belilaced cellar hole."

The spring/brook, the broken drinking glass/goblet, and the lilacs of "The Times Table" and "Directive" connect these two phases of the story in time and flow. The narrow-minded confusion caused by the pessimistic farmer can be overcome if someone less grim than he were to find the goblet and follow the instructions (it is "under a spell so the wrong ones can't find it"). It is unclear whether the farmer or the mare actually drank from the spring in "The Times Table," but in "Directive," the person or people being addressed are offered a promise for renewal, perhaps of the abandoned property, or the deserted town, or the people who might choose to live there once more, or perhaps of nature itself as it reclaims the abandoned farm. The stream provides a form of hope, not fully defined. If only you will partake of it, you might become versed in all the country things evident in and around this stream.

In poems with flowing water, people come and go from the landscape, but the streams remain and provide some degree of security. For example, a young couple walking through the woods in "West-Running Brook" notices a brook and the unusual direction it runs[30]:

> "Fred, where is north?"
>> "North? North is there, my love.
>
> The brook runs west."
>> "West-Running Brook then call it."
> (West-Running Brook men call it to this day.)

As the poem continues, the brook becomes the couple's mutual partner: "'We've said we two. Let's change that to we three. / As you and I are married to each other, / We'll both be married to the brook.'" A nearby brook can be a dependable source of water, perhaps also a place to fish or hunt for food. For farm families far from a village and far from neighbors, a brook could be indispensible.

The couple in "West-Running Brook" notices a standing wave in the water of the brook. After the narrator describes the stream in connection with birds, pools and alders, the husband and wife reach different conclusions about whether the wave was meant for them. The wife is sure it is. The husband says it isn't, and then he pretends to abandon any consideration of his wife's image and leave the brook to her: "'It is your brook! I have no more to say.'" His wife knows that he does have more to say, and asks him to speak. He replies with a speech on "contraries," going back "long, long before we were from any creature," describing "the stream of everything that runs away." But there is still more. After proclaiming multiple profound qualities for running water, he brings his focus back to this brook and to them, and they reclaim the brook and its name: "'It is most us.'"

The brook was near enough to their farm that they would always have it. This day, the brook became part of their marriage vows, a promise for a good life on their good farm, connected to a source that replenishes all that flows away, an implication of permanence that contrasts with the intermittent flow in "Hyla Brook." The literal wave "standing off this jut of shore" embraced the couple in a process more subtle than that of the figurative wave in "Two Look at Two" (lines 40–42), but the wave still represented love of the couple for the farm, with its stream, and love of the farm for them.[31] Frost used this simple brook to generate a range of metaphors about the ways that people and places bond with one another in the countryside. "West-Running Brook" may be his finest tribute to the value and significance of streams, especially those whose flow is unfettered.

Scythe, Meadow and Barn

> There were three in the meadow by the brook
> Gathering up windrows, piling cocks of hay
> "The Code"

Frost was in his teens when he learned how to mow meadows for hay. Haying was so time-consuming that farmers, farmhands and farm

Farming

families had to temporarily abandon other tasks: "they turned from everything to hay" ("From Plane to Plane").[32] Among things related to agriculture, Frost wrote about haying more than anything else except "farms" in general and orchards in particular. Few subjects led Frost to more contradictions and contrasts than making hay.

Frost considered the whispering of a scythe to be special somehow, perhaps because of the efficiency of cutting so much with one stroke with so little sound. "Mowing" is one of Frost's best-known early poems, and whispering was key: "There was never a sound beside the wood but one, / And that was my long scythe whispering to the ground. / What was it it whispered? I knew not well myself; / Perhaps it was something about the heat of the sun, / Something, perhaps, about the lack of sound— / And that was why it whispered and did not speak." "Whispered" appears again in the last line, and "whispering" is in line 32 of "The Tuft of Flowers" further on in *A Boy's Will*. He could hardly get enough of it. "Hiss" and "hissing" were for the wind and snow, while whispering was reserved for the scythe. Tim Kendall explores this wonderfully enigmatic sound at length.[33]

Frost said, "My favorite implements (after the pen) are the axe and the scythe, both of which besides being tools of peace have also been weapons of war."[34] With his penchant for contradiction and multiple viewpoints, Frost was fascinated by the awful contradictions of the scythe.

The curve of the scythe was one of the features that made it special. In his notebooks, Frost picked out one shape in particular: "Curl most significant thing in nature. Things return upon themselves."[35] The blade of the scythe is not circular and doesn't completely return upon itself, but the mower returns the curved blade repeatedly against the meadow grass, the scythe whispering again and again. Since its timeless invention, the curve of the scythe blade has brought the cut stems together and initiated the process of gathering the hay ("The scythe concaves the hollow").[36] Within the cycle of the seasons, within the phases of a curved, crescent moon, the scythe harvests in summer what is needed in winter. The curl or curve of the blade is essential.[37]

In sharp contrast, the grinding of a scythe blade generates multiple levels of discord in "The Grindstone." Having worn its wheel out of round, the narrator complains about the grindstone's resistance to his turning. Then the two men can't agree on how fast to run the wheel, how hard to press the blade, or when to stop: "Mightn't we make it worse instead of better? / I was for leaving something for the whetter. / What if it wasn't all it should be? I'd / Be satisfied if he'd be satisfied." Like the oblate wheel and the disagreeing men, the poem comes to an awkward stop, the last rhyme strained and perhaps not "all it should be." And if the blade is not "all it should be," the mowing might not be so efficient or satisfying next time. But neither the memory nor anticipation of that satisfaction brings any agreement to the sharpening.

Haying by hand was not easy. The work was tedious, rain could ruin the hay, and the farmer had to judge whether the hay had dried properly. Hay that was too wet would rot. Rotten hay was useless as animal feed, and rotting hay could reach such a high temperature (unlike "The Wood-Pile") that it might ignite and burn down the barn.[38] John, the farmer in "The Housekeeper," neglected his hay: "He's got hay down that's been rained on three times." Left in the field that way, the hay is worse than useless because it smothers the plants below it and endangers later cuttings. A competent farmer wouldn't waste a hay crop. John should have known better and should have done better. Years earlier, perhaps he would have done better, but time takes its toll on those for whom farming is "spiritually crippling."[39]

Frost used haying by competent farmers and farm hands to explore social attitudes and interactions in "The Code." One farmer should trust another, especially if that farmer had grown up farming. There is no need to point out the obvious. "'The hand that knows his business won't be told/ To do work better or faster—those two things.'"

When someone violates the code, they can expect a reaction, sometimes simple, sometimes harsh. Novices and impatient folks learn or are reminded the hard way. After a farm hand used a load of hay to bury a farmer who had stated the obvious, he is asked to reflect on his potentially lethal response:

> "Weren't you relieved to find he wasn't dead?"
> "No! and yet I don't know—it's hard to say.
> I went about to kill him fair enough."
> "You took an awkward way. Did he discharge you?"
> "Discharge me? No! He knew I did just right."

In retrospect, the code was obvious to both parties, a portion of the unwritten rules of everyday life. Other codes appear in other poems. In "A Time to Talk," a person doesn't shout at a passing neighbor. Instead, one takes the time to stop working, walk out to the road and talk in a normal voice. When gardening, though, "men work alone, the lots plowed far apart" and they remain silent ("The Strong Are Saying Nothing"). That's just how it's done.

Making hay, essential and exhausting work, brings the code into play as much as any activity on a farm. A single farmer can make hay, as Frost's narrator was doing by himself in "Mowing." Help made the task go more quickly, but any farmer or farm hand knew full well how to do the whole thing alone. He (they were nearly all men) didn't need to be told. The narrator in "The Tuft of Flowers" heads out to the meadow alone to turn the hay that another man had cut earlier:

> But he had gone his way, the grass all mown,
> And I must be, as he had been—alone,
>
> "As all must be," I said within my heart,
> "Whether they work together or apart."

Each man was doing his part of the haying, but one after the other as the process required (one to cut the hay early on a dewy morning, the other to turn it later so it dries). The mower had departed and was not even in earshot when the narrator arrived. But the mower had left a tuft of flowers: "A leaping tongue of bloom the scythe had spared/ Beside a reedy brook the scythe had bared." The mower had been deliberate and even counter-productive in mowing the reeds and leaving the flowers, as Frost explained in a letter to Louis Untermeyer: "Call your attention to the fact that the author of A Tuft of Flowers forestalled the cynic by having the mower mow the reeds which are worse forage than butterfly weed: item that it is the country custom to mow everything."[40]

The narrator in "The Tuft of Flowers" presumes, at first, that the mower had thought of nothing but himself when he left the flowers:

> The mower in the dew had loved them thus,
> By leaving them to flourish, not for us,
>
> Nor yet to draw one thought of ours to him,
> But from sheer morning gladness at the brim.

Yet the narrator is delighted to find the flowers, and is glad to share them with a butterfly. He imagines, then, that he can hear the whispering of the mower's scythe:

> And feel a spirit kindred to my own;
> So that henceforth I worked no more alone;

Stopping by Woods

...

"Men work together," I told him from the heart,
"Whether they work together or apart."

The code has been honored and fulfilled, this time beyond expectation. Nothing is said, but much is understood. It is not about the talking—it is all about the doing.

Of course, the code is not always that simple. In "Mowing," the felling of the orchises is a sign of accomplishment, but in "Rose Pogonias," the sparing of blooming orchises is a cause for celebration (see "Subduing the Land"). As a farmer, Frost was faced with this choice every year. Bring in the hay and the cows won't starve next winter, but leave some flowers and we can enjoy the summer. There is a way to have both hay and blossoms, but it comes with a risk. If the farmer delays mowing until the meadow is no longer "so confused with flowers," a hay crop can still be cut—unless the weather turns wet and prevents haying for the rest of the season. Are the flowers worth the risk? The mindscape becomes as much of a patchwork of contrasts as the landscape.

Frost reveled in such complexities. In a letter to John Bartlett, Frost wrote, "Could a man as farmer mow for weeds as poet he calls buttercups and daisies? Chew it over." Robert Faggen examined this "struggle for life" at length, quoting a book by Grant Allen that mentioned "buttercup stems" and "daisies."[41] Frost had read Allen's book years earlier, and it was almost certainly the source of his wording in the letter.

It is not just the pretty plants that are endangered by the scythe. Though spared by the cutting bar, a nest of birds is still imperiled by exposure in the mown field ("The Exposed Nest"). While the scythe in "Mowing" only "scared a bright green snake" (which presumably slithered away unharmed), one can imagine how many animals were not missed but sliced or chewed up by mowing, whether manual or mechanized. How much wildlife suffered so livestock could eat in winter?

After the scythe has done its job and after the hay wagons "brush the mow with the summer load" ("The Need of Being Versed in Country Things"),[42] the mown meadow becomes a dramatically different place. All that remains is a "headless aftermath" of stubble ("A Late Walk"), stubble that brings to mind "the memory of one absent" ("Waiting") and that fosters lament as the snow comes on ("Desert Places"). Any sense of accomplishment has vanished with the winds of seasonal change, and the theme in "Desert Places" becomes despair as the snow buries all evidence of the intense activity of haying: "A blanker whiteness of benighted snow/ With no expression, nothing to express." With a rhyme scheme not quite as interconnected as in "Stopping by Woods on a Snowy Evening," but with longer phrases that dwell on emptiness, the stubble in "Desert Places" comes to represent longing instead of harvest. As grim as stubble is, the narrator can sink even further and "scare myself with my own desert places" watching the stubble sink below the snow. Frost's tendency toward depression, well documented in Jay Parini's biography, was worst when he was inactive, but much less serious when he was working. In poems about haying, the inactive, dormant fields produce despair, even in the company of other people, while the activity of mowing is more positive, even when faced with difficult choices of flowers versus hay, and even when someone is forced to mow alone. In many ways, the annual cycle of haying was a parallel of Frost's own cycle of mood.

Feeding the Cows

Haying made it possible to feed livestock in those seasons when pastures were covered with snow or mud. The livestock that mattered most to Frost were cows ("I must not be gone from my cows very long").[43] Frost took an unconventional approach to dairying. A sign on the barn at Frost's farm in Franconia, New Hampshire, claims that Frost trained his cows to be milked at noon and midnight in keeping with his typical day.[44] At least sometimes, his approach worked: "We had two cows come in this week, so that we are swimming in milk already." In these productive times, Frost and his children named the milk cows fresh each day so that the milk would be fresh.[45]

But what became of the calves? The calf in "The Pasture" is fetched away from its mother so that the mother can be milked: "I'm going out to fetch the little calf / That's standing by the mother. It's so young / It totters when she licks it with her tongue." Robert Hass argued that fetching the calf is a sign that the calf is failing somehow because "it totters." Frost is retrieving the calf, Hass says, because the calf needs help.[46] But what is the reality of calves on a small farm in New England? First, all newborn calves totter when their half-ton mother licks them. It's a big tongue against a small body. Second, the farmer wants to collect milk from the mother. If he doesn't fetch the calf, the calf will drink the milk. The calf can drink formula instead, and the farmer can milk the mother cow for the family and perhaps for trade or sale (though Frost was sure that his cow noticed she is being milked by a human rather than feeding her calf).[47] Separating the calf from its mother is merely part of dairying.

But Hass correctly identified a farm family's foreboding about calves. In his notebooks, Frost imagines himself as a calf being taken to market, probably never to return to his mother or his farm.[48] The fate of calves at a market never appears in his poems, but it does in his letters. Frost and his children never named the calves "for fear of learning to love what must soon be slaughtered."[49] The realities of an agricultural life could be stark.

Calves that remained on the farm were put to use. Male calves could become oxen and provide motive power for the farmer. A local resident in "The Mountain" is driving his oxen so slowly that a visitor thinks, "It seemed no harm to stop him altogether." Their subsequent conversation tells a story about the mountain, and about the people who live around the mountain but rarely climb it, at least not all the way to the top. The slow oxen are a small but essential part of this detailed narrative about the countryside.

Female calves on the farm would be raised for years of dairying. While most cows led mundane, repetitive lives, Frost imagined a few that didn't. One highly unconventional cow in "A Cow in Apple Time" eats apples instead of grass, escapes over walls and stops giving milk. With cows like that, it isn't surprising that some farmers would give up on dairying. As the narrator points out in "Mending Wall," the resetting of stones has nothing to do with livestock because "here there are no cows."

In contrast, Frost turned fanciful about cows in his last collection of poems, *In the Clearing*. In "Lines Written in Dejection on the Eve of Great Success," the narrator imagines that one of his cows had participated in a nursery rhyme: "I once had a cow that jumped over the moon." A few lines later, he claims, "That was back in the days of my godmother Goose" even though the rhyme is not from Mother Goose. No matter—the clever reworking of the well-known rhyme evolves into a public fight between the cow and the farmer, and then escalates into a final comment on affixing blame for war. The ending is a long way from the farm, but distant wars inevitably encroach on farms and farmers.

The nursery rhyme theme continues in the next poem, "The Milky

Way Is a Cowpath," in which one character is to "believe it was the cow's / That overshot the moon." The last stanza returns to Earth with a practical summary of Frost's experience as a farmer, raising multiple generations of poultry and dairy cattle "for what they didn't earn." Frost probably lost far more money as a farmer than he ever earned, partly because, as he freely admitted, he was not a particularly good farmer.[50] But his income from farming was far less important to him that the opportunity to live on a farm in the countryside. A man of words and ideas, sounds and sense, it was the idea of farming more than the practice that drew him to it. In his preface to the poetry of *This Is My Best*, Frost said that his choice of poems from *A Boy's Will* and *North of Boston*, "brings out my inclination to country occupations."[51] The ultimate "country occupation" was farming, and throughout his life, whenever he could, he used farming, his own or that of others, to immerse himself in the countryside and become a country poet.

Frost, and every other farmer in New England, had to make the right choices if they were to have any chance of success. Some choices could be made after calm contemplation, like the traveller in "The Road Not Taken."[52] But many other choices were forced on farmers by the relentless march of seasonal change. Seeds planted too early would freeze. Seeds planted too late wouldn't have time to mature. Frost and other farmers had to determine when the time was right ("Putting in the Seed")—each year might be a little different. They also knew that firewood had to be split in spring so that it could dry in time for winter ("Two Tramps in Mud Time"); green wood didn't burn well in the stove. Nearly every facet of farm life depended on the seasons of the year. In the next chapter, we will see that farmers were not alone in their dependence on seasonal change.

Seasons

"Brush the mow
with the summer load"

Year after year, the cycle of seasonal change repeats nearly everywhere on Earth. In New England, spring, summer and autumn constitute the annual growing season, but each part of the growing season requires different work for farm families. No poem describes the seasonal changes in farm life better than "A Hundred Collars." The character Lafe notes the change in activity he sees as he makes his rounds collecting subscription dues for a newspaper:

> I like to find folks getting out in spring,
> Raking the dooryard, working near the house.
> Later they get out further in the fields.
> Everything's shut sometimes except the barn;
> The family's all away in some back meadow.
> There's a hay load a-coming—when it comes.
> And later still they all get driven in:
> The fields are stripped to the lawn, the garden patches
> Stripped to bare ground, the maple trees
> To whips and poles. There's nobody about.
> The chimney, though, keeps up a good brisk smoking.

All living things in New England, human and otherwise, must cope with seasonal change. Each year, there are periods of plenty, times of scarcity, and conditions that can kill. Ecological succession surges during the growing season and pauses every winter. Seasons dictate the growth, behavior and life cycles of organisms, and the planting, tending and harvesting by farmers. New England even has a fifth unofficial season: mud time. Each seasonal transition is predictable (up to a point) and requires some level of preparation.

Seasons

More than 180 of Frost's poems mention, or are set in, one or more seasons of the year, and in many of these poems, seasons play a key role. In about forty poems, Frost starts in one season and then switches to another, though not always in chronological order ("The Need of Being Versed in Country Things" is one of these. The first mention of a season is "the summer load" of hay, but the poem shifts to phoebes tending their nest and lilacs renewing their leaves, both of which begin in spring). In about a dozen cases, he returns to the first season or moves on to a third. The season might have to be inferred from the events in the poem (the type of flower blooming, the kind of farm work going on, the form of precipitation), but usually, Frost identifies which season it is.

Few of these poems are limited just to a description of seasonal change. As Nina Baym pointed out, "seasonal imagery can be used for many purposes." For Frost, the conditions and events of the seasons usually set the stage, or became metaphors, for something else (and the shorter the poem, the darker its mood tends to be).[1] The seasons themselves and the images they inspire are unavoidable components of the New England environment.

A handful of poems address seasonal change in general. In "Last Word of a Bluebird," a poem "as told to a child," the year-round resident crow explains the autumn departure and winter absence of the bluebird. The poem is heavily anthropomorphic but otherwise accurate: birds do migrate with the seasons, and when the cold passes (as it always does) "perhaps" the birds will return in spring (the crow doesn't make an absolute promise to a child that the birds will survive).

Frost describes several ways that the moods of humans change in the face of seasons, especially the seemingly endless winters of New England. "There Are Roughly Zones" starts with the inevitable talk about the weather ("We sit indoors and talk of the cold outside") and the bad luck of an intense cold snap, when the wind increases while the temperature drops to "so many below" (lines 15–17). But this farm family also acknowledges that they might have doomed their young peach tree by trying to grow it so far north. Was this hubris in the face of New England winters?[2] They won't know until spring arrives: "The tree has no leaves and may never have them again. / We must wait till some months hence in the spring to know."

In "The Onset," the narrator bemoans the "hissing on the yet uncovered ground" as the wind blows snow over the dead, susurrant leaves. He describes himself as someone who, in winter: "Gives up his errand, and lets death descend / Upon him where he is, with nothing done / To evil, no important triumph won, / More than if life had never been begun." The narrator's first reaction to the onset of winter is despondent regret about all that has not been accomplished, and now it is too late as we watch winter "death descend." The mood is as dark as that in "Desert Places."

But then the poem takes a radical change in direction, promising the spring overthrow of snow and ice and the failure of death to prevent renewal:

> Yet all the precedent is on my side:
> I know that winter death has never tried
> The earth but it has failed:
> ...
> Nothing will be left white but here a birch,
> And there a clump of houses with a church.

A similar sequence appears with even greater contrast in Frost's notebooks, in which he compares being "stepped on and crushed flat by the weight of winter" to "summer when it had its season / Of dance."[3] The inevitability of seasonal change makes it safe to be optimistic about the melting of snow in spring. It happens every year. With that hope in mind, Frost reminds us that the crushing weight of winter is not permanent. There is always death in winter, but there is also always new life in spring. There will be remnants and reminders of one season in another, of course, with white birch trees and white buildings—things natural and things human—lingering in the summer. It is Frost's version of yin and yang, things cycling together with just a little bit of each contained in the other. And from the reality of the seasons, Frost can pursue more profound questions of human experience, such as evil, regret and death. The seasonal cycle is a useful stage for any number of poetic explorations.

Frost wrote in his notebooks that "man begins where summer leaves off,"[4] so this chapter will examine each season in turn, ending with the season when Frost said we begin. But first, we will consider the inevitable but unpredictable surprises of unseasonable events.

Surprising Weather

As seasons change, the duration of daylight hours is completely predictable, but the weather is much less so. A.J. Herbertson summed it up succinctly (though without much punctuation): "Climate is what on average we may expect weather is what we actually get."[5] Living things in New England (or anywhere, for that matter) have to be able to tolerate not just the average conditions but also the extremes and the unexpected. While living in Franconia, New Hampshire, Frost experienced "the freezing of one bitter sky in mid–June" in which he lost "all our seed and a month's growth" including his "favorite tomato." In response to excessive rain, he wrote, "We easily fall into bitter apostrophe when the weather goes wrong."[6] Unseasonable events were frequent and sometimes maddening intrusions into his everyday life, so it is not surprising that such events should appear in several of Frost's poems.

In the transitional season of spring, things are not always spring-like, even within a single day. "Two Tramps in Mud Time" is set in April, but sunshine makes it feel like May, while clouds turn it into March. The clouds release a few flakes of snow, revealing that "winter was only playing possum."

In "Our Singing Strength," we see how a multispecies flock of birds copes with a substantial late-season snowfall: "Now was seen how these liked belated snow.... They could find nothing open but the road." The only place not obstructed by snow is the road on which the drover (the narrator) is traveling; the road retains heat from previous sunny days and can melt the snow, but the surrounding plants have cooled too much and the snow clings. The birds fly off the road to avoid the cart, but snowy fields and snowy trees force them back to the "open" road. They continually fly farther along the road in the direction the drover is going because they can't seem to figure out that they could return to the road behind him and escape his advance: "One such storm in a lifetime couldn't teach them / That back behind pursuit it couldn't reach them; / None flew behind me to be left alone." The flock keeps moving, slowly driven down the open road, singing as they go. The drover imagines that, even under the strain of slow pursuit, their songs have the collective power, gathered by an accident of weather, to bring on the growth of spring, to "sing the wild flowers up from root and seed." The poem takes the observation of an unusual, unseasonable event and turns it into a magical experience. The birds can, just with their voices, charm the plants up from the ground. The beauty of their songs will accompany the beauty of the flowers.

In the depth of winter, a warm day can set things free. Wildlife emerge on a sunny day that turns an alder swamp into a garden ("A Winter Eden"). Some of the animals may feed on the bark of trees, but the warmth lasts only a short time and the damage will be slight. Inanimate objects can be freed as well. The right combination of sun and snow ("A Hillside Thaw") can turn a slope into a cascade of "ten million silver lizards out of snow!"

But to a farmer, unseasonable weather can be a threat. "A night of frost" at the wrong time, in the midst of the peak of the "flowery burst," can kill the blossoms in an orchard, leading to a fruitless summer ("Peril of Hope"). At the other extreme, premature warming in winter ("Good-by and Keep Cold") can damage or kill a tree because of water loss above ground that their roots cannot replace from frozen soil[7]: "No orchard's the worse for the wintriest storm; / But one thing about it, it mustn't get warm."

Frost's poetic characters in "The Mountain" consider at length the paradox of unseasonable temperatures. A spring that emerges high on the slope seems to defy the season, staying cold in summer and warm in winter: "Warm in December, cold in June, you say?" Yet the poem is describing no more than the thermal inertia of water; it heats and cools slowly, the source well insulated deep underground, and lags behind the season. And the characters in the poem say just that: "I don't suppose the water's changed at all. / You and I know enough to know it's warm / Compared with cold, and cold compared with warm. / But all the fun's in how you say a thing."

The temperature of the spring water changes little or not at all with the season, and just feels warm or cold in contrast to the temperature of each season (Robert Faggen points this out in his lengthy exploration of the poem). Human sensory perception is an important part of the story[8] and it triggers the imagination, the joy of "how you say a thing."

Frost knew that seasonal change was inevitable, but he also knew that there could be surprises. A cold snap, a warm spell, or a spring that refused to change were familiar things in unfamiliar times or places. In his notebooks, Frost noted how poetry took advantage of such incongruities: "All poetry does is try to catch you off your guard with reminders of old sights and sounds."[9] Few things catch people off guard more significantly than extreme or unexpected weather, events from "old" seasons that we thought were over.

Winter

> We sit indoors and talk of the cold outside.
> "There Are Roughly Zones"

In New England, winter is the season that, in its own right, is most likely to be lethal. Living things can freeze to death. As "the cold creeps as the fire dies at length" and "drifts are piled" against the house and barn, the narrator in "Storm Fear," one parent of a three-member family, worries about their ability to survive the storm on their own: "And my heart owns a doubt / Whether 'tis in us to arise with day / And save ourselves unaided." People and animals can get lost in storms. Frost's characters face the challenges of a blizzard briefly in "Willful Homing" and at greater length in the narrative poem "Snow." For the man caught in a nighttime blizzard in "Willful Homing," "It is getting ... time he drew to a house," but in the end, his ability to "come to a door" is uncertain: "He may fumble wide of the knob a yard or more" and end up "a little late" in joining those who are concerned about his fate. But missing a knob by "a yard or more" could mean missing the house altogether in blizzard conditions. "A little late" might here be a euphemism for "dead."

In "Snow," the storm is raging, but still the character Meserve insists on taking his horses home, despite the invitation of Helen and Fred Cole to stay at their house, and even against the advice from his wife over the telephone: "'My dear, I'm coming just the same.'" The Coles argue about stopping him, and either can't or won't. Meserve gradually convinces himself to leave because it is downhill to his home, because conditions really aren't that bad, and finally because of his manhood: "'Well, there's—the storm. That says I must go on. / That wants me as a war might if it came. / Ask any man.'" Then he gathers his horses and heads home, leaving the Coles to fret about his fate in the storm, feeling sure that he has died and unsure whether they are to blame. In the end, Meserve gets home with the horses (confirmed by telephone: "'Hello, Meserve. You're there then!— and your wife? / Good!'") and everything is fine—except the bruised psyches of the Coles. Winter, with its opaque snowstorms, provides Frost with a transparent window into anguish, indecision and guilt. The snow has taken its toll.

Storms can be strong enough to test the strength of houses and barns, driving snow against the "lower-chamber window" ("Storm Fear"), or when "every gust... / Is a threat to the house" ("There Are Roughly Zones"). Shelter is a necessity in winter storms, yet the wind entices the inhabitants of shelters to come outside ("Storm Fear"; "Wind and Window Flower"). In the end, the ferocity of the weather makes the invitation easy to resist. In "Winter Winds" and "An Old Man's Winter Night," Frost recommends sleeping inside one's shelter as a way to cope with the cold and dark, whether of winter, or dementia, or both.

Gripped by the long winter, it is not surprising that people welcome any sign of the end of it. Frost's brief ode "To the Thawing Wind" asks the warm rain not only to melt the snow and ice, but also to "melt the glass and leave the sticks / Like a hermit's crucifix." Is the glass too much like ice? Does the hermit seek a religious conversion in spring? He goes on: "Burst into my narrow stall; / Swing the picture on the wall; / Run the rattling pages o'er; / Scatter poems on the floor; / Turn the poet out the door." The confinement of winter has gotten personal. The poet needs to escape, at nearly any cost, even the loss of his poems. Make it end! Let me out!

However, winter is not all about fear and longing, as Frost elegantly describes in "Dust of Snow":

> The way a crow
> Shook down on me
> The dust of snow
> From a hemlock tree
>
> Has given my heart
> A change of mood
> And saved some part
> Of a day I had rued.

The crow, the tree, and a dusting of snow all intersect to relieve the burden of that winter day. "The way" it happened mattered to the narrator, while other living things serve as essential parts of the process. He might not be able to find relief from winter on his own, but snow, that inevitable product of winter cold, can combine with the flora and fauna of the season to do the trick. In eight short, deceptively simple lines, Frost relieves the grip of winter.

The snowy landscape also provided Frost with an opportunity for slapstick. "Brown's Descent" imagines a farm so steep that Brown slides, lit lantern in hand, for two miles from his home to the bottom of the mountain. "Walls were all buried, trees were few" so there was nothing to stop him from sliding down the slope of ice. Neighbors who observe his descent are thrilled by the "signals" of light woven by his wildly waving lantern on the way down—somehow, he never loses his grip on his light. When he finally comes to a stop at the base of the slope, Brown the "Yankee" is stoical: "'Well—I—be—' that was all he said, / As standing in the river road / He looked back up the slippery slope / (Two miles it was) to his abode." Rather than waiting "Until the January thaw" (too far in the future, too unpredictable), Brown "took the long way home/ By road, a matter of several miles." "Brown's Descent" is one of the most literary pratfalls in history.

In several poems, Frost includes the winter setting of a poem even though, on the surface, it seems to play no part. Winter appears in passing in the first and fifth stanzas of "A Blue Ribbon at Amesbury," but is absent in the other twelve. Why mention it at all? Frost had probably learned from his years of raising laying hens that cold could damage the comb and wattle of a chicken, making it unsuitable for showing at a fair.[10] But in this poem, here is a champion hen that has defied winter, "an almost perfect bird" with "her coral comb." These blue-ribbon qualities in winter are even more impressive than a summer victory.

Why bother mentioning snow in "The Middletown Murder" when the main topics are adultery, revenge and country justice? Maybe Walt's attempted escape is slowed by the slippery snow, making Jack's aim that much more accurate. Maybe the "dirt and snow" together suggest to the reader a more vivid contrast with the spilled blood. These are details, to be sure, but they enrich the story.

According to Natalie Bober, Frost first encountered winter ice in Massachusetts after his family moved from San Francisco. A thimble he had filled with water froze on a windowsill, and he and his sister put the ice on the hot stove and watched it dance as it melted. Frost used that image in his preface *The Figure a Poem Makes*: "Like a piece of ice on a hot stove the poem must ride on its own melting."[11] Winter ice generated a metaphor for poetic quality.

Outside the house, we find ice forming and melting, night and day, in several poems. The effect ranged from subtle to spectacular. Icicles stay frozen in place on the eaves of a house at night ("A Winter's Night"; "An Old Man's Winter Night"). In the latter poem, the narrator says that the old man "consigned to the moon" the task of keeping "his snow upon the roof, / His icicles along the wall to keep." Keeping the icicles frozen in place on a moonlit night causes less disturbance than daylight would to a mind whose memory is fading. In "Beyond Words," the collection of icicles on the eaves is an "armory of hate," but it's an "armory" of ice that can't last forever: "You wait!" Eventually, the sun will break the icicles free. This inevitable melting will provide the narrator with a satisfying seasonal vindication (until the next winter inevitably allows the icicles to form yet again).

Just as sunlight melts icicles, it can melt snow into midday rivulets ("A Hillside Thaw"). They don't last for long, though, and the nocturnal moon again turns things solid. "The sun's a wizard / By all I can tell; but so's the moon a witch." After moonrise, "the swarm was turned to rock" in the cold.

Up on the mountain ("The Mountain"), the spring that flows all year produces ice in winter: "'One of the great sights going is to see / It steam in winter like an ox's breath, / Until the bushes all along its banks / Are inch-deep with the frosty spines and bristles— / You know the kind. Then let the sun shine on it!'" The sun makes the ice a chandelier of reflection and refraction. Frost leaves unsaid (but probably understood) that if the sun lingers long enough, the ice will melt back into the spring.

The ice definitely melts, cracks and falls from the bent "Birches," as Frost admits (feigning lack of intention) in his truthful explanation of the bent groves of small white trees:

> Loaded with ice a sunny winter morning
> After a rain. They click upon themselves
> As the breeze rises, and turn many-colored
> As the stir cracks and crazes their enamel.
> Soon the sun's warmth makes them shed crystal shells
> Shattering and avalanching on the snow crust—
> Such heaps of broken glass to sweep away
> You'd think the inner dome of heaven had fallen.

The narrator goes on to claim that he prefers to explain the bending of birches by the swinging by small boys—and perhaps small girls as well in "Wild Grapes." But he clearly delights in the visual effects of the ice.

In "Birches" and "To the Thawing Wind," the ice-glass metaphor reaches for something celestial. If only "the Thawing Wind" could melt the glass along with the ice, it would leave a "hermit's crucifix" of the window frame. The ice from the birches is from "heaven" and the narrator in "Birches" would like to climb a birch tree "*toward* heaven." What is up there, anyway? The birch would bend long before the swinger could find out, and no matter how warm the wind, it will not melt glass. Glistening ice and shiny glass inspire hope that remains unfulfilled.

In another poem ("After Apple-Picking") there is a window actually made of ice: "I cannot rub the strangeness from my sight / I got from looking through a pane of glass / I skimmed this morning from the drinking trough / And held against the world of hoary grass. / It melted, and I let it fall and break." This ice does not sparkle or delight. Instead, it distorts the farmer's view and leads him to a slumber made restless by dreams of endless apples.

The ice in "After Apple-Picking" foretells the coming of winter, but ice can also linger into spring ("Two Tramps in Mud Time"): "The lurking frost in the earth beneath / That will steal forth after the sun is set / And show on the water its crystal teeth." Shiny, glittering, slippery and sharp, Frost presented ice in its many moods.

As winter replaces autumn, Frost notes the decline of plants and animals in the cold and snow. Winter has meant the demise of some animals along with the leaves, including "My Butterfly" whose broken wing was among the leaves under the eaves: "It seemed God let thee flutter from His gentle clasp" ending "that reckless zephyr fling ... of thy dye-dusty wing!"

Many birds survive the end of autumn by migrating south before winter, like the bluebird in "Last Word of a Bluebird." The summer bird that sang in the tree "with an angelic gift" has, in "Looking for a Sunset Bird in Winter," departed for a warmer climate, leaving behind only a single dead leaf.

Other birds remain in New England in winter, of course, but they usually travel in flocks. In "A Winter Eden," competition for mates gives way to the collective search for food: "So near to paradise all pairing ends: / Here loveless birds now flock as winter friends." In "Winter Ownership," a flock appears out of nowhere: "A sudden flight / Of tiniest birds goes by like a charge of shot." The "small bird" in "The Wood-Pile" is agitated because it is alone, away from its flock. The bird doesn't sing, but it does its best to fly away from approaching danger, and to stay hidden. But it is impossible to do both. I agree with Robert Faggen's inference that the bird in "The Wood-Pile" is "probably a white-tailed junco." Northern juncos have conspicuous white feathers on the edges of their tails and typically gather in small flocks in the winter.[12]

Much of the time in winter, animals are quiet, sometimes very quiet.

Stopping by Woods

The snow in "Desert Places" appears to have blanketed the farm and woods so thoroughly that "all animals are smothered in their lairs." Frost knew that snow did not really smother animals in winter, but the fresh snowfall had indeed smothered their tracks and made it seem as though all the animals had vanished. If they weren't dead, where were they?

On a warm day in winter, however, the animals become obvious. In "A Winter Eden," a sunny day briefly releases birds and rabbits from the embrace of winter. But were they fooled into thinking winter was over, especially the rabbits emerging from safe dens? Are they at risk? We ask this because "To a Moth Seen in Winter" bemoans the hopelessness of a single insect sitting out on an unseasonably warm day. The moth appears to have made a fatally flawed decision to become active: "Nor will you find love either, or love you." Yet the moth may not be quite so doomed as the speaker supposes. With "The wings not folded in repose, but spread," this moth might have been releasing pheromones, potent scents that allow other moths to find it from quite far away. Even in cold air, the volatile lure could travel hundreds of meters downwind. If there were a male moth of the same species active at the same time, it could have been drawn in after the narrator left the scene. Such unseasonable emergences are rare, but for some species they are successful, perhaps essential, even against these odds.[13]

Plants die or decline in various ways in winter. In "Reluctance," even the late-blooming flowers have faded: "The last lone aster is gone; / The flowers of the witch hazel wither." On the farm in "Desert Places," a field succumbs to the snow: "But a few weeds and stubble showing last." There is also snow in the woods, and one detail appears in "Reluctance" that is repeated in later poems: "The leaves are all dead on the ground / Save those that the oak is keeping." Oak and beech trees (both in the plant family Fagaceae) often retain brown, marcescent leaves into the winter.[14] Leftover leaves appear briefly in "Winter Ownership" ("Through a withered-leaf-clad oak") and in "A Late Walk," a poem of autumn:

> A tree beside the wall stands bare,
>   But a leaf that lingered brown,
> Disturbed, I doubt not, by my thought,
>   Comes softly rattling down.

These tardy leaves can be deceptive to the wishful thinker. In "Looking for a Sunset Bird in Winter," the tree that had held the bird in summer now holds on to a leaf: "No bird was singing in it now. / A single leaf was on the bough." In "A Boundless Moment," "A young beech clinging to its last year's leaves" in March is mistaken for "the Paradise-in-Bloom" that should not appear until May. In each case, Frost eventually clarifies the initial confusion engendered by lingering leaves. As he stated in *The Figure a Poem Makes*, a poem "ends in a clarification of life—not necessarily a great clarification, such as sects and cults are founded on, but in a momentary stay against confusion."[15] But the clarifications in these two poems— it's not a bird or a flower, but a dead leaf—are also disappointments, especially in winter, a season filled with disappointments. The narrators had hoped for something better.

As the leaves come off the trees, they blow around, pile up and decay. Leaf loss is mostly an autumn phenomenon (e.g., "November") but Frost carries it into winter as well, especially in "A Leaf Treader." The narrator describes the death of leaves and his unwillingness to follow their lead as they pass him by in their descent. But the narrator doesn't speak during autumn. He reveals at the end of the poem that he is treading through the snow, and thus belatedly explains how "I have safely trodden underfoot the leaves of another year." In other poems from winter, those leaves that had not been trodden "lie huddled and still" ("Reluctance") or "under the eaves" ("My Butterfly"). The ultimate fate of these leaves is decay, one form of waste that Frost addressed frequently.

The fates of single trees in winter appear in a few of Frost's poems. Frost used a storm-felled tree to initiate an exploration of human goals and directions ("On a Tree Fallen Across the Road"). He reverses the question about what happens "if a tree falls in the forest" by giving the tree the ability to pose a question to humans: "But just to ask us who we think we are / Insisting always on our own way so." The poem quickly leaves the tree behind, but the dramatic winter event of a fallen tree has gotten our attention.

Frost usually mentioned "woods" and "forest" to describe a setting, with little if any judgment or emotion. However, he lived in rural New England in the early twentieth century and thus had to use wood for fuel, lumber, tools and more. In the last poem of his last collection, "In Winter in the Woods Alone," he described the harvesting of a maple tree as merely a matter of fact: "I see for Nature no defeat / In one tree's overthrow." Harvesting wood was a matter of necessity, especially in winter, for cooking food and staying warm. When a young man cuts a Christmas tree from the narrator's property ("To a Young Wretch"), the sentiments of the season produce a willingness to forgive and "Help me accept its fate with Christmas feeling." Whether for décor or fuel, one tree doesn't make that much difference.

Or does it? The story in "There Are Roughly Zones" is strained with anxiety over a single peach tree that might be succumbing to the cold and wind ("There is nothing much we can do for the tree tonight"). What will be lost if the tree dies? Peaches, of course, but also the wager they placed by bringing such a tree so far north, as well as whatever confidence they have in their own judgment as farmers. In contrast, another (or the same?) farmer displayed good judgment with the location of an orchard in "Goodby and Keep Cold": "I don't want it stirred by the heat of the sun. / (We made it secure against being, I hope, / By setting it out on a northerly slope.)" However, even that placement doesn't make things certain: "something has to be left to God." The life of a farmer is a full of risk and hope. Winter tests both in the extreme.

Spring

For whom would a poem on Spring be by?
"A Cloud Shadow"

Frost wondered who would write a poem of spring, yet thirty-one of his poems start in spring. He looked forward to spring after winter because the New England winters could be so confining ("To the Thawing Wind") whereas spring is so lush ("A Prayer in Spring") and full of anticipation despite the mud ("Pussy-willow Time").

Spring, however, is also brief in its transition from winter to summer. Frost recognized the fleeting nature of spring, especially the color, in "Nothing Gold Can Stay," making the duration of new leaves much shorter ("an hour") than it actually is. He used just one line to address the failure of Paradise ("So Eden sank to grief"), and in just eight lines, demonstrated that spring is a perfect metaphor for things impermanent.

Puddles are among the most ephemeral features of spring. Ruts and footprints fill with water in mud-time: "That every footprint's now a pool, / And every rut a river cool" ("Pussy-willow Time"); "In every wheelrut's now a brook, / In every print of a hoof a pond" ("Two Tramps in Mud

Time"). The rain and melted snow have nowhere to go in the saturated ground, so every available depression fills with water.

In "Blue-Butterfly Day," Frost describes butterflies that alight on the mud by the puddles in a road: "But these are flowers that fly and all but sing: / And now from having ridden out desire / They lie closed over in the wind and cling / Where wheels have freshly sliced the April mire." The butterflies that survived the winter have emerged to mate. Their subsequent behavior, as Frost describes in the last two lines, is consistent with a process called "puddling." Male butterflies of several species, including "blues" (family Lycaenidae) drink from puddles of water and gain dissolved sodium from the soil or protein from dung. Frost's blue butterflies might have been drinking fluids from the mud (and dung) of the "freshly sliced April mire" in the road. When lycaenid butterflies "puddle," they close their wings above their bodies. On windy days, butterflies in this posture would be "closed over in the wind" while they "cling" to the ground. Robert Faggen concluded that the butterflies on the road were dead, but if so, how did they cling? Maybe they were stuck in the mud and Faggen is right, but I think the puddling hypothesis has merit, especially in light of the precision of Frost's description.[16]

Puddles don't last long in a dry wind ("Let's Not Think"), but more substantial pools retain water long enough to supply water for trees ("Spring Pools") or spring peepers ("Pea Brush," "Hyla Brook"). Vernal pools are the inevitable result of snowmelt and spring rain on an irregular topography. The inland portions of New England have ranges of hills and old mountains, plus a variety of landforms left by glaciation. On a smaller scale, the soil has become uneven over the years, sometimes due to animal burrows, but more often as a result of storms that softened the ground with rain and uprooted trees in the wind. The result is an array of pits (depressions that once held the roots) and mounds (the accumulations of soil from the upturned roots).[17] Every spring, many low spots fill with water. By mid-summer, the water is gone.

In "Spring Pools," the vernal pools are not connected to "any brook or river" that could drain the water away. The quiet pools serve as mirrors of the sky above: "These pools that, though in forests, still reflect / The total sky almost without defect." The surface shows the "total" sky except for the minor "defect" of the bare branches. These liquid reflections will also "shiver" in the wind (Frost described shivering more fully in "Let's Not Think").

Stopping by Woods

Before the leaves emerge and produce a closed canopy of "dark foliage," there is sufficient sunlight reaching the forest floor for "watery flowers" (often called spring ephemerals) to grow quickly and bloom. They can't last long because the trees will "blot out" the light, so they grow fast, die young and leave as many seeds as possible (though they are nearly all perennials that will emerge again the following spring from the same roots or bulbs). Adelson and Elder discuss "perennation" and other aspects of "Spring Pools" at length.[18]

The buds on the trees need water to swell and grow: "The trees ... have it in their pent-up buds / To darken nature and be summer woods." Many buds will produce leaves that intercept the sunlight and darken the ground beneath (other buds produce flowers, a distinction Frost toyed with in "A Winter Eden"). Swelling and growing requires water, and buds get the water "by roots to bring dark foliage on." Tree roots draw the water from the soil, and indirectly from the pools, in the process of transpiration. But trees have no pumps or hearts, so water movement is driven by events at the cellular level high up in the tree. As the weather warms in spring, the winter storage of starch in the buds breaks down into sugar, raising the concentration of dissolved molecules in the bud tissues and simultaneously lowering the concentration of water in the buds. There is a higher concentration of water in the xylem cells of the wood near the buds, and as a result, there is net movement of water from high concentration (wood) to low concentration (bud), a process of random diffusion (osmosis). But water is cohesive, and when water moves into the buds, it drags more water with it, all the way through the hollow xylem vessels that are continuous through bud, branch, trunk and root. As the roots give up their water to the upper reaches of the tree, water from the soil is pulled in to replace it. Thus do the soil and, eventually, the pools give up their water. The pool water is indeed "not out by any brook or river, / But up by roots."[19]

In "Spring Pools," Frost turns the trees into a dark and malevolent force that destroys "These flowery waters and these watery flowers," the twin faces of spring beauty. His is a vision in keeping with "Hansel and Gretel" and "Peter and the Wolf," where evil lurks in the forest. Fear is a popular reaction to the unknown, and Frost found a way, rooted in plant physiology, to give his readers new reasons to fear those dark trees. They ruin everything about spring.

Frost's main point, however, is not the dark but the loss of flowers. For Frost, flowers are a source of beauty and pleasure, often the goal of an action or search (e.g., "The Quest of the Purple-Fringed"). Their loss would diminish his joy. Thus he says of the trees, "Let them think twice before they use their powers / To blot out and drink up" the light and the water that the flowers need. They are about to destroy something wonderful. Make them stop!

Of course, nobody can stop the trees from their developmental march through spring. The seasons progress whether we like it or not. Frost, with his interest in astronomy, knew that the seasons were dictated by the predictable orbit of a tilted Earth around the Sun. In "Acceptance," he accedes to the inevitability of the circadian rhythms of each day and night ("Let what will be, be") and he knew that seasonal change was equally inevitable (though it might be "treason" to "accept the end of ... a season" ["Reluctance"]). But wishing against certainty may be the ultimate action of life itself, in the face of inevitable death.

Farmers also wish that the spring could last longer. In "A Prayer in Spring," the narrator doesn't want to confront autumn just yet: "Oh, give us pleasure in the flowers today; / And give us not to think so far away / As the uncertain harvest; keep us here / All simply in the springing of the year." The reluctance to anticipate a harvest is much darker in "The Strong Are Saying Nothing." In that poem, the uncertainty of harvest is made equivalent to the uncertainty of the afterlife: "There may be little or much beyond the grave." Spring is the season for planting, but the weather of the growing season, from spring through autumn, is so unpredictable that farmers cannot be sure of what each year will bring. Farmers would prefer to continue "springing" and not look ahead to harvest time. It is easy to imagine disaster because it has happened before. Hope must be balanced with realism. Some say a prayer, others say nothing at all. Why tempt fate?

Yet Frost gives glorious reasons to tempt fate in other poems that celebrate renewal and growth. Nina Baym claims that one of these, "Putting in the Seed," is Frost's only "spring poem which is entirely affirmative."[20] I would argue that "Pussy-willow Time" and "Evening in a Sugar Orchard" are two others, but I still like her choice because of its exquisite description of seed germination: "The sturdy seedling with arched body comes / Shouldering its way and shedding the earth crumbs." And so much more comes before that concluding couplet. Spring is a time of petals, passion, love, sex and birth, and this poem has it all, yet stated indirectly as Tim Kendall points out, "saying without saying."[21] Mark Richardson, however, could not resist saying that the poem is clearly about insemination and that it contains "phallic" images.[22] While those things may be true, the agronomic setting helps keep the sexual temperature under control (vegetables are hardly Dionysian). Overall, I agree with Baym that "Putting in the Seed" is "entirely affirmative." Frost affirms that spring is a season of growth and promise, and then the poem ends. Enough said.

Spring is also when bluebirds return to breed ("Last Word of a Bluebird").[23] They "chime" in "pussy-willow time" ("Pussy-willow Time") and are part of a multispecies spring flock in "Our Singing Strength." Their appearance in April is described in two poems, "The Bonfire" and "Two Tramps in Mud Time." In the former: "The breezes were so spent with winter blowing / They seemed to fail the bluebirds under them / Short of the perch their languid flight was toward." In the latter: "A bluebird comes tenderly up to alight / And turns to the wind to unruffle a plume." Spring bluebirds seem delicate, even fragile, barely suited for such early arrival. Yet here they are. In his prose, Frost suggests that bluebirds derive strength and protection from their choice of nests: "Ballads lead their life in the mouths and ears of men by hear-say like bluebirds and flickers in the nest holes of hollow trees."[24] Fragile birds can survive when surrounded by wood. With their distinctive color and April arrival, Frost was intrigued by the paradoxical nature of bluebirds.

Also set in springtime, but focused on livestock instead of birds, what is the underlying tone in "The Pasture?"

> I'm going out to clean the pasture spring;
> I'll only stop to rake the leaves away
> (And wait to watch the water clear, I may):
> I sha'n't be gone long—You come too.
>
> I'm going out to fetch the little calf
> That's standing by the mother. It's so young,
> It totters when she licks it with her tongue.
> I sha'n't be gone long—You come too.

Robert Hass claimed that it "is not simply an invitation to communion and leisure,"[25] and as far as leisure goes, he is obviously right. Clearing the leaves from the spring and fetching the calf are hardly acts of leisure. The leaves are messy, and even a newborn calf is hard to lift. But these are chores of spring, of new life and a fresh growing season. Frost wants his wife to go with him for the short time that it will take to complete the chores so that they can share the joy. The day must be pleasant or he wouldn't ask her along. The call for communion is not just present but emphatic.

It is also not the only time Frost used this phrase. In a 1915 letter to his friend Louis Untermeyer, Frost described an imaginary home on Hudson's Bay where he says he would live with his fishing boat, his dog, his wife and no neighbors. He ended the description with an appeal that Untermeyer would definitely have understood: "You come too."[26] Even in an imagined life, this exclusive invitation expressed Frost's admiration and respect—even love—for his friend. At its heart, "The Pasture" embraces the growing season and the companionship of farming and friendship.

Spring inevitably gives way to summer, but when summer arrives, Frost still hasn't forgotten about spring. He uses the contrast of summer to illustrate the lushness of spring. In "Hyla Brook," Frost reminds the reader of the breeding frogs and water flow of spring. The stream will "have gone groping underground / (And taken with it all the Hyla breed." By summer, Hyla Brook was "a brook to none but who remember long." A visitor might not realize, nor an impatient person remember, how quickly things changed with the seasons. The cool mist of spring and the water in the brook are but memories in summer. Frost *wants* us to remember, however, and not be fooled by the diminished flow of summer. He also wants us to be reminded by the mid-summer silence of "The Oven Bird" that, for flowers, "mid-summer is to spring as one to ten." Warblers are not dependent on flowers, but they follow the same seasonal rhythm. Spring is a time of resurgence and reproduction by plants, frogs and birds. As the growing season advances, "mid-summer" is a time of plenty and therefore a time of growth, but it is also the beginning of the end.

Summer

> Loud, a mid-summer and a mid-wood bird.
> "The Oven Bird"

Frost included summer in his poems more often than any other season. Though summer was often simply the setting in which something happened, Frost did take advantage of the summer weather to explore and observe the landscape as a whole. In two poems, "Summering" and "Happiness Makes Up in Height for What It Lacks in Length," Frost focuses on the image of a perfect summer day, made even more special in contrast to either the noise of farm work when the "wains were out" or dismal weather with "mist and cloud." The sun and warmth of summer days can be exquisite moments for the residents of New England.

As pleasing as summer days might be, summer nights could be magical. In "In a Vale," "The fen had every kind of bloom," maidens "came every night with the mist" and "bird and flower were one and the same." The young narrator, while living in the vale, learns the mysteries of birds and flowers: "And thus it is I know so well / Why the flower has odor, the bird has song." Frost, best known as a realist, had a mystical streak throughout his life.

The gardens, vales and woods of summer are indeed exquisite places for birds. The narrator claims to have enticed the birds to "A Summer's Garden," acknowledging that he needed their songs far more than they needed his garden. In "Midsummer Birds," the birds (swallows?) are busy feeding in the air, but they are quieter in summer than during the mating season of spring, almost blending in with the ripening plants just below them. In contrast, a thrush at dusk ("Come In") is singing so late in the evening that it makes itself conspicuous. With so many summer birds, Frost noticed those that did something different.

As warm and song-filled as summer is, no season is perfect. In Frost's own life, the summer of 1896 held considerable joy because it was the season for his delayed honeymoon with Elinor, but it was also a time of distress after his good friend Carl Burell was seriously injured.[27] We see an analogous contrast in the summer fantasy "Spoils of the Dead." Despite the ominous title, the poem begins with fairies and flowers:

> Two fairies it was
> On a still summer day
> Came forth in the woods
> With the flowers to play

But the flowers guide the fairies to a corpse. Though the fairies "were not afraid," humans know what these flowers signify:

> When *you* came on death,
> Did you not come flower-guided
> Like the elves in the wood?
> I remember that I did.

The beauty of the blossoms makes death that much more poignant.

In Frost's poetry, flowers appear in at least three dozen poems set in summer, sometimes as an incidental item but usually as a significant part of the story. ("Summering" is unusual in not mentioning flowers, perhaps because it was an early poem.)

In "Flower Guidance" and "Forest Flowers," Frost admonishes anyone who would pick a flower. In "The Subverted Flower," the male character "lashed his open palm/ With the tender-headed flower," which is a prelude to the revelation that he is a brute. In all three poems, the destruction of a flower has serious consequences. It is not surprising, therefore, that the survival of flowers would be celebrated. The narrator in "Locked Out" is delighted that all but one of the flowers locked outside the house each night remained unmolested. Flowers are to be respected and protected.

However, if nobody is there to notice, or if picking is for a good cause, flowers might be expendable. In "Asking for Roses," if the person who grew the roses is not home, then it is, by default, permissible to pick them. If you grow your own flowers with the express goal of picking them ("A Summer's Garden"), then go ahead. On an old farm gone to ruin ("The Generations of Men"), it is permissible to ask a cousin (and potential mate) to "'Pick me that flower.'" If an apprentice is trying to please her injured mentor, she can pick a pair of orchids, leaving behind the rest for seed ("The Self-Seeker"). If your stay is brief and the flower insignificant, you may also get away with picking flowers ("On Going Unnoticed"). In a "little hour" in the woods, you manage to find the modest "coralroot flower" and pick it "as a trophy of the hour." If you leave quickly enough, you will get away with this theft.

Part of the sense of accomplishment in "Mowing" includes striking down flowers. If you work alone in the meadow, the scythe can take precedence over the "feeble-pointed spikes of flowers / (Pale orchises)." But only four poems later in *A Boy's Will*, a mower working alone had left "The Tuft of Flowers" that the narrator and his butterfly companion are pleased to find:

> But he turned first, and led my eye to look
> At a tall tuft of flowers beside a brook,
>
> A leaping tongue of bloom the scythe had spared
> Beside a reedy brook the scythe had bared.

In this case, the flowers had been spared by the scythe, and that was all to the good. In spring or summer, Frost's preferred rule was the preservation and appreciation of flowers.

Pollination, and all that it implied, was a specific aspect of flowers that seems to have fascinated Frost. Bees ("A Prayer in Spring"; "The Strong Are Saying Nothing"), butterflies ("The Tuft of Flowers"), or both ("A Summer's Garden"; "Pod of the Milkweed") visit flowers, spread pollen and make seeds possible. But it isn't always simple. If the flower is cut or bent, the pollinators will have difficulty finding the flowers ("The Tuft of Flowers"; "Range-Finding"). If conditions are too cold and wet, insects won't be able to fly to the flowers ("A Line-Storm Song"). In each case, the visitation of blossoms serves as a springboard for larger questions, sometimes answered, sometimes not.

In the Clearing, Frost's last collection of poems, opens with a detailed exploration of pollination in "Pod of the Milkweed." The milkweed flowers are "coming out," blooming in such profusion that the event should be "sung about." The pollinators heed the call and fight each other for the nectar: "One knocks another off from where it clings. / They knock the dyestuff off each other's wings— / With thirst on hunger to the point of lust. / They raise in their intemperance a cloud / Of mingled butterfly and flower dust." The overarching question in this case, though, is the inefficiency of the process, the focus in the second part of the poem. Even though many flowers were "passionately trod," the result from dozens of flowers in each cluster is just "one pod." After all that effort, it turns out that "waste was of the essence of the scheme." With so much furor, passion and combat, why is there so little result? What can account for so much apparent waste? The question "must be fairly faced." And in an appended note, we are promised that it will be: "*And shall be in due course."[28] It turns out that the process isn't as wasteful as it first seems, and Frost included an answer to the question of waste in a draft of the poem in his notebooks: the single pod is "bursting full of fertile seed."[29] Thus the question is "fairly faced" with abundant silken seeds that blow away from each ripe seed pod. (Of course, each "fertile seed" has an infinitesimal chance of successfully germinating and producing a mature plant, another conundrum of waste explored in "One Favored Acorn," "Waste of Cod Fish Eggs" and "Wanton Waste.")

What might be Frost's best-known questions stemmed from the attempted pollination of an aberrant flower (the white heal-all) by a moth in the night. The observer in "Design" wonders why a normally blue flower was white, why the spider chose this flower, and what steered the moth into the jaws of death. The answer? "What but design of darkness to appall?"

The question of the moth's movements is the easiest to answer: the moth was seeking nectar, and was probably serving as a pollinator as it moved from flower to flower of the heal-all. The spider is the culprit here, ambushing the moth before it could feed or transfer pollen. The spider exploited the instinct of the moth to visit white flowers (white is the most reflective, conspicuous color at night), but the spider itself was acting only on its own instinct when it climbed to the top of a plant. When it got there, it found flowers and enough visiting pollinators to encourage it to lie in wait. Ever patient, the spider finally got its meal when this moth flew in.

Stephen Jay Gould used "Design" as an example of a "contingent detail" in nature, an unlikely confluence of events that might not happen again were time to be turned back and repeated.[30] There was nothing unusual about the white spider or the white moth; that particular moth was just unlucky to have visited a flower occupied by a spider. The really "contingent" aspect of the story was the white flower: "What had that flower to do with being white, / The wayside blue and innocent heal-all?" Heal-all flowers are nearly all violet with white petal tips (simplified to the single syllable "blue" to fit the meter of the line—close enough), with only the rare flower being fully white.[31] Here was a strikingly unusual, specific concurrence from which Frost derived his final question, a question at once cosmic, unique, yet hesitant. That question—indeed, the entire sonnet—is astonishing.

Frost's most direct questions about biology of pollination are in "A Summer's Garden." Frost observes the insects that visit his flowers: "But so my flowers brought the insects winging, / The butterflies, the neighbor's murmuring bees." Yet the garden withered in autumn, leaving him to wonder: "The lives I entertained where are they now?" What became of all the blossoms, bees and butterflies that were here just yesterday?

Frost was far from the first person to wonder about the process of pollination. Plants give away nectar and pollen just so they can be fertilized. How can this exchange possibly work? Even if the right pollen ends up in the right place, how can it be worth the cost? It is inefficient and wasteful. It also depends on insects, tiny, fragile animals that cannot be active in winter. How can they make a living from resources that are available only briefly? Where do they go?

Stopping by Woods

The answers are not that hard to figure out, though they might not be immediately obvious. Plants use a small percentage of their available energy to make pollen, nectar, and the flowers themselves. In the end, despite the show of colors and proliferation of pollen, the plant ends up with a net gain in seed production. Petals and pollen are expendable in the cause of reproduction. They are merely the cost of doing business.[32]

Many insects, on the other hand, can make their livings from flowers, and then they become dormant during the winter months. Their eggs, larvae, pupae or adults wait out the cold until the next growing season. They take their cues from day length and/or temperature to become active or to enter dormancy at the right times.[33] To a human observer, the absence of winter activity does not seem normal. We are mammals, and more than that, we are a species of mammal that doesn't happen to hibernate. Our durable bodies and long life cycle make it hard to comprehend one or more generations being completed within a single year. To the casual observer, the insects simply appear and disappear as if by magic. To an experienced naturalist like Robert Frost, their appearance was simply one more facet of seasonal change.

Summer in New England is all too brief. Few things are as precious as a warm summer night when we can be out looking at stars and star-like features in the dark. Some people get carried away. The participants in "The Bonfire" gather brush so they can "burn it as one pile" and then "before it burns out / It will have roared first and mixed sparks with stars." The star-like sparks will be spectacular, but only as long as the fire lasts. In a similar fashion, though by dissimilar means, the "Fireflies in the Garden" make a "starlike start" but then "can't sustain the part." The momentary brightness of the embers or insects reminds us of the momentary nature of the seasons. The fireflies are especially enjoyable in the benign conditions of summer, when we can be out in the garden without fear of frostbite and the bugs do all the work. But they "can't sustain the part" and summer can't last as long as the stars. The actual stars in the heavens change so slowly that "Still it wouldn't reward the watcher to stay awake / In hopes of seeing the calm of heaven break" ("On Looking Up by Chance at the Constellations"). Seasons are not nearly as persistent as the positions of the stars in the heavens. Summer, like the flashing of the fireflies, will be gone before we know it.

After reciting the last portion of "Reluctance" to Amherst College alumni, Frost said that his reluctance to accept "the end ... of a season" in the poem was "that pain at the end of summer."[34] That pain could be eased somewhat by something as simple as the blooming of a flower. As summer comes to a close, late-season blossoms lure people out into the country-side. In "The Quest of the Purple-Fringed," the narrator eventually finds the elusive "far-sought flower." Satisfied with his quest and resigned to the inevitable change of season, he heads back: "Then I arose and silently wandered home, / And I for one / Said that the fall might come and whirl the leaves, / For summer was done."

Autumn

> It was the tree the autumn fire ran through
> "Maple"

For Frost, leaves were a major theme of autumn, including their color, descent, dispersal and decay. He sometimes equates color change with fire: "burning maples," a maple tree on his farm named "Torch," "autumnal blaze" in "Winter Has Beaten Summer in Fight,"[35] and in three lines in "Maple": "It was the tree the autumn fire ran through / And swept of leathern leaves, but left the bark / Unscorched, unblackened, even, by any smoke." Frost knew that the forests near his farm in Franconia, New Hampshire, sometimes burned, so he might have also known that the thin bark of maples makes them vulnerable to real fire.[36] Did that make each "autumn fire" more special because it left the maple trees alive?

Early in the season ("October"), the leaves "have ripened to the fall" and the narrator asks that the process be delayed: "Slow! Slow! / For the grapes' sake, if they were all, / Whose leaves already are burnt with frost, / Whose clustered fruit must else be lost— / For the grapes' sake along the wall." This request for a seasonal suspension parallels a similar request in "Spring Pools," and it is equally futile. Soon, as the cold descends, the "amethyst" grapes, high on their vines, will shrivel and turn brown. Still, one can wish for an unseasonable stretch of warm weather long enough to allow the fruit to survive for harvest. Just a little more time, please!

The tone is more accepting of seasonal change in "In Hardwood Groves," in which the narrator describes the seasonal cycle as "The same leaves over and over again!": "Before the leaves can mount again / To fill the trees with another shade, / They must go down past things coming up. / They must go down into the dark decayed." The dead leaves "*must be pierced by flowers*," the spring ephemeral flowers (so highly favored and mourned in "Spring Pools") that grow before new leaves emerge in the canopy. As the sharply-pointed shoots of the flowers emerge from the soil early in the spring, some of them grow up through holes in the dead leaves, appearing to have "pierced" them with their sharp tips. On the rare occasion when this occurs, a plant can actually get strangled by the dead leaves and be unable to open, facing a challenge similar to that of the trillium plants underneath piles of birch branches in "Pea Brush."

The autumn mood is playful in "Going for Water" as the moonlight streams through bare branches of trees. The anticipation of the water gatherers becomes even more positive when they can hear the brook and confirm that their chore will be successful. In this poem, Frost describes a combination of work and joy, perhaps best known in "Two Tramps in Mud Time" ("where love and need are one"), but in "Going for Water" there are shiny gems and metals:

> A note as from a single place,
> A slender tinkling fall that made
> Now drops that floated on the pool
> Like pearls, and now a silver blade.

But autumn, like silver, tarnishes with time and the mood grows somber. Returning to his farm in Derry in the autumn of 1907, Frost wrote, "I can't look at my little slope of field here with leaves in the half dead grass, or at the bare trees the birds have left us with."[37] This same despondency appears in some of his poetry. "A Late Walk" mourns the passing of summer:

> And when I come to the garden ground,
> The whir of sober birds
> Up from the tangle of withered weeds
> Is sadder than any words.

The end of the poem makes what little it can of what remains.

> I end not far from my going forth,
> By picking the faded blue
> Of the last remaining aster flower
> To carry again to you.

It is time for the couple, faced with things "sober" and "withered," to prepare for winter. "Sorrow" is "My November Guest" and it has arrived to stay a while. The time has come to "close the windows and not hear the wind" ("Now Close the Windows") and wait for spring.

All but one of the autumn poems from *A Boy's Will* consider things of the season and not much more. They are often beautiful, even moving, but so is autumn. In the last poem of *A Boy's Will* ("Reluctance") and in later poems, Frost went further. "Reluctance" is mostly about the onset of winter, but at the end, it looks back on the transition from autumn:

> Ah, when to the heart of man
>   Was it ever less than a treason
> To go with the drift of things,
>   To yield with a grace to reason,
> And bow and accept the end
>   Of a love or a season?

Seasonal change is inevitable, so is there any sense in not accepting it? Will remembrance or reminiscence suffice to avoid "treason," or must we pine, grieve or rage against the end? And must we consider "the end of a love" to be as inevitable as the end of a season? Is there any "reason" to link love and a season this way? Or is it all about the love *of* a season that has ended? Frost has left us with a wonderfully irrational question.

The narrator in "Misgiving" (*New Hampshire*) describes the wind and the leaves in three stanzas to set up his own wish about immortal experience in the fourth. The leaves tend to travel in a wind "That drops them no further than where they were." This is *not* the metaphor he wants for his own afterlife: "I only hope that when I am free, / As they are free, to go in quest / Of the knowledge beyond the bounds of life / It may not seem better to me to rest."

The autumn leaves in "Bereft" (*West-Running Brook*) reveal the secret of a man alone in his house and in the world: "Word I had not one left but God." The leaves have fallen and blown away, exposing the narrator in all his lonely vulnerability. A reader might wonder whether the man will live to see a new crop of leaves next year.

Frost could be fanciful as well as serious. If humans begin in autumn, as his notebooks say, then let them celebrate that beginning. "Clear and Colder" (*A Further Range*) provides a witch's recipe for "Fall Elixir," a mix of summer, winter and snow, stirred by the wind, that is ready to serve in autumn: "Wait and watch the liquor settle. / I could stand whole dayfuls of it." Humans "love" the confluence of seasons that constitute the Elixir, consuming the essence of the annual cycle. They accept the inevitable change of seasons and take satisfaction in having prepared for the winter ahead: wood is cut and stacked, hay is in the barn, garden produce is dried or canned, apples and squash are in the cellar, and the farm is battened down against the coming cold. Fully prepared, New Englanders (along with the "Gods above") can fortify themselves with the Elixir, perhaps their most pleasurable preparation for the change in season.

In contrast, Frost was at his most serious in "November" (*A Witness Tree*) when "a year of leaves was wasted." In this and other poems, Frost describes the waste and decay of leaves. The dependable seasonal occurrence of leaf fall provided an opportunity to explore other types of waste in human lives: too little sleep, too much crying, too much ignoring what really matters. Waste was one of Frost's most common themes, but few poems encapsulate it in so many ways: decay, time, pleasure, and finally war. These are not equivalent types of waste: we can't avoid the "waste" of time in sleep, and we can deprive ourselves of pleasure, but how should we think of the loss of the wasted leaves? The consequences of these types of waste, individually and in isolation from the others, seem trivial. If we focus solely on waste in our personal lives, however, we will end up ignoring something of monumental wastefulness: war.

In the context of everyday New England, Frost knew well the perseverance required to prepare for winter. The harvest and hay had to come in, food had to be preserved, the wood had to be cut, split, seasoned and stored, and the buildings had to be tightened up for the cold, wind and snow. The fire of autumn color could be enjoyed, even celebrated, but it couldn't be allowed to become a distraction. A mild day was a welcome interlude, but it wouldn't last. Preparation was essential.

The physical preparations for winter were completed in autumn by people coming together, working together and depending on each other, especially within families. They were braced for the change: "Winter here this morning—snow on the roof and a wind that says, Time to bank up the house" (October 10, 1916). When Frost wrote in his notebook "Man begins where summer leaves off,"[38] it is likely that he was alluding to the manifestation of strength and cooperation that became so apparent and so necessary throughout rural New England in autumn. With the harvest in place from the seasons of plenty, New Englanders could endure the season of want. But one fact was as reliable as the cycle of seasons: it wasn't going to be easy.

Agrarian Diaspora

*"From too much dwelling
on what has been"*

In an interview with Jay Parini, Robert Penn Warren described Robert Frost's experience in New England: "It's as though he were dropped into the countryside north of Boston from outer space, and remained perpetually stunned by what he saw."[1] What was so stunning about the region north of Boston?

By the time Frost arrived in New England in 1885, an agrarian diaspora had been underway for decades and would continue into the twentieth century. People had been leaving the land since the mid–1800s because of the depletion of firewood and timber, the lure of inexpensive, fertile and rock-free land to the west, or the rise of industry in the cities. While Lawrence, Massachusetts (where Frost attended high school) was growing at a nearly exponential pace in the 1880s, many of the surrounding rural towns were in decline, losing as much as 30 percent of their population between 1860 and 1900. During that same time, nearly half of the towns in Vermont decreased in population, and hill farms were usually the first to be abandoned. Many of these rural communities would not return to their former population size until the 1980s.[2]

Most of the departing farmers could not find buyers for their inferior property, as was the case for Brad McLaughlin in the "The Star-Splitter": "Few farms changed hands; so rather than spend years / Trying to sell his farm and then not selling, / He burned his house down for the fire insurance." Unlike Mr. McLaughlin, most farm families simply left their land, houses and barns "forsaken" ("The Need of Being Versed in Country Things"). After "The mountain pushed us off her knees" ("The Birthplace"), much of the landscape remained untended by humans. There will be nobody around to check the fences when "her great weight creaks the barbed wire in its staples" ("The Bear"). If her "great weight" pulls some of the wires off of the staples on the fence posts, soon there will be nothing left of the fence but a single "strand of wire" ("The Need of Being Versed in Country Things"). Did the young horse ("The Runaway") or the apple-crazy cow ("The Cow in Apple Time") run wild across the countryside after sneaking through the fences of their farms, or were they free to roam after being abandoned along with someone's property, with no fence to contain them or nobody to "take him in"? What will become of "the teams that came by the stony road" when they no longer "drum on the floor with scurrying hoofs" bringing hay into the barn, and when they "no more" pull wagons full of hay that "brush the mow with the summer load" ("The Need of Being Versed in Country Things")? And what will become of the meadow that is no longer mowed?

When Frost came to New England, he found a patchwork of occupied and deserted farms. The scale of desertion was so stunning that it appeared in some of Frost's earliest writing. *Petra and Its Surroundings*, an essay Frost published in his high school bulletin in 1891, ended with the line "To-day, all is ruin but the tombs that honey-comb the cliffs, and the city is a city of the dead."[3] In contrast to the vitality of San Francisco, rural New Hampshire was dotted with the "ruin" of empty farms, so much so that the utter desolation seen in Petra seemed an appropriate analogy. His essay was a confluence of his classical education in high school, his memory of California, and his observation of deserted, ruined property all around him.

Frost began working on his own farm in Derry, New Hampshire, in 1900. During his frequent walks "botanizing" around Derry, he saw first hand what happened to the farms that had long been abandoned, or that were newly deserted after the departure or death of his neighbors. "Ghost House," the second poem in *A Boy's Will*, starts with the decay of an old homestead, "That vanished many a summer ago, / And left no trace but the cellar walls." Cellar holes became common as the wooden structures above the stone foundations collapsed and rotted away ("The Cellar Hole" was the original title of "The Generations of Men"[4]). Over time, old cellars became so overgrown that they were easy to miss, but Frost knew how to spot them. In "Directive," he describes a cellar disappearing under the lilacs as "slowly closing like a dent in dough." (Thoreau described cellar holes and old wells as dents in the ground, so it is quite possible that Frost, an admirer of Thoreau's writing, could have borrowed the term from *Walden*.[5]) Wherever Frost went in the countryside, he found the dents in the soil, or the flowers planted by their former owners, or collapsing stone work: "forty years / Can do a good deal to bad masonry" ("A Fountain, a Bottle, a Donkey's Ears and Some Books").

Frost also saw houses that didn't wait for decay but succumbed to fire. In contrast to "The Star-Splitter," the cause of the fire in "The Need for Being Versed in Country Things" is not mentioned, but it could have had any number of origins. With so few people around, especially in the middle of the night, the fire could burn unhindered: "The house had gone to bring again / To the midnight sky a sunset glow. / Now the chimney was all of the house that stood." The whim of the wind allowed the barn to survive the fire, but the remains of the farm—the chimney, the pump, the fence and the barn—are left in disorder and disarray, whether burned or not.

Disorder

There is no question that death, decay and disorder are prominent in Frost's poems. His countryside is full of diminished things like abandoned farms, decaying woodpiles or passing seasons, so much so that he wonders "what to make of a diminished thing" (summer in this case) in the last line of "The Oven Bird." Frost's recurrent themes of waste and decline have prompted several authors to claim that he was writing about entropy, the thermodynamic degradation of all forms of energy to heat (a formal definition is given by Robert Hass[6]). Irving Howe speaks of "the certainty of physical dissolution" and Nina Baym insists that the decay in "The Wood-Pile" is "unmistakably" a reference to thermodynamics.[7] She and Hass both consider "West-Running Brook" to be a description of entropy[8]:

> The stream of everything that runs away
>
> ...
>
> It seriously, sadly runs away
> To fill the abyss's void with emptiness.

Though these lines can be read as a simple and elegant description of entropy, are these lines, and the other alleged examples of thermodynamics in Frost, solely about entropy? The laws of thermodynamics, including entropy, apply to processes in a closed system at a microscopic scale (molecules, atoms and subatomic particles). There has been considerable debate about how, or even whether, entropy applies to large-scale disorder, and with regard to a disordered landscape, the answer is no.[9]

Frost's world of decaying farms is neither microscopic nor a closed system, so entropy is not the dominant process in play. Instead, Frost focuses his attention on the energy transformations that are most important in the landscape. For example, several lines in "West-Running Brook" demonstrate that the character named Fred grasps the water cycle: "The sun runs down in sending up the brook." If the brook had been in a closed system (that is, without any solar input), the water cycle would decrease as less and less water evaporates, precipitation decreases and finally, all the water is in the ocean. At that point, the stream would no longer exist.

On Earth, streams continue to flow because there is an external energy source—sunlight—that evaporates water ("sending [it] up") and moves it around in the wind. When water vapor rises into the atmosphere, especially over land, it condenses, falls, and continuously replenishes the stream. In a closed system, entropy would bring things to a halt, but in an open system, water can run as long as the external supply of energy is available. When Fred says, "the sun runs down," he might be referring to the long-term decline of the sun's energy, or perhaps only to the decline of sunlight each evening. Either way, he is acknowledging that the cycle will continue as long as sunlight is available. Thus, the flowing water of West-Running Brook is "the tribute of the current to the source."

With regard to the renewal of ecosystems on land abandoned by humans, solar energy is also essential. Sunlight drives photosynthesis, the conversion of simple molecules into complex molecules, which in turn leads to the complexity of living organisms and ecosystems. Frost labels the apparent disorder of a field of weeds on an old farm as "waste" in "The Last Mowing" and in "Something for Hope" ("wasteful weed"). But biologically speaking, the weeds are thriving, living things, highly ordered and complex, growing and not declining. Human disorder allows an increase in the order of other species. And Frost's use of the word "waste" actually celebrates extravagance, not deterioration: the "wild" things in the field are beautiful, complex and highly ordered flowers with precise and colorful blossoms.

Continuing to Leave the Land

As the twentieth century began and Frost found himself living on his own farm, people continued to leave the land. Frost mentioned "Abandoned farms in the hill country" in his notebooks, wrote of an abandoned school house in the mountains of New Hampshire, and noted in a 1917 letter to Amy Lowell, "My address is Amherst Mass, though really we are living in the abandoned town of Pelham so close to the woods that if the woods burn our house must go too."[10] Frost was swimming upstream when he moved into the countryside instead of out. From his farm, he could observe what happened after most people left the land and only a few remained, the connections among families and friends having been stretched or broken. The characters in his poems were part of the history of the landscape as they endured their isolation (or, more pessimistically, their predicament).[11] Frost found these recalcitrant people fascinating, even if they burned their property for the insurance, and especially if they used the insurance money to buy a telescope ("The Star-Splitter").

Frost explicitly described the decline of the rural population in several poems. The citizens around "The Mountain" are aware of their dwindling numbers: "'There is no village—only scattered farms. / We were but sixty voters last election.'" And if people aren't careful, their pessimism can make it worse. The narrator in "The Times Table" knows how tenuously people are holding on to their farms. It won't take much to send them on their way, whether by emigration or death, and "close a road, abandon a farm / Reduce the births of the human race." Don't tempt fate with a "sigh" of resignation.

But in many places, it is already too late to keep people from leaving. One of the characters in "A Fountain, a Bottle, a Donkey's Ears and Some Books" is surprised to find a sturdy house empty: "I never saw so good a house deserted." Another empty house, "The Black Cottage," has lost its original owner: "'Everything's as she left it when she died,'" and there is little prospect that her sons will continue to use the cottage in the summer, much less maintain it as it begins to deteriorate. The floorboards are coming loose, "bees" nest in the walls, and the exterior appears "fresh painted by the shower a velvet black," the result of moldy siding turning dark in the rain. It's only a matter of time before the structure succumbs like so many others.

Some families still retain a connection to their deserted property.

Stopping by Woods

The Stark family plans to visit their ancestral home with its cellar hole, "To stand together on the crater's verge" ("The Generations of Men"), but a rainy day deters nearly everyone and only two family members arrive. As it turns out, the emptiness has a value for these cousins. They can meet, talk and plan for their future together, hopeful that inbreeding will not become an issue. The adjacent brook "roared" as they conversed, and the noise meant that only they could hear their shared words, just in case any other family members might be nearby, ready to warn them against their marriage. Is their union the best way to produce the next generation? Perhaps it is the only way that their family can continue.

One doesn't have to worry about being overheard in "The Census-Taker." The single house is "the only dwelling in a waste cut over / A hundred square miles round it in the mountains." People removed everything of value in and around the building and thus had no other option but to leave. The census taker's "melancholy" has increased with each new discovery of so many places with so few people, but now his depression "is extreme where they shrink to none at all. / It must be that I want life to go on living." In this desolate, ruined place, there is so little life that one cannot be hopeful. Hope can only reside elsewhere.

There are gravestones ("stones out under the low-limbed tree") of "mute folk" beside the "Ghost House," the house itself having been reduced to its foundation with only "ruined fences" around it. Frost gives one of these gravestones a voice and spirit to tell the tale of change. We hear of the family members who had lived and died here on a working farm, but that was in the past. Now it is just one more homestead, a "vanished abode" beside its "disused and forgotten road," that has rotted down to rock.

A whole community has disappeared in "Directive" and become little more than a scattering of abandoned foundations "in a town that is no more a town." But the poem quickly focuses on one property: "There is a house that is no more a house / Upon a farm that is no more a farm." One of these lines is repeated later as readers are directed to "weep ... for the house that is no more a house / But only a belilaced cellar hole." We are asked to mourn this abandoned house with its funereal flowers, the lilacs, already in place—put there, in fact, by the people we are to mourn. Robert Faggen noted, "Lilacs in their beauty belie the destruction and death upon which they grow." He also proposed a broader "ironic implication: nature does not yield a source and does not permit recovery of the past."[12] But whose recovery is not permitted?

Just as humans are asked to weep over a cellar hole in "Directive," humans would be expected to weep over the burned-out house in "The Need of Being Versed in Country Things." But in the barn that survived the fire, the phoebes do not weep:

> For them there was really nothing sad.
> But though they rejoiced in the nest they kept,
> One had to be versed in country things
> Not to believe the phoebes wept.

Nor do the phoebes sigh, even though their calls are "like the sigh we sigh," and even though the farmer's equating of a "sigh" with "death" ("The Times Table") seems to transform each call of the phoebe from a sigh of mourning to a sigh of warning. These sighs are what we think we hear from an exhaling horse or a calling bird because we suffer "from too much dwelling on what has been."

Faggen is right that humans are not going to recover their past among the ashes, but the flora and fauna that were here before the farm (plus the lilacs brought in by the farmers) are now recovering *their* past. The phoebes "rejoiced" because they had a new home, now free from human interference. People who are "versed in country things," who, in Faggen's terms, "suspend the anthropocentric"[13] and realize that a lost homestead is found habitat, will believe that the phoebes do not weep and do not sigh, and that the sighing and weeping are ours alone. The lesson of "The Need of Being Versed in Country Things," is not to be anthropocentric.

Frost's perspective was sometimes anthropocentric, sometimes not, but his examination of the agrarian diaspora in multiple poems encompassed both the human and non-human components of the landscape, making it possible to comprehend, and perhaps take comfort in, the return of other species previously excluded by farming. If we have, as instructed in "Directive," found the goblet and filled it in the stream, then we can "drink and be whole again beyond confusion," and thus we will "be versed in country things." Faggen is right, but only from a human perspective, not from the perspective of the birds, lilacs and elms. The resurgence of nature is not the recovery of *our* past, but it is of *theirs*. As Frost acknowledged in the last line of a highly anthropocentric poem, "The Times Table," the departure of humans will "bring back nature in people's place." We will explore this resurgence of nature next.

Ecological Succession
"They rejoiced in the nest they kept"

When farms were abandoned, the inevitable result was ecological succession, the invasion of fields, pastures and meadows by weeds, shrubs and trees.[1] Henry David Thoreau coined the term "succession" to describe changes in the forest after the disturbance of the landscape by humans.[2] Thoreau focused almost exclusively on trees, but others have described the initial dominance of herbaceous plants, followed by a "shrub stage" and then trees. Weeds, shrubs and trees all begin to grow once the land is no longer farmed, but weeds grow more quickly than woody plants and are initially the most conspicuous vegetation. There are many types of herbaceous plants that can invade agricultural land, and the species in any particular location are often a matter of chance, though climate, soil, and previous land use can favor certain species over others. Among these weeds are the flowers that Frost spoke of frequently.

Weeds are not dominant for long, however. Shrubs, including hardhack (*Spiraea tomentosa*, also called steeple bush), meadowsweet (*Spiraea latifolia* or *Spiraea alba*), juniper and raspberry, are so predictable in succession that they are sometimes called "pasture shrubs."[3] Another shrub, sweetfern (*Comptonia peregrina*—not a fern but a flowering plant), can thrive on exhausted soil because its roots form associations with nitrogen-fixing bacteria.[4] Each winter, the shrubs retain their woody height while the weeds die back to the ground. The weeds begin to decline as the shrubs get taller, overtop the herbaceous weeds and cast more shade.

While the weeds and shrubs are growing, so are trees. Like the shrubs, they maintain their height each year, adding more the next. Unlike shrubs, trees grown from seeds have a single stem and keep growing taller. They will eventually overtake the other plants around them and begin to form a canopy. Then most weeds and shrubs that grew in the open will die out, to be replaced by those that can survive on early spring sunshine or on sunflecks that sneak between the canopy leaves.

Not all trees grow at the same rate, however. Paper birch is one of those that becomes conspicuous early in forest succession, and it grows only where it is not shaded by other trees. White pine and balsam fir also grow quickly, especially in pastures where resinous seedlings had previously been avoided by grazing livestock. Oaks, maples and hemlock grow more slowly, but their saplings can eventually work their way into the canopy if taller trees die and let in light.[5] There is no single end point or climax to the succession process (though the concept of climax was in vogue among many ecologists in Frost's time[6]). There is considerable variation in the soils and topography of New England, so no single species of tree can take over a whole region. In addition, there are natural disturbances (storms are most important) and an assortment of human activities that frequently restart the successional clock, keeping weeds, shrubs and pioneer trees in the mix.[7]

Wildfires are rare in New England except in some parts of the boreal forest in northern Maine and in well-drained sandy soils along parts of the coastline. Elsewhere, fires can spread among dead leaves and other debris in dry, windy weather. In all of these plant communities, nearly all of the fires are caused by human activity, and nearly all of them burn along the ground without killing mature trees (seedlings, on the other hand, are easily killed by the flames). For thousands of years, Native Americans set fires deliberately in parts of New England and thereby reduced the density of underbrush (except in wetlands where fires did not burn well). Today, fires are less frequent than in pre-colonial times, which has allowed fire-susceptible species, such as maple, to increase in abundance at the expense of some fire-resistant species like white oak.[8]

Succession involves not only the plants—the weeds, shrubs and trees that fill in when agriculture ends—but also the animals that live among those plants. A shift from farm to woods takes decades, and as the habitat changes (conditions, food, nest sites, etc.) the result is a change in the resident birds.[9]

Today, New England is mostly covered in trees, the result of a successional process that Frost knew well. Colin Nickerson described the present state of the region's forests with a nod to the region's poet: "The woods are lovely, dark, and back."[10] But when we compare presettlement vegetation (based on the composition of pollen left in lake sediments) with what we see today, the effects of agriculture, logging and other human activities are still evident. Now, the abundance of tree species is less tightly correlated with climate and soil than it was before European colonization. And not surprisingly, there are measureable effects of climate change on the distribution of plants in the regrown forest. Successional change continues, and human activity sometimes drives it in unprecedented directions.[11]

Frost and Ecological Succession

Frost described every phase of ecological succession in New England.[12] If mowing missed a patch of meadow ("A leaping tongue of bloom the scythe had spared" in "The Tuft of Flowers") or if the meadow was no longer mowed at all, herbaceous weeds flourished in the absence of "mowers and plowers" ("The Last Mowing"). The "tumultuous" flowers overtaking a meadow and going "wild" in early succession could be celebrated ("The Last Mowing"). From a farming perspective, flowers were "lovely blooming but wasteful weed" because plants with colorful flowers were poor food for livestock compared to grass ("Something for Hope"). But couldn't farmers appreciate both the flowers and the forage? Regarding weeds springing up on farms, Frost wrote to George Whicher, "Don't farm hard enough yourself to lose the ability to see it partly from the weeds' point of view."[13]

With time, woody species grew large enough to become conspicuous. Raspberries grew up around the cellar holes in "Ghost House" and "The Generations of Men," taking advantage of whatever light was available. Blueberries quickly filled in a burned pasture in "Blueberries," literally rising out of the ashes. Two species of *Spiraea* shrubs, meadow sweet and steeple bush (both are avoided by livestock), take over from "edible grass" (edible for grazing animals, that is) in the first four lines of "Something for Hope."[14] Not only are these shrubs not good plants for livestock to eat, they are coarse and firmly rooted, making them formidable weeds if one were trying to reclaim the land for gardening or farming. *Spiraea* species do produce colorful flowers, though, so it's not a total aesthetic loss.

Trees live long enough and eventually grow large enough to take over a piece of open land. In lines five through eight in "Something for Hope,"

Frost continues his description of succession as a steady process of replace-ment, one stage to the next, trees replacing shrubs. Though he lists maple first, birch and spruce grow faster and will become conspicuous earlier in succession than maple. Given more time and the deaths of some of the fast-growing trees, maple will reach the canopy.

In "The Last Mowing," Frost bemoans the arrival of trees that will shade out the flowers. Mowing prevents woody tree seedlings and saplings from growing as tall as weeds, but when mowing stops, the trees can con-tinue to grow and eventually stake their "shadowy claim" (line 10). When the trees grow tall and develop full canopies, flowers that were abundant early in succession will die out in the shade.

Frost's poetry is laced with references to flowers, so it is not surprising that he considered the brightly flowering weeds of early succession to be special, and that he sometimes wished that the trees would not eliminate them (a wish analogous to that regarding seasonal change in "Spring Pools").

In other poems and in his notebooks, Frost focused on the trees, especially when it came to the disappearance of people and the growth of trees in their place. In unpublished verse from the notebooks, the trees grow back as soon as a farmer dies: "When he himself would scarce be underground/ Before his field would all go back to woods." Only living, active farmers can forestall the encroachment of trees: "The only reason why the [illegible] grass / Can keep the better of trees / So close we mow the grass."[15] The town of Bow, New Hampshire ("The Generations of Men") is "A rock-strewn town where farming has fallen off, / And sprout-lands flourish where the ax has gone." Trees in the woodlots, having been cut at least once, had refused to die and instead sent up sprouts that would, in time, form the "sprout-lands" of multi-stemmed trees. The same has happened to apple trees in "Ghost House": "The orchard tree has grown one copse / Of new wood and old where the woodpecker chops." The "copse" or coppice is "a thicket of small trees or underwood periodically cut for economic purposes."[16] Apple wood is dense and makes good fire-wood, a practical reason to make a "copse" out of an orchard.

The mountain slope of "The Birthplace" was the site of a family farm, but not forever: "The mountain pushed us off her knees. / And now her lap is full of trees." In "A Fountain, a Bottle, a Donkey's Ears and Some Books" (published in 1923[17]), "Old Davis" promises to show his friend a fountain that he saw in 1885 on the mountain: "No doubt it's grown up some to woods around it." Such regrowth is exactly what we would expect after nearly forty years. The location of the stone wall in "Mending Wall" makes no sense in terms of active farming: "There where it is we do not need the wall: / He is all pine and I am apple orchard." Nobody would expend the effort to build a wall between pines and an apple orchard; the pine trees must have grown up where a field, meadow or pasture had been abandoned. "The Times Table" bemoans a pessimistic attitude that will "reduce the births of the human race, / And bring back nature in people's place." Such attitudes can be blamed for abandoned property like that in "Directive" with a sign saying "CLOSED." Frost anthropomorphizes the woods that are growing back in a mere two decades: "Where were they all not twenty years ago? / They think too much of having shaded out / A few old pecker-fretted apple trees." Each of these poems acknowledges, sometimes with a sense of loss, sometimes not, that the departure of people from the rural landscape has allowed forest succession to reclaim the land, even overtopping the orchards that had once seemed so durable.

Not all trees had to wait for people to leave the land. Since the beginning of settlement in the seventeenth century, a few trees had managed to survive along the fences and stone walls that bounded the farms and homesteads. At these margins, the ample sunlight allowed trees to spread outward with long, low branches that were not shaded out by neighboring trees.[18] In "Ghost House," Frost notes, "Those stones out under the low-limbed tree," and in "A Dream Pang," there are "low boughs the trees let down outside." Today, these broad trees with big limbs are a common sight along many stone walls of New England. Such trees, with unobstructed sunlight, would have produced an abundance of seeds that rained down on the adjacent fields, germinating into seedlings that could, at some point, take advantage of departing farmers. In "Into My Own," Frost wishes that those seedlings were already as large as their parents, "those dark trees / So old and firm they scarcely show the breeze." The lines of large trees stand along the edges of fields as "the merest mask of gloom." He wants all the trees to be that large so that they "stretched away unto the edge of doom." It is a dark wish so that "into their vastness I should steal away." Frost knew that small trees would eventually grow as large as "those dark trees," but his mood made him impatient for someplace to "steal away." His mood would need to be satisfied with imagined succession.

As forest succession proceeded in New England, there were parallel changes in the bird fauna. In at least two of Frost's poems, "Come In" and

"Never Again Would Birds' Song Be the Same," we can find evidence of the effect of succession on birds. When reading "Come In" today, it seems odd that the narrator responded to hearing a thrush by exclaiming, "hark!" Their songs are nice to hear, but are not that unusual. For example, I hear more than one veery singing every spring, and I've heard wood thrush songs in rural New England and residential neighborhoods of Ithaca, New York, and Worcester, Massachusetts.

But I doubt that would it have been odd to say "hark" a century ago. In Frost's time, the woods were less contiguous and had smaller trees than they have today. By then, only long-abandoned fields would have tall trees, and they would be part of a patchwork that included shorter vegetation and active farms. His woods had sufficient open space to favor bluebirds, but wood thrush and veery would have found less suitable habitat and their songs would have been heard less often. When surprised by a rare and beautiful bird song, "hark" seems an appropriate exclamation.

Today, with larger expanses of mature trees, New England has fewer bluebirds but more wood thrush and veery. Since 1966, wood thrush in Massachusetts have declined in abundance for several reasons, including deforestation in their tropical winter habitat,[19] but over the past century, their expanded breeding habitat in the resurgent forest may well have kept the decline from being even worse.

Frost mentioned other birds that preferred open ground. Nighthawks nest in open areas, while whippoorwills nest among trees that have little or no underbrush.[20] They hunt insects in the dim light of evening and morning and have distinctive calls. Frost included both in several poems. In "Waiting," as evening deepens toward night, "the last swallow's sweep" over the "stubble field" gives way to "the bat's mute antics" (the flying mammals that share the crepuscular sky with birds) and then "the nighthawks peopling heaven," each with a "vague unearthly cry." In this setting, the birds do not detract but actually assist the narrator in focusing on "the memory of one absent." Frost must have experienced scenes like this among his many evening walks, and he seems to have used them both as source material and as times of contemplation. The countryside that supports these birds is comforting and secure, unlike the rising cities that are spreading into the rural areas and turning "the note of the evening hawk" into a distant memory ("The Parlor Joke").

An evening transition nearly identical to that in "Waiting" occurs in "Ghost House":

Stopping by Woods

> Night comes; the black bats tumble and dart;
> The whippoorwill is coming to shout
> And hush and cluck and flutter about

But here, the narrator is a ghost, the occupant of the old house. The ghost shares the house with a host of resurgent plants, flying animals and "mute folks." The decay of the house seems "slow and sad" but all the beings and souls are "As sweet companions as might be had." The flora and fauna are benefiting from an abandoned building as clearly as the phoebes in "The Need of Being Versed in Country Things" and the birds at the end of "The Thatch." But as succession fills in the nesting habitats of nighthawks and whippoorwills, their calls will become less frequent.[21]

It is possible that Frost was also telling a tale of succession in "Never Again Would Birds' Song Be the Same." The setting of Eden from Genesis is, of course, a garden, a landscape modified by deliberate management (divine, in this case). Eve arrives, and her voice somehow changes the voices (songs) of birds. This modification of bird songs wrought by Eve "persisted in the woods" and "never would be lost." Had the "garden," the manipulated, managed landscape, become a "wood"? Had ecological succession replaced the cultivated with the wild? If so, then the poem could be describing the response of birds to the regrowth of the forest. The bird songs in the wood are not the same as the bird songs in the garden because the birds are not the same species, and thus the title makes ecological sense: "Never Again Would Birds' Song Be the Same." Though I cannot be sure that Frost deliberately included succession as an underlying theme in this poem, it strikes me as a reasonable possibility.

A Landscape Patchwork

The patchwork of farms and wild vegetation produced by abandonment and succession was complex and ever changing. In *A Boy's Will*, Frost described this complexity in two poems with different perspectives, one human, the other mythic. The human observer in "The Vantage Point" has options: "If tired of trees I seek again mankind." The farms and villages where humans live and toil are visible in one direction. But later, "I have but to turn on my arm, and lo, / The sunburned hillside sets my face aglow" with a forested scene full of birds and insects. The mosaic of the rural landscape is on a sufficiently small scale to be visible from this single vantage point. (Frost initially titled this poem "Choice of Society,"[22] which might have referred to the role of humans not only in viewing but also in producing the mosaic.)

Six poems later, Frost imagined how Pan would look at this same landscape, "At wooded valley and wooded hill" ("Pan with Us"): "In all the country he did command / He saw no smoke and he saw no roof. / That was well! and he stamped his hoof." The trees had nearly taken over from the farmers, with just a few souls living off the land ("And the world had found new terms of worth"). These stragglers have to cope with the resurgence of Nature, the inevitable result of succession. Pan approves.

But Pan viewed this resurgence "on the height of naked pasture land." The only way a pasture can remain open is with human use, the grazing of livestock. The work of grazing animals is clearly evident, including "the fruited bough of the juniper" that flourishes because the "half-wild steer" eats nearly everything except juniper.[23] The influence of livestock on juniper also appears in "The Vantage Point," in which the narrator goes "to a slope where the cattle keep the lawn. / There amid lolling juniper reclined").

Pan might not see any humans at the moment, but the presence of the pasture allows him to infer that someone comes to the pasture "to salt the half-wild steer" and that there are "homespun children with clicking pails / Who see so little they tell no tales." This suggestion of the presence of things is similar to that in some Chinese paintings. When asked to depict a monastery in a wooded landscape, one artist included only a monk gathering water in a landscape of trees and mountains. Where was the monastery? It had to be in there somewhere, of course, or there wouldn't be a monk by the stream.[24] Inference alone is often enough.

Pan is a wonderfully complex and appropriate observer, standing in a pasture that feeds his favored sheep, while admiring the woods that constitute his favored wildness. Yet the patchwork of farms, forest, flowers and fields turns out to be too complex even for a deity that Frost considered to be an essential part of "the One God."[25] At the end of the poem, Pan lies down, overwhelmed by multitasking and unable to decide what music to play: "What should he play?"

As Pan contemplates his decision, he absent-mindedly "raveled a flower and looked away." Why would Frost include such a detail? Because

Frost wants to express his preference for early successional flowers over late successional trees. Pan may have favored the wildness in this landscape, but Frost did not favor Pan, destroyer of blossoms, and may have taken some pleasure in the confusion of a deity who would defile a flower.

Despite his appreciation of early successional flowers, Frost understood the inevitable nature of succession and the effects of the process on humans and non-human species. As George Bagby has pointed out, Frost's early poetry emphasized the human view of succession, and only later did he express doubt of an anthropocentric view.[26] We get the human perspective throughout "The Times Table." When a horse sighs, the farmer claims that each sigh brings "a death." Then the narrator fears that the farmer's claim, however true, will cause roads to close, farms to be abandoned and birthrates to fall, all of which will "bring back nature in people's place." The demise of humans is to be mourned, but the last line does admit that something will take the place of people, and that there won't be a vacuum once they're gone.

In "Something for Hope," Frost becomes an advocate of using succession as a guide for living on the landscape of New England: cut the trees for lumber, use the cleared land for a farm, but then abandon the land and be patient as the trees regrow and complete the cycle. Rather than fight it, Frost is recommending that people have the foresight to adjust their lives to "a cycle we'll say of a hundred years." If people worked within the cycle instead of against it, he argues, then there would be more reason to hope. At this time scale, however, patience must extend beyond a single human lifetime, perhaps an unrealistic expectation.[27]

In "Blueberries," patience is rewarded much more quickly. Blueberry bushes fare poorly in the shade of trees, producing little or no fruit. When humans tend blueberries, they ensure a good yield by preventing the surrounding vegetation from shading the bushes. Robert Faggen focused on blueberries as a commodity because a farmer "has taken care to produce them."[28] The blueberries in this poem, however, were not tended at all. Instead, they were just a happy accident. A patch of woods had been logged off and the dry pine slash burned ("The fire ran and burned it all but the wall"). Two years later, there were blueberries in the burned-over land because there was sunlight, plus ash from the fire for fertilizer:

> "And presto, they're up all around you as thick
> And hard to explain as a conjurer's trick."

"It must be on charcoal they fatten their fruit.
I taste in them sometimes the flavor of soot.
And after all, really they're ebony skinned:
The blue's but a mist from the breath of the wind."[29]

Like the burst of flowers after mowing, the flush of berries after a fire won't last long. One brief notebook entry almost certainly laments how succession results in "no blueberries any more"[30] after trees shade out the shrubs. In "Blueberries," though, there is less concern for returning trees than for hungry neighbors. Everyone will be wanting fresh berries.

Yet even in the haste of preparing to gather this bounty of fruit, the characters in "Blueberries" take the time to enjoy the new berries: "You ought to have seen how it looked in the rain, / The fruit mixed with water in layers of leaves, / Like two kinds of jewels, a vision for thieves." Picking blueberries in the rain is just too messy, but one can admire them when the drops of water refract the bright points of light.

Throughout his poetry, Frost took different points of view regarding succession, as he did with seasonal change, sometimes admiring it and other times wishing it would cease. It is not surprising that he had complex feelings about such a complex process. The spatial mosaic of farms, active and abandoned, was constantly changing as some of his neighbors left or died, and the deserted properties were at various stages of being reclaimed by the forest. Frost watched each stage happen, sometimes with admiration, sometimes with regret. He loved the flowers that sprang up in fields and he wished they could persist ("The Last Mowing").[31] He was familiar with the shrub stage of succession and titled his penultimate collection of poems *Steeple Bush*, a hardy species of *Spiraea* with bright pink blossoms. He also knew that the rise of "maple, birch and spruce" trees ("Something for Hope") was inevitable: "the not mowing brings trees on" ("The Last Mowing," line 8). When shade from the canopy of mature trees eliminated flowers and shrubs, it could shade his psyche: "Petals I may have once pursued / Leaves are all my darker mood" ("Leaves Compared with Flowers"). In contrast, the bright white bark of birch trees was a source of joy ("Birches," "A Young Birch," "Wild Grapes"). Mostly, though, Frost was matter of fact about the regrowth of trees in New England: "In youth I looked for flowers / Where now I look for trees."[32] He accepted the trees because he had no choice as the landscape filled up with them (and he could "leave the world" on his botanizing walks to visit those blossoms that were able to survive beneath trees, the "Forest Flowers"). Only storms that toppled trees, or the infrequent cutting of fuel or timber, could reset the successional clock. "One had to be versed in country things" to grasp the inevitability of ecological succession, and to explore this transformation in verse as deftly as Frost.

Life Cycles
in a Resurgent Nature
"For them there was
really nothing sad"

Various species of plants and animals will be able to complete their life cycles at different times within the long span of ecological succession. Along the way, individuals grow and age, conditions change, and failure is frequent. But as long as suitable habitats exist, species that need those habitats can succeed. Frost noticed how species rose and fell in abundance over time and from place to place. Those that caught his attention became part of his poetry, sometimes in cameo roles, sometimes as the center of attention. Some of these species became actors in multiple poems, much as Henri Matisse turned objects in his studio into actors within different drawings or paintings.[1]

Each vignette is part of the larger story of environmental transformation: white birch and wild grapes thrive in the sunlight of early succession. Ferns, a diverse group of species, can be found anywhere from full sun to deep shade, typically with broad fronds that might be hiding something from view. Alder shrubs prefer wet, swampy soils, and often provide refuges for wildlife. Lilacs, planted as ornaments around houses, persist, at least for a while, after those who planted them have departed. Maple trees, in contrast, start slowly but can eventually tower over all but the other members of the forest canopy. Birds, like ferns, can be found almost anywhere but face a daily challenge: how to make it through the night (or, if nocturnal, through the day). These species, along with every other creature, will not live forever, either in whole or part, and their remains sustain the decomposers. Decomposition, in turn, fuels new growth that replaces the old.

The stories in this chapter range from full sun through shade into the soil, each habitat hosting different characters. But first, how shall we refer to them? What names should apply?

Names and Naming

When Frost used names for the plants and animals in his poems, they could be specific or generic, rarely formal, and occasionally cryptic: a hummingbird was "the meteor that thrusts in with needle bill" in "A Prayer in Spring"; autumn was "that other fall we name the fall" in "The Oven Bird"; a woodpecker was "a feather-hammer" in "A Winter Eden"; and the reader was supposed to make "One Guess" from clues about a grasshopper in "Ten Mills." On occasion, he avoided using names entirely, either because the name was unknown (the flower that "hadn't a name" in "Blueberries," line 66) or because names were unnecessary to appreciate a riot of bountiful blossoms: "I needn't call you by name" ("The Last Mowing"). And in at least one case, he removed a couplet about names ("Tuft of Flowers").[2]

Frost played with names when ambiguity made it possible. "Wild Grapes" opens with a puzzle: "What tree may not the fig be gathered from? / The grape may not be gathered from the birch? / It's all you know the grape or know the birch." Grape vines climb birch trees, so grapes can indeed be harvested by climbing birch trees. But what about figs? Surely figs can be found only on fig trees. And it was surely a fig tree that Zaccheus climbed to be able to see Jesus (Luke 19:4), except that the tree is named "sycamore" in the King James Bible, and the tree he climbed appears in Frost's poem "Sycamore." In New England (and elsewhere in North America and Europe) there are sycamore trees (in the genus *Platanus*), but they are not fig trees and bear no figs. Yet around the Mediterranean Sea, there are fig trees with the formal name *Ficus sycomorus*, a name that has been Anglicized to the common name "sycamore" (even though figs and sycamores are not even in the same family of trees).[3] So what sycamore may not the fig be gathered from? Good question.

Though Frost hardly ever used the formal "scientific" names for living things, those names were usually derived from Latin or Greek, and thus they would have meant something to him because of his training in classical languages. But he rarely used Latin and Greek for *any* reason in his writing, and he rarely used a formal name for any species in his poetry unless, like Calypso or Clematis, it was also widely used in English. After all, the farmers and villagers who lived in rural New England did not use formal names. Common names were plenty good enough. Frost pointed this out to his friend Sidney Cox, "I needn't qualify as a specialist in botany and astronomy for a license to invoke flowers and stars in my poetry."[4]

There were other reasons to stick with common names. In "In White," a poem that he later revised and retitled "Design," Frost did attempt to use a formal name, but chose an archaic form (at least in some versions of the poem): "The blue Brunella every child's delight."[5] "Brunella" substituted a "b" for the "p" in *Prunella*, the actual formal name. Perhaps Frost had not seen the botanical spelling in print but only inferred it from hearing the name spoken (who hasn't, at some point, confused the sounds of B and P?). Whether someone pointed out the problem or he discovered it himself, he decided it was better to play it safe.

Brilliantly (and mercifully), Frost changed the line so that it returned to the common name: "The wayside blue and innocent heal-all?" The result was one of the best lines in one of his most profound poems. Neither Brunella nor *Prunella* would have helped. Here and in most contexts, formal names were too long, too unfamiliar or too arrhythmic to be part of the sound of Frost.

There were three exceptions to this pattern, two minor and the third significant. Frost could not avoid using *Cypripedium reginæ* in "The Self-Seeker" because the Broken One was a botanist and used such names in his study of orchids. In "Time Out," the genus *Maianthemum* fits the poetic rhythm far better than any of the available common names. The third formal name is *Hyla* in "Hyla Brook" and "The Bonfire." *Hyla* is a genus of frogs that includes spring peepers (*Hyla crucifer*). *Hyla* has an almost musical quality that flows more smoothly than "peeper" (though Frost did use "peeper" in "The Onset" and "peeping" in "Pea Brush"). For these frogs of spring, either name would do, but *Hyla* was just too nice to pass up. Sad to say, *Hyla* has been officially supplanted by *Pseudacris*,[6] a name I cannot confidently pronounce. Change is not always good.

The process by which the name *Hyla crucifer* was changed to *Pseudacris crucifer* followed the rules of zoological nomenclature.[7] In a broader sense, "nomenclature" drew Frost's ridicule in "Lucretius Versus the Lake Poets" ("college nomenclature") and in "Kitty Hawk": "Some have preached and taught / All there was to thought / Was to master Nature / By some nomenclature." To Frost, some names defied common sense. How could

115

apples, pears and plums all be considered roses ("The Rose Family") when it was obvious that "The rose is a rose"? On the one hand, he almost certainly recognized the similarities of structure among the blossoms of the apples, peaches, cherries and strawberries in and around his farms. These traits are the unifying characteristics of Rosaceae, the rose family. Yet even now, botanists have not definitively answered Frost's speculation: "What will next prove a rose." Estimates of the number of species in the rose family range from 2,000 to nearly 20,000.[8] Such uncertainty does not inspire confidence (although much of it stems from the large size of this cosmopolitan family in which new species continue to be discovered).

But much more important than mere names was the process of naming that Frost perceived as pigeonholing and oversimplification. Nature was being reduced to "Pretty Scenery" when Frost thought it should include "the Whole Goddam Machinery" ("Lucretius Versus the Lake Poets"). Science, with its formal nomenclature and precise rules for assigning names, was too constricting and too limiting. Where was the metaphor? Where was the art? Frost refused to be bound by any rules that limited his vision. Instead, he used his own rules, and his own creative imagination, to make sense of the countryside in which he lived, worked, walked and observed. He needn't call everything by name.

Birch

After farms have been abandoned for a few years, young trees begin to grow above the weeds and shrubs. White birch thrives in these sunny conditions, and whenever Frost mentions birch in a poem, we see the early-successional pioneer status of this species. Birch trees are among those thrusting upward through the shrubs in "Something for Hope." The tips of the trees in "Birches" dip down "to the withered bracken" ferns, early successional plants that persist among the birches.[9] Birch tips also dip into sweet fern and hardhack in "Wild Grapes" (line 33). Successional shrubs and ferns on the ground, plus sun-loving grapes high in the birch branches (also in lines 163–4 of "New Hampshire"), indicate that the grape vines and birch trees grew as the vanguards of this forest glade when sunlight was abundant. They could not have grown so high in the shade of other trees.[10]

In Frost's time, white birch was widespread on land allowed to go wild, and he gave birch trees a prominent role in at least six poems. Birches were swung in winter ("Birches"), cut in spring ("Pea Brush"), climbed for grapes in autumn ("Wild Grapes"), conspicuous in the growing season ("The Onset"), and generally admired ("New Hampshire," "A Young Birch"). Their prominence was clear evidence that farms had been giving way to trees before 1900.

In "Birches," Frost explains how both swinging and ice will bend young birch trees low, but only ice will "bend them down to stay." What becomes of these bent trees, "their trunks arching in the woods / Years afterwards, trailing their leaves on the ground"? When mature oak trees are bent by ice, their growth slows in the shade of taller trees and they try to compensate by growing thicker wood and vertical branches on the upper side of the bend.[11] Will bent oaks or bent birches ever be able to rejoin the canopy, or are they doomed to die and allow others to thrive? These are questions for ecologists as well as poets.

The most striking feature of paper birch is, of course, its white color: "And climb black branches up a snow-white trunk" ("Birches"); "The birch begins to crack its outer sheath / Of baby green and show the white beneath" ("A Young Birch"); "Nothing will be left white but here a birch, / And there a clump of houses with a church" ("The Onset"); "One day my brother led me to a glade / Where a white birch he knew stood alone" ("Wild Grapes"). Young or mature, in any season, white birch bark deserved our attention.

There are exceptions to the inclusion of white with birch. White bark is not mentioned in "Pea Brush" because the birch trees have been cut down and left as "stumps still bleeding their life away," nor in "New Hampshire" where the description is merely presaging "Wild Grapes" where white bark is mentioned twice.

"White," by itself or in contrast to darker things, appears in many of Frost's poems, but birches are special in their brightness and their sharing of his wife's maiden name. They are so steadfastly white (or if not yet, they will be soon, with more growth), and so abundant in second-growth forest (especially around 1900) that they have become a New England icon, made that much more iconic by their prominence in the poetry of Robert Frost. Today, white birch is in decline because they cannot survive in the shade of other trees. Frost captured for us the time when birches reigned supreme.

Grapes

Like white birch, grapes are native to North America. While it is true that indigenous American grapes do not lead to great wine, their roots, grafted to old-world vines, saved nearly all the vineyards of Europe from lethal infestations of an insect, the grape phylloxera.[12] And even pedestrian wine was safer for New England colonists to drink than water that might be contaminated by human waste from an outhouse too close to the well.[13]

Ripe purple grapes are attractive and appealing but often hard to get. Two poems in *New Hampshire* address some of the problems in harvesting grapes. First, grapes of the Granite state are borne high up on birch trees: "Her unpruned grapes are flung like lariats / Far up the birches out of reach of man" ("New Hampshire"). But how can white birches produce purple grapes, fruits not their own? Because, as Frost knew, the sun-loving birch trees were perfect ladders on which sun-loving grape vines could twine: "It's all you know the grape, or know the birch" ("Wild Grapes").

In "Wild Grapes," we see that picking these elevated grapes can be hazardous, especially for a small child who doesn't "weigh anything." The girl recounts the story of how her older brother climbed the birch and "threw me down grapes to miss and scatter / And have to hunt for in sweet fern and hardhack" (two species of early-successional shrubs, thriving in the sunlight). To make the harvest more efficient, he bends the tree down within her reach, but instead of grabbing the grapes, she grabs the birch and "it caught me up as if I were the fish." Having started off wasting the scattered grapes in the weedy undergrowth, she suddenly finds herself fearing for her life. But then she perseveres through primal instinct ("I had not taken the first step in knowledge; / I had not learned to let go with the hands") and clings to her lifeline long enough for her brother to rescue her. "And the life I live now's an extra life / I can waste as I please on whom I please." This modern-day "Eurydice" would have the luxury of living twice, having survived the temptation of the grapes.

Not all grapes are out of reach, of course, but then there is another problem: neighbors. Grapes are one of the fruits that draw people across walls and boundaries of deserted farms (and maybe occupied ones as well), and the new owners of an old farm in "In the Home Stretch" speculate about their neighbors: "'I doubt they have left many grapes.'" They fear that it might be too late to find any fruit, just as other people fear it might soon be too late to pick the "jewels" in "Blueberries."

118

But even grapes that are not sought can cause anxiety. In "To Earthward," the mere odor or "musk" of grapes is a painful reminder of sweet love "that seemed too much." The scent, the wine and the hangover of heartbreak are the dark side of grapes, the fruit of Dionysus, the source of indulgence and excess, or the headache that reminds us of things once possessed but now lost.

Grapes can overrun, confuse and entangle farms as well as lives. Fences are sunny (on at least one side) and vines thrive on these human constructions just as they thrive on birches. In "Ghost House," "O'er ruined fences the grapevines shield" with vines so thick that they nearly replace the fence. In the confusion of tangled stems, some of the vines eventually die and accumulate as long strands of dry wood, perfect for carrying a fire. Their flammability explains the efforts of the narrator in "The Bonfire" to keep a roadside fire from reaching the "grape vine entanglement."

Frost's poems show us how grapes can be enticing, but often at a cost. The fruit befuddles, the vines ensnare, obscure and burn, and the harvest can be dangerous. Perhaps it is best that those grapes high up in the sun-drenched birches remain "out of reach" ("New Hampshire"). For Frost, "out of reach" seems to have become out of mind; after the heartache of "To Earthward" in *New Hampshire*, he did not write about grapes again. It was as if the sun-loving vines had finally been shaded out and faded away.

Ferns

Living in fields and forests, ferns appear early in succession and persist within the forest understory, often thriving where other plants might struggle to gain a foothold.[14] Sometimes they blend in, other times they are conspicuous in their abundance or in contrast with their surroundings. Outcrops of rock abound in New England, especially along streams ("The Falls") and on mountains ("The Mountain"), and these are inevitably homes to ferns. Frost inserted ferns in his poems in a fashion similar to their insertion in the landscape: rarely dominant, but often important, a verdant Greek chorus that is never far from the action.

Frost's interest in ferns was serious enough that he pressed the frond of a small fern in one of his notebooks.[15] His interest in ferns was also long-standing. Anyone taking a tour of Frost's farmhouse in Derry, New

Hampshire (where Frost lived from 1900 to 1909), will likely be shown a former library book that has Frost's signature on the check-out card. The card is for *How to Know the Ferns*, a book that Frost was said to carry with him when he walked in the countryside.[16] There is no question that he did know his ferns. In a 1918 letter to the president of Amherst College, Frost compared the interruption of peoples' lives by World War I to the interrupted fern (*Osmunda claytoniana*).[17] At age 81 in 1955, during a walk in Vermont with Reginald Cook, he dismissed the ferns along the trail: "'Oh, they're all the common ones: the hay-scented and lady ferns!'"[18]

Despite his familiarity with these plants, only bracken fern or brake (*Pteridium aquilinum*) is identified by its common names in four poems. In eleven other poems and two pieces of prose, the ferns are merely "ferns," their uniformity allowing Frost to bypass the names in his field guide to ferns. Frost seems to have used the field guide less as a source of names than a companion (perhaps an excuse) to walk in the woods, something he sought to do as often as possible. How, then, did he use ferns in his poetry?

In "A Servant to Servants," some botanically-inclined visitors are camping at a farm so they can look for ferns near Lake Willoughby.[19] The woman serving their meal wonders aloud: "Our Willoughby! How did you hear of it? / I expect, though, everyone's heard of it. / In a book about ferns? Listen to that! / You let things more like feathers regulate / Your going and coming. And you like it here? / I can see how you might. But I don't know!" She goes on to tell the visitors an extended tale of her life and family. Tim Kendall gives a succinct overview of the source and significance of her narrative,[20] and it is the narrative that is the point of the poem. Frost uses ferns as bait for an audience so that the servant's story of confinement and madness can be told. But as the servant's narrative lengthens and her audience seeks a way to depart, the ferns become an excuse for them to leave. As the visitors seek escape, the servant turns the pleasantries of their departure into one more articulation of the depth of her despair. Scattered throughout the poem, ferns act as a small but essential part of the supporting cast.

Ferns are sometimes so ubiquitous in New England that they can hide just about anything. In a children's story from the decade when Frost's family lived on the farm in Derry, "Margery" is mostly hidden from Papa and the other children "over in the ferns" next to the yard.[21] When Frost wrote that he would wear an interrupted fern around his hat in honor of those whose lives were interrupted by war, he noted that "it would cover me up."[22] In "The Hill Wife," the wife impulsively decides to cover herself up and hide from her husband: "She stood, and then she ran and hid / In the fern. / He never found her, though he looked / Everywhere." The ferns played their sylvan role, shielding the lonely, childless wife; her success in hiding among the ferns ends the marriage. Readers are left to imagine her fate among the ferns.

Readers also remain uncertain about a nest that has lost its cover of ferns and other plants ("The Exposed Nest") that withered after being cut down by a mower. First a child and then the child's parent discover the nestlings "left defenseless to the heat and light." They use the wilted ferns as best they can "and gave them back their shade."[23] Then they "turned to other things" and never checked to see whether their repairs allowed the mother bird to return or the nestlings to survive. Only later did the narrator wonder whether their efforts had been successful.[24]

Ferns can hide things in other ways. They often thrive as weeds around objects constructed of stone, such as the "well-curbs" in "For Once, Then, Something." The narrator's reflection in the well was surrounded by "a wreath of fern and cloud puffs." When looking into a well or pond or puddle, the most obvious sight is the reflection of the sky and surrounding plants. With some concentration, though, deeper things can be perceived through that reflection. But as the narrator begins to discern something white (there is that color again), he loses sight of it. The object disappears from sight because a fern, acting as more than mere reflection, released a physical intrusion: "Water came to rebuke the too clear water. / One drop fell from a fern, and lo, a ripple / Shook whatever it was lay there at bottom." The verdant periphery of ferns (Parini likened it to a poet's crown of laurels[25]) produced a drop of water from its lush fronds that disturbed the perception of the narrator, preventing him from identifying something, whatever it might have been, hidden below. So mundane yet so prevalent, the green leaves joined with the water surface to maintain the secrets of the well. What might be hiding down there?

Within the forests of New England and elsewhere, the seeming monotony of ferns gives the impression of something primitive and ageless. No flowers, no seeds, no obvious means of propagation, yet so abundant, ferns are living fossils. In "A Line-Storm Song," Frost presents ferns as a benchmark for antiquity: "To the ancient lands where it left the shells / Before the age of the fern." The frilly self-similar leaves of fossilized ferns grew in forests inhabited by land animals older than dinosaurs.[26] Anything that occurred "before the age of the fern" must be old indeed.

But even ferns die and wither, and some dead ferns, including bracken, retain their dry, dead leaves. Though merely incidental in "Birches" (line 14) and "The Onset" (line 20), dry "brake" in "The Bonfire" helps carry a fire that the narrator barely manages to keep from spreading into the forest. Some ferns have significance beyond their green lives.

In 1948, Frost wrote *A Romantic Chasm* as a preface to the British edition of *A Masque of Reason*. In it, he mentioned a demonstration of the "internationality of ferns" by Jack Haines, who showed him a "spleenwort" (*Asplenium*) "up a small cliff," a location reminiscent of the fern habitat in "The Mountain." Though he never used the names spleenwort or *Asplenium* in his poetry, Frost knew what the fern was and was happy to be "boosted" up to see a spleenwort "by matchlight."[27] Finding this particular type of fern had enriched his botanizing if not his rhymes. In his poetry, whether in full sun or deep in the forest, generic "ferns" were nearly always good enough.

Alders

Alders (*Alnus*) are abundant shrubs that take on a supporting role in an array of Frost's poems. They often grow in thickets in New England, rarely reaching tree size or shape (different species elsewhere can be more tree-like). They can grow well in places where other plants struggle because they host clusters of nitrogen-fixing bacteria in nodules on their roots.[28] They prefer soils that range from damp to wet. On the wet end of the scale, alder swamps are habitats for several species of wildlife, at least partly because their tangle of stems provides shelter and protection. On a warm winter day, some of the inhabitants emerge briefly from the swamp to romp in the sun ("A Winter Eden"). But when a young hunter "lurks" with his hound at the edge of a swamp, the alders defy the hunter's sight and the hound's nose (as long as the "yelps" of the hound don't terrify a "hare" so much that it bolts into the open: "The Rabbit-Hunter").

Just about any farm in New England can have some alders somewhere ("In the Home Stretch," line 197) because the topography is irregular and therefore dotted with wet areas where alders thrive. Where there are bodies of water, whether still or flowing, alders often inhabit the edges, like "the far shore alders" along "West-Running Brook" (line 26). If the conditions are just right, and if one is sufficiently patient to "skirt the margin of alders for miles and miles," the reward might be "purple spires" of flowers "'Neath the alder tree" ("The Quest of the Purple-Fringed"). Just be prepared for dampness underfoot.

There are times when alders defy expectations. Patches of alders should be wet enough to serve as a barrier against fire, and by themselves, they nearly always are. But if grapes have climbed the alders years ago and since died, the "alder and grape vine entanglement" could carry fire across damp ground ("The Bonfire").

Sometimes alders occupy a space next to a stream or pond where members of a farm family might like to go fishing or have a picnic. To accommodate the family, the farmer must try to clear away the inconvenient shrubs. The alders, with their profusion of stems, appear to have other ideas: "I've known ere now an interfering branch / Of alder catch my lifted ax behind me. / But that was in the woods, to hold my hand / From striking at another alder's roots." The alder's resistance to destruction, though only seeming to be conscious, probably contributes to their success (along with a preference for wet habitats that humans usually avoid). No wonder that alders continue to populate New England to this day.[29]

As with ferns, Frost nearly always referred to alders in a generic way, with just the name "alder." In part V of "The Hill Wife," however, he includes the sentence "And once she went to break a bough / Of black alder." What is black alder? There is a species known as black alder in Europe (*Alnus glutinosa*) that has been introduced to North America, but it is rare or absent in New Hampshire and Vermont. Among species indigenous to New England, the name black alder sometimes refers to a type of holly (*Ilex verticillata*) that is more often called winterberry because its bright red fruits ripen in September and persist through the winter. Winterberry grows in swamps and damp soils, so it might be found growing with alders. But why would a lonely wife seek to "break a bough" from this shrub?[30]

If berries were present on the shrub, her motives might have been medicinal. These fruits are occasionally used as a folk remedy for fever (hence one common name: fever-bush), though a large dose would be potentially toxic.[31] Did she seek the bough for a cure, or to induce sickness as a way to get attention or sympathy from her distant husband? Or did she seek it as a poison that would help her escape her marriage? It is also possible, of course, that she was simply attracted to the bright red fruit. Whatever the reason, there is no certainty that her intent to break the bough was fulfilled. Instead, she chose to hide among the ferns and never return to her husband.

Though less ubiquitous than ferns, alders serve a similar function—hide or obscure things in the landscape. And while ferns can easily be brushed aside, woody alder thickets are difficult to penetrate and thus hold on to their secrets more tightly. Alders and ferns add a touch of mystery to the countryside and to Frost's poetry, giving the reader something unknown or unseen to contemplate.

Lilacs

Lilacs (*Syringa*) are not native to New England but are often planted as ornamental shrubs in many parts of North America. Pretty they may be, but they are durable as well, surviving long after the people that planted them have left them behind.[32] Thus they join with a resurgent native flora in the process of succession.

Lilacs appear in only two of Frost's poems ("The Need of Being Versed in Country Things" and "Directive"), and the draft of a third ("The Times Table"),[33] but what lilacs lack in frequency they make up in importance.

Lilacs persist after a farmhouse has burned down in "The Need of Being Versed in Country Things," leaving a barn that becomes home to phoebes: "Yet for them the lilac renewed its leaf." The lilacs, a remnant of the farm, can now spread unhindered and grow new leaves, just as the phoebes can recover some of their past by restaking a claim to the barn.

In "Directive," an abandoned farm includes a house that is now nothing but a cellar hole (surrounded by many others) with discarded toys under a pine tree. Frost asks the reader to mourn for "the house that is no more a house, / But only a belilaced cellar hole, / Now slowly closing like a dent in dough." The lilacs, once there for show, are now taking over the cellar hole, growing around it, filling it up with dead leaves, branches and flowers. Its roots displace and dislodge the stones of the cellar walls, letting in the soil. The lilacs decorate one of Frost's most creative domestic images, "now closing like a dent in dough." This "dough" won't bake, but will harden instead as it merges back into the land. And the lilacs will remain as a reminder of what was. They are the link of the past and present.

With regard to "Directive," Robert Faggen argued: "Lilacs in their beauty belie the destruction and death upon which they grow, the former dwelling of another creature, and in this respect are elegiac in the tradition not only of *Walden* but also of Whitman's poem 'When Lilacs Last in the Dooryard Bloomed' and Eliot's reference to Whitman in the opening of 'The Wasteland [sic].'"[34] The two poems mentioned by Faggen (Whitman's "Memories of President Lincoln" [1866] and Eliot's "The Waste Land" [1922]), along with "Lilacs" by Amy Lowell (1925), preceded the publication of "Directive" (1946). However, "The Need of Being Versed in Country Things" was first published in 1920[35] and would have had only Whitman as a potential reference. Kendall argued that Frost disliked Whitman's reduced adherence to poetic form,[36] so it is an open question whether the lilacs in "The Need of Being Versed in Country Things" were inspired by Whitman's poem.

There are other options for the provenance of lilacs in "Directive" and in the draft of "The Times Table." One possible source is Henry David Thoreau, who in Walden referred to old cellar holes as dents and noticed the proximity of lilacs: "Still grows the vivacious lilac a generation after the door and lintel and the sill are gone." Thoreau was an influence and inspiration throughout Frost's life, so it would not be at all surprising if "Directive" drew some of its imagery from Walden.[37]

Another possible source for lilac imagery preceded both "The Need of Being Versed in Country Things" and "Directive." Lucinda Carleton included her poem "The Old Cellars" in a chapbook of poetry about lilacs and roses. George Monteiro is uncertain whether Carleton's verse could have inspired Frost's references to lilacs, but it is an interesting hypothesis.[38]

A third possible reference is from Amy Lowell. Lilacs appear in "Directive" in precisely the same setting as those in Lowell's "Lilacs," a poem that begins with a clear reference to Whitman and then includes an old house and cellar (italics added): "Lilacs in *dooryards* / Holding quiet conversations with an early moon; / *Lilacs watching a deserted house* / Settling sideways into the grass of an old road; / *Lilacs*, wind-beaten, staggering under a lopsided shock of bloom / *Above a cellar* dug into a hill." I doubt that the similarities between "Lilacs" ("Lilacs watching a deserted house," "cellar") and "Directive" ("house that is no more a house," "belilaced cellar hole") are accidental. Frost expressed admiration for Amy Lowell's poetry when writing to her directly or when telling his daughter Lesley how to prepare to meet with Lowell, should an invitation to do so be forthcoming. According to Jay Parini, however, Frost disparaged her poetry in private conversation. In 1925, Frost begged off attending a dinner in Lowell's honor, but then felt guilty when she died shortly thereafter. He wrote a brief tribute to Lowell for the *Christian Science Monitor*, and then wrote to Louis Untermeyer, "I didn't rise to verse" in her honor.[39] But twenty years later, Frost appears to have risen to verse in "Directive," with its striking similarity to Lowell's poem. Whatever he thought of her poetry in particular and free verse in general, perhaps he found the images in "Lilacs" highly compelling.

Another less certain reference might be worth considering: Lowell's repeated mention of the heart-shaped leaves in "Lilacs" might have been derived from the almost caring (loving? heartfelt?) growth of the lilacs in "The Need of Being Versed in Country Things": "Yet for them [the phoebes] the lilac renewed its leaf." If Lowell was indeed referencing Frost, then there could be a circle of lilac images connecting these poems and these poets.

Maple

Trees become the dominant form of vegetation after flowers and shrubs have flourished in the sunlight. There are dozens of tree species in New England that differ in shape, habitat, growth rate, phenology, utility and prominence in ecological succession, and throughout his life, Frost observed the changes of individual trees and of trees in the landscape. Trees in the titles of poems offered inspiration at home ("Tree at My Window"), encouragement to leave home ("The Sound of Trees") or contemplation away from home ("Stopping by Woods on a Snowy Evening"). Trees could obstruct ("On a Tree Fallen Across the Road") or disappoint ("Christmas Trees"), but they could also provide resources to keep a farmer alive ("In Winter in the Woods Alone").

Frost also examined every stage of the life cycle of trees. From seeds ("One Favored Acorn") to seedlings ("Maple") through sapling stage ("A Young Birch") all the way to death ("On a Tree Fallen Across the Road"), trees were important points of entry into explorations of the landscape. Frost even used the structure of tree wood as an analogy for the vitality of countries: "there are certain countries that are in the dead wood, certain countries that are in the live wood, and we are in the cambium layer," the layer that produces the new cells of new growth.[40]

Frost mentioned apple trees more often than any other type, but all apple trees in North America were derived from those brought over from Europe. Apple orchards were part of many farms and have already been discussed in that context. Next in line after apples was maple.

Sugar maple (*Acer saccharum*) grows slowly, but still manages to be a dominant species in northern New England, and it was one of the trees that Frost used repeatedly as the starting point for his metaphors.[41] Maple is so important that Frost imagined a family that named its daughter Maple. The poem "Maple" does not seem, at first, to be about maple trees at all but only about a girl who is named for a maple tree. As the poem jumps around in time and place, however, the life cycle of maple trees becomes central to the mystery of the girl named Maple.

Maple's mother had died shortly after giving birth without explaining why she chose the name Maple. Maple's father explains the name as best he can for his young daughter: "'I don't know what she wanted it to mean, / But it seems like some word she left to bid you / Be a good girl—be like a maple tree. / How like a maple tree's for us to guess. / Or for a little girl to guess sometime. / Not now—at least I shouldn't try too hard now.'"

As the mystery unfolds, the theme of names and naming (discussed in depth by Robert Faggen)[42] intertwines with Maple's connection to actual maple trees. A maple seedling has two leaves, mentioned explicitly late in the poem (line 150), but also implied much earlier as the two pages (leaves) of the bible marked by her mother with a maple leaf (lines 65–68). By failing to replace the maple-leaf bookmark, Maple loses those two leaves of the seedling, the leaves of her childhood. She has grown beyond mere seedling stage.

A maple seedling lives under the canopy of other trees, and Maple lives her life surrounded by other people. A young maple tree can survive in the shade, but it cannot grow unless it gets sunlight. This light comes when neighboring trees die, in whole or in part, and let sunlight through gaps in the canopy. A young tree cannot move into those gaps; the gaps have to form in the right place, a matter of luck. The right trees have to die for a young maple to grow. If these trees don't die, or at least lose large branches, the young maple will never have enough light to grow and reach the canopy.[43]

Early in "Maple," the father's inability to explain her name leaves

127

Stopping by Woods

Maple in the dark, a darkness like that from the shade of canopy leaves. For Maple, the darkness is not fatal, though, but transforming: "What he sowed with her slept so long a sleep, / And came so near death in the dark of years, / That when it woke and came to life again, / The flower was different from the parent seed." Maple, the girl, is not rooted in this darkness. She has lost her symbolic roots (her family) as her mother and then her father fail to resolve the mystery of her name. Her mother who named her has died, and her father is at first unable and later unwilling to provide any insight. Without roots, Maple is not fixed in place like her namesake. Just as the narrator in "The Sound of Trees" plans to break free of the influence of trees and leave them behind, the rootless Maple has broken free and is able to move. She pulls out of the dark shadows of ignorance cast by her parents and searches on her own. Thus her "name with meaning" does not completely rule her life but is merely one of the things that "ruled *in* her life" (italics added) and she moves off to seek the light. Maple grows because she receives light from a looking glass, a house with a sunny cellar, her school, the city, and the upper stories of an office building. She grows in the presence of the light, like a maple tree, and matures in the society of adults (approaching the height of the canopy). Finally, another light appears and she is recognized while taking dictation:

> "Do you know you remind me of a tree—
> A maple tree?"
>
> "Because my name is Maple?"
>
> "Isn't it Mabel? I thought it was Mabel."
>
> "No doubt you've heard the office call me Mabel.
> I have to let them call me what they like."
>
> They were both stirred that he should have divined
> Without the name her personal mystery.
> It made it seem as if there must be something
> She must have missed herself. So they were married.

Now fully mature, Maple and her husband search for the tree that inspired her name (the themes of names and trees continue to intertwine): "Once they came on a maple in a glade, / Standing alone with smooth arms lifted up, / And every leaf of foliage she'd worn / Laid scarlet and pale pink about her feet." Like the fallen red apples in "Unharvested," the leaves (upper sides scarlet, lower sides pink) are "wasted" ("November") but not "trodden black" ("The Road Not Taken"). Could this tree, its cool flames on the ground, be the source of her name? "But its age kept them from considering this one. / Twenty-five years ago at Maple's naming / It hardly could have been a two-leaved seedling." Earlier in their search, Maple had decided, more than once, to live without the pursuit of the mystery. After finding this smooth, bare tree, and fallen red leaves, she makes her final, emphatic decision: "'We would not see the secret if we could now: / We are not looking for it any more.'" From here on, we learn no more of her story.

"Maple" is so complex in part because Frost's observations of maples trees are mixed within the metaphors, not presented in advance. The factual foundation of autumn, seedlings, and life in the forest is laid down late. Frost allows (forces?) readers to explore the truth of maples along with Maple, to share the joy, the discovery, and the frustration. Unlike "Design" and many other poems where the observations are described before the development of metaphors, in "Maple," the reader gets to play along.

Tim Kendall[44] explored the web of metaphor and mystery in "Maple," relishing the obvious and the obscure, admitting in the end that much remains hidden and much remains for speculation by the reader. For example, is Maple's ultimate decision to abandon her search the result of repulsion from the resemblance of the red leaves to the blood of her dying mother?[45] Perhaps. But perhaps we are pushing the metaphors too far.

In 1931, Frost wrote: "All metaphor breaks down somewhere. You don't know how much you can get out of it and when it will cease to yield." The person-as-tree, "name with meaning" metaphor goes only so far. Maple begins as a child (seedling) but loses her two leaves and is left in the dark under the canopy of adults. So far, so good. But unlike a tree, she is able to move into a sequence of sources of light that she needs to power her growth. Had she been truly rooted like a tree, her growth would have been much less certain. Most maple seedlings die without ever getting light from a random gap in the canopy. They do not experience the "happy chance" (line 169) of getting enough light (Faggen points out the role of chance throughout the poem).[46]

Had the maple metaphor applied at every step, then Frost's antepenultimate line would make sense: "better a meaningless name" because the "name with meaning" would have almost certainly doomed Maple to a short life in the dark. Instead, she becomes an adult because she is a human being, not a tree (Faggen notes the irony of the phrase "better a meaningless name").[47] A life that could have been written in despair in the darkness of shade is instead an emergence from the dark into the company of other people in the light. The child is named Maple, but being a child instead of a tree, she succeeds. In Frost's New England, most people survived, but most maple seedlings did not.

"Maple" and several other poems set maples in different seasons of the year, especially autumn, winter and spring. Mature maple trees in summer are mentioned in only two poems, and in both cases, the inclusion is fleeting. In "Something for Hope," maples appear briefly as one of the trees that replace shrubs in the process of ecological succession (line 6). In "The Bear," "maple" rhymes with the "staple" of barbed wire on which the bear leaves a tuft of fur (line 8).

There is much more to be said about maples in other seasons. "Evening in a Sugar Orchard" is set near a sugar-house with its fire burning in the season of rising sap, "a lull in March.... Among bare maple boughs." The sap swells the buds with water as the leaves and flowers resume growth after winter dormancy (described in "Spring Pools").[48] But the narrator dismisses the confection being made and asks instead, "'O fireman, give the fire another stoke, / And send more sparks up chimney with the smoke.'" The narrator wants stars, flying, glowing stars that can animate the fixed stars of heaven: "The sparks made no attempt to be the moon. / They were content to figure in the trees / As Leo, Orion, and the Pleiades. / And that was what the boughs were full of soon." The syrup can last a long time in the sealed containers, but sparks fly from the sugarhouse, out among the bare trees, only during sugaring. Let's enjoy these fleeting points of light while we can before the trees leaf out.

After the maples are done with their leaves in autumn, the leaves change color "In one autumnal blaze" ("Winter Has Beaten Summer in Fight"), and the hillsides are covered with "burning maples,"[49] "the tree the autumn fire ran through" ("Maple"). Frost shows us how sugar maple trees begin and end their annual growth in the company of fire.

In most of the poems that include maples, the trees are bare. Maple trees in "A Hundred Collars," "The Onset," "Maple," "A Summer's Garden" and "Winter Winds" have shed their leaves. When maple trees are cut for firewood ("Good-by and Keep Cold," "In Winter in the Woods Alone") it takes place in winter. The maple trees in "A Boundless Moment" and "Evening in a Sugar Orchard" have yet to leaf out. And of course, the maple wood stacked so neatly in "The Wood-Pile" is not merely leafless but dead.

Green maple trees interested Frost far less than trees that were changing or bare. He liked to wonder, and these bare trees gave him much to wonder about. How could they change so much and so often and still survive? How could they make it through the winter, standing out in the cold, naked and exposed, in temperatures that would quickly kill a naked human? Where did they get all that color and then lose it? And how could such fragile seedlings produce trees so large, so strong and so abundant? These are all important questions for botanists, plant physiologists and ecologists. They are also the questions that stimulate poetry: "all nature does is to keep throwing out hints for us to take in science or art."[50]

Birds

Within the dynamic landscape of New England, birds have to be able to find habitats that fulfill their requirements and allow them to reproduce. Here I will consider two aspects of avian habitats, nesting and perching at night, within a sequence of farms and successional vegetation.

The nests of birds are distinctive, sometimes vulnerable, often defended by the parent birds, and above all, essential for breeding. In three poems, Frost describes human intrusion upon bird nests and hinted at possible outcomes. "The Exposed Nest" is set on an active farm where a hay mower has barely missed the nest of a ground-nesting bird, leaving the nestlings alive but at risk. The only people who seemed to care about the young nestlings were a parent and child, but they "turned to other things" and forgot to return and learn the fate of the birds. Have one or both parent birds returned to tend the nest? The reader never finds out. The message is clear: farming had provided a suitable habitat for building a nest, but then it endangered the nests of those birds who could not foresee that their habitat would be mowed.

Other ground-nesting birds thrive in open, early-successional habitats such as the one shared with flowers, butterflies and spiders in "Range-Finding." Even though a long-range bullet has "cut a flower beside a groundbird's nest," the nest remains intact, "and still the bird revisited her young." The day-to-day resilience of the bird and its nest allows the parents and offspring to survive single bullets. But what if there are soon to be more bullets? The reader is left to wonder.

Blueberry bushes have sprung up in a burned pasture in "Blueberries" and people picking berries have kept a bird away from its nest: "For complaining it flew / Around and around us." But the pickers moved on, leaving the reader to conclude that the bird was able to return quickly to the nest. Hope seems justified because picking berries is not nearly as destructive as mowing or gunfire, and shrubs provide a tangle of cover for the nest.

Frost knew enough about birds to notice that, among the flocking birds in "Our Singing Strength," many would migrate elsewhere and there were "really a very few to build and stay." Only those birds that could find suitable sites would stay and build their nests. Phoebes were among those that could find a good site ("The Need of Being Versed in Country Things") and "they rejoiced in the nest they kept" in an abandoned barn of a deserted farm. With humans gone and their structures left behind (or left alone for the breeding season like the woodshed behind my house), these birds have increased opportunities to produce another generation.[51]

The discovery of a hidden nest symbolizes the process of revelation in poetry. In a letter to Everett Glass, Frost wrote, "The subtlest thing as a bark-and-lichen mimicing [sic] nest of the hummingbird, should be obvious when pointed out." Hummingbird nests are subtle indeed (I have seen only one, and a friend had to point it out to me) but once discovered, they are delightful to behold. The poet strives to produce that same kind of delight in readers by revealing what was previously hidden.

Bird nests become metaphor in "The Death of the Hired Man" in which hay, loaded by an experienced farm hand, is reminiscent of multiple nests: "He bundles every forkful in its place, / And tags and numbers it for future reference, / So he can find and easily dislodge it / In the unloading. Silas does that well. / He takes it out in bunches like big birds' nests." Bird nests have a pattern and structure to them, and Silas's care and organization made his "bunches" fit that image. His loads of hay, though large enough to hang over the sides of the wagon,[52] were not random piles of dry grass, but something planned. Silas, however, would not live long enough to construct nests of hay ever again.

Among mature trees in a forest, humans are less likely to find or disturb nests, but birds have other requirements that must be met. Most birds are diurnal creatures, active during the day, quiet in the dark. Their vision and hearing were not built for navigating in the night. We are used to seeing birds active during the day, but where do they go each night when it gets dark? I once watched a diffuse, seemingly endless flock of birds pour out of the sky into a large cattail marsh at dusk. On occasion,

I've seen large numbers of crows all headed in the same direction just before sundown. I often notice the diminuendo of bird songs as night falls. The birds have gone away, out of sight, out of hearing. But where?

Frost paid attention to the answer. There is an anthropomorphic description in "Acceptance" as a bird that has stayed out just a little too long manages to find "his remembered tree" and "twitters softly, 'Safe!'" The bird has found his nighttime perch, his rest and respite for the dark hours. The character Meserve in "Snow" (line 226) compares his chances in the blizzard to "the small birds at roost" on their perches that winter night: "And yet tomorrow / They will come budding boughs from tree to tree," having survived despite being so tiny and vulnerable. If they can survive the storm, so can he. In "In a Vale," Frost gives a mystical description of a place to which the last nocturnal maiden returned at dawn: "Back to the place from which she came— / Where the bird was before it flew." The bird flew during the day, and this nighttime place was its perch.

Once on their perches, birds are better off staying put than fumbling for a new perch in the dark. The narrator in "Come In" states this fact. It is "Too dark" for the thrush "To better its perch for the night, / But it still could sing." Joseph Brodsky, however, focused just on the dark and missed the safety of the perch: "'The woods' are 'too dark' for a bird because a bird is too far gone at being a bird.... Thus, our bird is doomed; no last-minute conversion ('sleight' is a conjuring term) is feasible."[53] Brodsky is right that no change of perch is feasible, but he is mostly wrong. The bird is not doomed because it is already secure on its perch, chosen earlier when there was sufficient light. In the dark, the thrush has no reason to change to another perch. The thrush is merely singing in "the last of the light of the sun," not moving around. The bird is just fine. As for the singing, it is alluring, inviting the listener to "come in."[54] Brodsky argues that Frost has equated the pillars of straight tree trunks to the pillars of a church, and that the call of the thrush is now the call to prayer, an invitation to come into the church to lament his losses in the dark.[55] But the analogy is imperfect (Frost says "almost"). There is no reason for the listener to go in. Though the woods do resemble columns in a dimly lit church, this resemblance is not sufficient for the star-gazer to lament. The thrush is safe for the night, the sun will rise again in the morning, and the human listener has merely stopped to listen to the music. He is enjoying the sound, not mourning a loss. True, he notices that the setting resembles a place for mourning, but the last four lines make it clear that there is nothing to mourn, that he has not been asked to mourn, and he wouldn't mourn "even if asked." He is still "out for stars" and has only paused momentarily to listen to the thrush. Now that "the last of the light" of the day has faded, the listener is free to go on his way and view the stars, secure in the knowledge that the bird is secure on its perch and free to sing its enticing melody a few more times.

But Brodsky's concern about birds leaving their perches is wholly justified in a different poem, "The Thatch." As the narrator endures an unexplained winter standoff with someone inside the cottage, he unexpectedly disturbs birds roosting in the thatch where they had previously built their nests: "I flushed birds out of hole after hole." On that night of cold winter rain (likely to freeze before sunrise), these birds may well have been "doomed": "They could not go flying about in search / Of their nest again, nor find a perch." We never learn the fate of the birds he disturbed that night. Driven from their perches, even though unintentionally, many—maybe all—of them must have perished, exposed in the freezing rain. Our only comfort is knowing that the disaster will not be endlessly repeated because the cottage, years later, has deteriorated badly and become uninhabitable for humans, as miserable inside as outside. Were any birds to inhabit the remains of the thatch, they would not be disturbed by any human occupants. Thus the abandoned cottage becomes a parallel of the abandoned barn in "The Need of Being Versed in Country Things." Both empty structures, allowed to decay for lack of human ownership, have become safe homes for birds. Nature flourishes among human detritus, whether in England or New England.[56]

Decomposition

> With the slow smokeless burning of decay
> "The Wood-Pile"

Any discussion of life cycles has to acknowledge the inevitability of death. When living things die, they become a source of energy for scavengers, detritivores and decomposers. Frost focused most often on the last of these, the actions of bacteria and fungi, and he wrote about the decay of leaves more often than all other examples of decomposition. Each year, a new crop of leaves produces the sugar that is the basis for tree growth. In autumn, of course, the leaves on deciduous trees (along with some of the needles on conifers) change color, die, fall off the tree, get moved around, and decay.

The wasting of leaves begins with their fall from the tree, and Frost described the falling of leaves multiple times. In "October," there is a two-beat emphasis on the "waste" of leaf fall after they "ripened" with color: "O hushed October morning mild, / Thy leaves have ripened to the fall; / Tomorrow's wind, if it be wild, / Should waste them all." In "A Summer's Garden," "Leaves race across the bare beds none knows whither," and on a wet and windy day in "November," leaves are "beaten down" so thoroughly that, by the end of that day, "A year of leaves was wasted." It does seem wasteful for trees to dump a "year of leaves," especially to someone raking them off of a lawn or garden ("Gathering Leaves").

But only once the leaves have fallen can the waste of decay begin. Speaking of leaves and roads, the narrator in "Closed for Good" addresses the trees beside a road: "'From you the road receives/ A priming coat of leaves.'" Because the only traffic on the road is the narrator on foot, the leaves decay slowly: "'The shape of leaves will show / Beneath the brush of snow.'" The lack of traffic was also significant in "The Road Not Taken": "And both that morning equally lay / In leaves no step had trodden black." Decay in early autumn had not yet been hastened by passing feet. But "A Leaf Treader" in winter made all the difference: "I have safely trodden underfoot the leaves of another year." Though it was probably too cold for the leaves to decay as soon as the Leaf Treader had passed, they would be positioned perfectly, in contact with the soil, to rot away in spring.

Rain, wind, snow and feet have driven the leaves into contact with the soil "In Hardwood Groves": "To make one texture of faded brown / And fit the earth like a leather glove." Soil is where the leaves get recycled: "They must go down into the dark decayed." Frost was familiar with the cycle of growth and decay, just as he was familiar with the cycle of the seasons, and he summarizes the cycle of growth in the opening line: "The same leaves over and over again!" This cycle is made possible by the decay of the old, the wasting of one year's foliage to supply the raw materials for the next. As George Bagby pointed out, Frost understood that "what might in isolation appear to be waste can be shown to be fruitful in a larger context," the cycle of reproduction, growth, death and decomposition.[57]

Decay is slower for leaves that end up in lakes or streams because of the lower levels of oxygen in water compared to air.[58] In "The Sachem of the Clouds," newly-fallen leaves practically clog a stream: "the brook lies wrapt in silence on its bed of autumn leaves." In Hyla Brook in summer ("Hyla Brook"), long after the autumnal infusion of dead leaves, "its bed is left a faded paper sheet / Of dead leaves stuck together by the heat." Over time, insects and other aquatic animals gradually break the underwater leaves into fragmentary detritus that accumulates on the bottom in calm water.[59] Beds of detritus will cloud the water when disturbed, but in a stream, the current will carry the fragments downstream, clearing the water at the point of disturbance. Only once, in "The Pasture," does Frost mention the transport of leaf detritus in a stream: "(And wait to watch the water clear, I may)."

The social decay of rural communities, as people died or departed from the land, was followed by actual decay. Empty wooden buildings rotted away and left cellar holes, and anything else that was wooden—tool handles, farm implements, sheds and firewood—decomposed along with the houses. Frost captured the essence of this decay in "The Wood-Pile." The narrator can tell from the gray color of the wood, the loose bark, the vine "round and round" the pile, and the weakened support at the end of the stack that the wood has sat here for several years. The absence of tracks in the snow indicates that nobody has been by for some time, even though it is winter, the season when this wood would be most valuable.

As the woodpile sits exposed to precipitation and rests on wet soil, it rots into the swamp with "the slow smokeless burning of decay." In six words, Frost perfectly encompasses the process of decomposition: slow (wood is difficult to break down), smokeless (enzymatic reactions of fungi and bacteria don't require fire) yet burning (oxidation). On a cool morning, a pile of wood chips will steam from the heat of decomposition. It appears to be on fire, but isn't. Frost's woodpile in the snow is not producing enough heat to actually "warm the frozen swamp" at all, much less produce steam, but the wood is still slowly decomposing in any part of the pile that is not frozen.

Once the narrator has inferred the age of the woodpile, facts give way to supposition. How could this pile have been left in the woods after it was so carefully cut and neatly stacked? Maple is excellent firewood, and it has been laid here for drying so that it will burn well. Everything about the pile speaks to good sense, except that the wood has been left to rot in a swamp. Why?

The land surrounding the woodpile had been abandoned decades earlier, long enough that the trees had grown large enough to harvest for firewood. Within that second growth of forest, someone had harvested some of the trees a few years ago, but then departed and not returned for the results of the harvest. How could someone waste all this wood and all this work? Were they lazy? John Lynen thought so: "The man who cut it can carelessly forget its practical value."[60] But anyone who has expended the energy to cut an entire cord of wood and then carefully stack it would not be "careless." Did the woodcutter have more wood than necessary? With cook stoves and cold winters, it was hard to keep up, much less get ahead. The narrator speculates: "I thought that only / Someone who lived in turning to fresh tasks / Could so forget his handiwork on which / He spent himself, the labor of his ax." What "fresh tasks" could distract a New Englander from such a fine woodpile? I think that the most likely explanation is that he was no longer a New Englander. He might have moved away to find an easier life, as so many had done before. Or perhaps, like the woodpile, he was fueling "the slow smokeless burning of decay"—he was dead.[61] Leaves, abandoned woodpiles, corpses—they all decompose.

By the time Frost concluded "The Wood-Pile" with his brilliant description of decomposition, the narrator is even farther from home than at the start of the walk in the swamp. The bird has come and gone, and the woodpile has presented a mystery full of clues but still with no clear solution. The woodpile, a wasted effort that would never warm a human soul, continues to waste away. It would, slowly and imperceptibly, molder down to minerals and ash, and its decay would, eventually, contribute to the soil and the growth of more trees. Waste for the woodsman would become a resource for the woods, part of the cycle of growth and decay that supported the return of the forest to post-agrarian New England.

Conclusion
"Versed in country things"

"The Need of Being Versed in Country Things" is one piece in a long narrative of environmental history that runs throughout the poetry of Robert Frost. Frost, both poet and naturalist, understood the flora, fauna and farm families of the New England countryside. His descriptions of that countryside, scattered among hundreds of poems, constitute a vivid and compelling narrative full of insights into a dynamic landscape.

This narrative of the countryside is important in two ways. First, many of Frost's images and metaphors arise from the narrative, and thus it is the foundation for much of his art. Second, the processes that are central to the narrative—seasonal change, agriculture, ecological succession and life cycles—are clearly evident today, making it possible for readers to experience the narrative for themselves and thereby connect with the poet and his poetry.

Narrative: Points of Departure

Frost took his "botanizing" walks in the countryside with what Louis Pasteur called the prepared mind. When he chanced upon things that were new or interesting, he would hold them in his memory for later use. Many of these observations appear in his poetry as descriptions of the countryside, and they resonate with readers because they are so thoroughly apt. He "found a dimpled spider, fat and white" in summer ("Design"), and he would like to "climb black branches up a snow-white trunk" of a young birch tree in winter ("Birches"). Wood decomposes "With the slow smokeless burning of decay" ("The Wood-Pile"). A long-abandoned house is just a cellar hole "Now slowly closing like a dent in dough" ("Directive"). Countless generations of birds—or of any living thing—come down to us, "On the long bead chain of repeated birth" ("On a Bird Singing in Its Sleep"). A newly-germinated pea seedling emerges from the soil by "shouldering its way and shedding the earth crumbs" ("Putting in the Seed"). A stream that flows, day after day, even after long periods without rain or melting snow, is "the tribute of the current to the source" ("West-Running Brook"). In Frost's descriptions, nearly every word is familiar, but the combinations are strikingly original. His creative juxtapositions turn mere accuracy into crystalline precision that entices the reader to accompany him on his deeper explorations.

The reader is also enticed by the accessibility of Frost's language. In his essay *The Unmade Word*, he wrote, "The word lies in our everyday speech, practical, hard and unliterary; and that's the way I like the word—there's where my fun with it begins."[1] "Everyday speech" helped to make Frost's poetry deceptively simple.[2] The language, the rhythm and the meaning all seem obvious on first reading. If Frost were only superficial, however, nobody would care about his poems half a century after his death. Frost started with simple words and played with them, just as his character in "The Mountain" explains: "But all the fun's in how you say a thing." Frost's "fun" lasted for decades. In 1948, he wrote: "the fun only begins with the spirited when you treat the word as a point of many departures."[3]

Rooted firmly in the reality of his observations, Frost's descriptions were his points of departure. From each description, his poetry radiated out in many directions, each direction serving as an entry into events, ideas and images that were often complex and profound. Irving Howe noted how Frost's observations preceded metaphor: "Frost's greatest poems, as it happens, are those which end upon a coda of reflection."[4]

There is no doubt that Frost's reflections were deliberate and disciplined efforts that produced what critics define as his art. It was a process, informed by Emerson, the Romantic poets and others, that became his own. We must not forget, however, that these reflections were born from his observations. The observations were just as deliberate and disciplined as his reflections, and without them, the reflections would never have happened. His unique ability to describe those observations helped make Frost distinctive, both in his own time and ours.

Conclusion

Some authors argue that a focus on description and reality misses the point of Frost's poetry. John Lynen claims, "One can become so interested in the 'reality' of Frost's New England or so concerned to see the local landscape as a reflection of the poet's own experience that one forgets to notice the art through which the regional world is presented." Jay Parini says much the same thing: "One must be careful when using poems, which are constructs of the imagination, as though they were mere transcriptions of a poet's experience."[5]

I'm sure that many readers miss the richness of Frost's art and imagination, but I am equally sure that many readers and critics have missed some of the "reality." His descriptions of the countryside appear to be so simple that they are easily overlooked. If readers miss elements of Frost's landscape, they will miss the full complexity beneath Frost's apparent simplicity. They will fail to notice that the skilled poet was also a skilled naturalist.

If readers miss the descriptions, they might also fail to recognize where description ends and metaphor begins. I suspect that many readers have interpreted some of his descriptions as metaphor, and have missed or misunderstood the transition from reality to imagery. Doing so has produced some confusion of fact with imagination, and obscured the connection between the two. Because reality was the basis for so many of Frost's metaphors, if we miss that connection, then we might fail to recognize the source of much of his art.

Frost's "fresh noticing of the details"[6] was essential to his poetry. His descriptions were the raw materials from which he could generate any number of metaphors, images, themes and speculations. As he said in his essay "The Figure a Poem Makes," a poem "begins in delight and ends in wisdom."[7] In poem after poem, "delight" is the description, rooted in observation, that gives rise to metaphorical "wisdom." Together, these pieces make a glorious whole.

Narrative: Engaging the Reader

From a mountaintop in New England, the view today is a vast expanse of trees. In among the trees we can spot towns (with their church steeples), roads, bodies of water, the occasional farm and sometimes a ski trail. But the tree canopy covers most of the land, giving little hint of what is below.

How can we look back in time, to the time of Frost and the time of his ancestors, with so much vegetation in the way?

LIDAR (**l**ight **d**etection and **r**anging) is a laser-based tool that archaeologists use to reveal old structures under the trees, shrubs, weeds and detritus of the forest. With our unaided eyes, we have trouble spotting the glacial grooves, rockshelters, old foundations and abandoned roads that were left by people and events of the past. LIDAR makes them jump out at us.

The poetry of Robert Frost often acts like literary LIDAR. It reveals unseen elements of the landscape, sometimes in their contemporary settings, other times as vestiges of the past, or hints of the future. The revealed elements form a narrative of environmental history that is vivid but uneven because it comes to us one poem at a time. Each poem gives the reader only a piece of the narrative, but words, subjects and themes appear repeatedly, connecting the poems into a whole. In Frost's work, it seems that the New England countryside is woven into the poetry as a recurring, complex character. It is not a character from fantasy but from everyday life as it was lived by the farmers, flora and fauna in a shared landscape. Generations came and went, there was extravagant success and utter failure, joy and depression, birth, growth, life and death, things familiar and things so altered that they were hard to recognize.

The narrative begins over twenty thousand years ago when ice was leaving its marks on New England. The rocks have striations gouged into their surfaces, tracing the path, northwest to southeast, of the glacial ice that once spread across all of New England ("Directive," lines 15–17). Today, "The Drumlin Woodchuck" has its "strategic retreat" on a drumlin, a teardrop-shaped hill that had been formed under a massive ice sheet.[8]

Once the ice melted back, First Nations people lived here for millennia, only to be killed and displaced by European settlers ("Genealogical") so that old-growth forest could give way to farms ("The Birthplace"). Some farm families tended their farms for centuries, heeding the rhythms of the seasons ("A Hundred Collars") yet fearful that extreme weather would ruin an entire crop ("Peril of Hope"). Starting in the 1800s, opportunities elsewhere lured farmers off their land, and their farms were left abandoned and untended ("The Star-Splitter," "The Black Cottage," "Ghost House"). The decline in population was sad for those left behind ("The Census-Taker"), but not for a resurgent nature ("The Last Mowing"). The contrast

141

of old and new, past and present, is striking and hard to fathom ("The Need of Being Versed in Country Things"): "For them there was really nothing sad. / But though they rejoiced in the nest they kept, / One had to be versed in country things / Not to believe the phoebes wept." Today, phoebes often nest in barns, each cellar hole is "slowly closing like a dent in dough" ("Directive"), and in a landscape that once harbored more farms that forest, "now her lap is full of trees" ("The Birthplace").

We also find old stone walls surrounded by second-growth forest, but despite being mute (like the stones in "Ghost House"), these stones find their own historical voice in Frost. The wall in "Mending Wall" is "there where it is we do not need the wall." There is no need for a wall because the "farm ... is no more a farm" ("Directive").

But years ago, there was plowing, and then the stones mattered. Plowing on a farm in "The Star-Splitter" was "there where he moved the rocks to plow the ground / And plowed between the rocks he couldn't move." The stones of the fields had to be moved out of the way of the plough blade, dragged in a stoneboat and piled along a boundary where they took up the least amount of space for the farmer and the neighbors. Out of the way and out of mind, the wall of stones became a refuge for trees that would otherwise have been grazed or mowed or tilled to death. The absence of neighboring trees allowed sunlight to reach the low branches of these trees. As a result of all that sunlight, these low branches survived and grew out from the wall, dropping seeds each year in the fields. Each year, plows or mowers or grazers killed the seedlings. But on most farms, farmers eventually discovered that "no plow among these rocks would pay" ("Something for Hope") and farming was abandoned. Once the farm is no longer a farm, each "low-limbed tree" in the walls ("Ghost House") continues to rain seeds on the unmanaged land. Without "mowers or plowers" ("The Last Mowing"), seedlings survive and head skyward, filling the openings between the walls, growing straight and lean in contrast to the "low boughs" ("A Dream Pang") of their stout, gnarly parents among the stones. As the trees grow tall, the stolid walls fall apart, but so slowly that the walls far outlast those who built them. None survives to tell the tales of when the walls were first laid down. Only the new tenants will take notice and decide whether to watch the stones settle into the Earth, or to pick up and pile up the fallen stones, perhaps with one's neighbor ("Mending Wall"). No, we do not need this wall now, ages and ages hence, but long ago, someone did. Thus each mute wall has a story to tell, and some of those stories appear in the poetry of Robert Frost, each a part of the larger narrative of the environmental history of New England.

Readers can participate in Frost's narrative by linking our own experiences with his. A summer stream full of leaves at low flow ("Hyla Brook") can transform into a torrent after a storm, washing the leaves downstream much more forcefully than in "The Pasture." Vernal pools harbor animals, so it is not just flowers that depend on them ("Spring Pools"). You might see deer picking at their food before emerging from the woods or crossing lakes ("Two Look at Two," "The Most of It"). In some years, sugar maple seedlings are so abundant on the forest floor that cows could not possibly lick them all up ("Maple"). Goldenrods often join steeple bush pushing up through grass, and then it might be white pine instead of maple, birch and spruce that overtops them both ("Something for Hope"). Winter ice in hollows does not always catch the sun, so it enchants us differently from ice crystals on peaks ("The Mountain"). And if you find a true bog, the ghostly spires of white orchids might surpass those in sunny meadows or thick cedar swamps ("Rose Pogonias," "The Encounter"). There is delight in connecting your own experience with that of Frost and contributing new pieces to the narrative.

Narrative: A Lesson for Today

Frost's poetic chronicle of the countryside tells us of a time that is fading but not quite gone, a time when birch trees were more common than they are now, when some rural farmers resisted the pull of the city or the Corn Belt, when an ax helve was carved by hand, and when oxen were the motive force on roads and fields. If we look carefully, the changes he described are still evident today. Dead birch trees, shaded out by maple and oak, lie on a forest floor between the walls, a few old cellar holes can still be identified peering out from the soil, and old roadbeds appear as long, flattened ribbons that interrupt the contours of hills. Some patches of forest have multi-stemmed trees in the canopy that sprouted years ago from stumps that remained after logging.

Much has changed of course: hay is cut and baled by machines, there are fewer barns in which birds can nest,[9] apple orchards are replaced by houses with vinyl siding, blue butterflies ("My Butterfly" and "Blue Butterfly Day") are increasingly endangered,[10] and the moonbeams of "Moon

Compasses" are obscured by haze and artificial light. Today, wild turkeys, beavers and coyotes are often seen or heard in the countryside, but they never appear in Frost's poetry, a strong indication of their rarity or absence when he lived in New England. Frost's response to hearing a thrush in "Come In" is "hark" because a century ago, the trees were smaller and the woods less contiguous than they are today. His woods were sufficiently open so that bluebirds were common but wood thrush and veery were rare. Today, with larger expanses of mature trees in New England, the opposite is true.

The countryside is still changing, still dynamic, even if the specific causes and characters are different from a century ago. Birches still flourish in patches of abandoned land. Hand-hewn wooden implements are now artisanal. Oxen compete at agricultural fairs. Cities continue to grow, but much of the urban workforce has chosen to live in rural areas, clearing many of the trees that had grown up on old farms, yet insisting on leaving some land "wild" for continued succession. These changes join with the continuum of disturbance that is an inevitable feature of the countryside. It is never static, no matter how many calendar photographs of New England might make us think it is.

To some extent, we can see ahead by looking back to notice where we've been. A history of the countryside can reveal the processes that will continue through today into the future. The details will change, and the relative importance of events will shift, but much will be similar. Ecologists can provide data on these processes, but we have Frost to thank for a language of the countryside that makes these processes vibrant and compelling. An aging orchard, a cedar swamp, a whippoorwill, a clump of bracken in a meadow—all of these things come sharply into focus when we read about them in Frost. And if we see any of them for ourselves in the landscape, whether on a hike or in our backyards, we become part of the continuity of the countryside, from Frost's time to our own. Our contemporary connection to the landscape has been illuminated and enriched by the delight and wisdom of New England's poet naturalist. His poems still teach us how to be versed in country things.

The Ongoing Narrative: A Sunset Glow

Not long ago, a house burned down in a neighboring town. In an age of smoke alarms and fire trucks, the level of destruction was surprising.

All that remained were the foundation and two chimneys, one large, one small. I immediately thought of the parallels with "The Need of Being Versed in Country Things," but also immediately noticed the differences. In this freshly-burned house, both chimneys stood straight from top to bottom and thus did not closely resemble the typical pistil of a flower. There is a new house being built fairly close by, so the land is not abandoned. There are hay fields nearby where tractors still mow the plants two or three times a year, let them dry, and then scoop them off the ground to squeeze them into hay bales, either small rectangles or huge rolls. Nobody uses wagons to haul loose hay that hangs down and brushes the mown stubble. The road is not stony (except for unpaved side roads or the tiny stones embedded in asphalt). Nobody uses teams of horses or oxen to work their farms. Nobody depends on an outdoor well with a hand pump. Stone walls are everywhere, but they are mostly in disrepair and thus utterly insufficient to contain cattle or goats or llamas or emus. Everyone who has livestock depends on fences, either wooden or wire, some of them electrified.

This scene was not a reenactment of "The Need of Being Versed in Country Things," but many of the essentials of the poem and of the time are the same. Houses burn down, farmers mow and gather hay, people are nostalgic about what has been, and phoebes find nest sites to rear their young. All of these elements are parts of the ongoing narrative of New England, even if there are fewer farmers and more commuters able to divide their time between city and country with the aid of fast transportation.

If we want to understand how the landscape has come to be as it is and how it continues to change, if we want something to hope for among trees that take a lifetime to mature, surrounded by the slow smokeless burning of decay, if we want to do more than sigh and weep from dwelling on the past, then we need to be versed in country things and rejoice in all the wonder that surrounds us, today and in the future. What better guide is there than the verse of Robert Frost?

Chapter Notes

Preface

1. Jay Parini. 1999. *Robert Frost: A Life* (Henry Holt, New York), 414.
2. David Orr. 2015. *The Road Not Taken* (Penguin Press, New York).
3. Benjamin J. Kaston. 1948. "Spiders of Connecticut." *State Geological and Natural History Survey Bulletin No. 70* (Hartford), 411–412; crab spiders hold captured prey vertically and do not wrap them in silk, so Frost's description of the spider is accurate, despite claims to the contrary: George Monteiro. 2015. *Robert Frost's Poetry of Rural Life* (McFarland, Jefferson, NC), 45–47.
4. Some heal-all plants do have flowers that are entirely white: Merritt Lyndon Fernald. 1950. *Gray's Manual of Botany*. 8th edition (D. Van Nostrand, New York), 1,225.
5. Robert Faggen. 2006. *The Notebooks of Robert Frost*, 127.
6. James H. Speer. 2010. *Fundamentals of Tree-Ring Research* (University of Arizona Press, Tucson).
7. John Elder. 1998. *Reading the Mountains of Home* (Harvard University Press, Cambridge), 42, 236–237.
8. Robert Bernard Hass. 2002. *Going by Contraries.* (University Press of Virginia, Charlottesville), 93.
9. Robert Faggen. 2006. *The Notebooks of Robert Frost*, 231–234.

Prologue

1. Richard Poirier and Mark Richardson eds. 1995. *Robert Frost: Collected Poems, Prose & Plays: "The Figure a Poem Makes"* (Library of America, New York), 778.

Introduction

1. Jay Parini. 1999. *Robert Frost: A Life* (Henry Holt, New York), see especially the afterword, 449–458; Richard Poirier and Mark Richardson eds. 1995. *Robert Frost: Collected Poems, Prose & Plays* (Library of America, New York), chronology, 929–955.
2. Jay Parini. 1999. *Robert Frost: A Life*, 22–24; Richard Poirier and Mark Richardson eds. 1995. *Robert Frost: Collected Poems, Prose & Plays*, 932.
3. Jay Parini. 1999. *Robert Frost: A Life*, 24–26, 443, 447; Lawrance Thompson ed. 1964. *Selected Letters of Robert Frost* (Holt, Rinehart and Winston, New York), 71, 167, 175, 377; Richard Poirier and Mark Richardson eds. 1995. *Robert Frost: Collected Poems, Prose & Plays*, 802.
4. The author's given name was Frances Theodora Parsons. *How to Know the Wildflowers* (Charles Scribner's Sons, New York). See Donald Sheehy, Mark Richardson and Robert Faggen eds. 2014. *The Letters of Robert Frost. Volume 1: 1886–1920*, 40; Jay Parini. 1999. *Robert Frost: A Life*, 56.
5. Richard Poirier and Mark Richardson eds. 1995. *Robert Frost: Collected Poems, Prose & Plays*, 936–938.
6. René Vallery-Radot. 1900. *La Vie de Pasteur* (Flammarion, Paris), 84: "dans les champs de l'observation, le hasard ne favorise que les esprits préparés" (translation by Mrs. R. L. Devonshire, Garden City Publishing, New York).

Chapter Notes—Introduction

7. Robert Faggen. 2006. *The Notebooks of Robert Frost*, 166.

8. Jay Parini. 1999. *Robert Frost: A Life*, 56.

9. Mark Richardson ed. 2007. *The Collected Prose of Robert Frost* (The Belknap Press of Harvard University Press, Cambridge), 296.

10. Donald Sheehy, Mark Richardson and Robert Faggen eds. 2014. *The Letters of Robert Frost. Volume 1: 1886–1920*, 448, 695, 285, 248, 193.

11. Robert Faggen. 2006. *The Notebooks of Robert Frost*, 112.

12. J.B. Harborne. 1982. Introduction to *Ecological Biochemistry* (Academic Press, New York), 87–90.

13. Donald Sheehy, Mark Richardson, Robert Bernard Hass and Henry Atmore eds. 2016. *The Letters of Robert Frost. Volume 2: 1920–1928* (The Belknap Press of Harvard University Press, Cambridge), 477, 571; Lesley Lee Francis. 2015. *You Come Too: My Journey with Robert Frost* (University of Virginia Press, Charlottesville), e-book location 679; Elina Garrison and Jay Gedir. 2006. *Ecology and Management of White-Tailed Deer in Florida* (Florida Fish and Wildlife Conservation Commission), 3.

14. In a 1915 letter, Frost wrote, "I have had a surveyor chain the farm"; Donald Sheehy, Mark Richardson and Robert Faggen eds. 2014. *The Letters of Robert Frost. Volume 1: 1886–1920*, 306.

15. Robert J. Cormier. 1977. *The New Book of the Proprietors of Common and Undivided Lands in Shrewsbury* (Transcription, American Antiquarian Society), 47.

16. Robert Faggen. 1997. *Robert Frost and the Challenge of Darwin* (University of Michigan Press, Ann Arbor), 94; a search of the internet for "white-tailed hornet" shows many sites that use that name, e.g., http://umaine.edu/home-and-garden-ipm/common-name-listing/bald-faced-hornet/.

17. Joseph Brodsky. 1994. *The New Yorker*. Sept. 26, 73.

18. Jeffrey Meyers. 1996. *Robert Frost: A Biography* (Houghton Mifflin, Boston), 217; Benjamin J. Kaston. 1948. *Spiders of Connecticut*, 411–412.

19. George Monteiro. 2015. *Robert Frost's Poetry of Rural Life* (McFarland, Jefferson, NC), 45–47.

20. Mark Richardson ed. 2014. *Robert Frost in Context* (Cambridge University Press, Cambridge), 54; *Prunella laciniata* is not included in *Gray's Manual of Botany* (Merritt Lyndon Fernald. 1950. 8th edition. D. Van Nostrand, New York), nor is it listed as occurring in New Hampshire (Frost's home state when he wrote "Design") by the U.S. Dept. of Agriculture: http://plants.usda.gov/core/profile?symbol=Prla7.

21. Thomas C. Bailey. 2001. *Robert Frost as Nature Poet and Naturalist*, 222.

22. Robert Faggen. 2006. *The Notebooks of Robert Frost*, 303.

23. Donald Sheehy, Mark Richardson, Robert Bernard Hass and Henry Atmore eds. 2016. *The Letters of Robert Frost. Volume 2: 1920–1928* (The Belknap Press of Harvard University Press, Cambridge), 53.

24. Mark Richardson ed. 2007. *The Collected Prose of Robert Frost*, 345; Donald Sheehy, Mark Richardson and Robert Faggen eds. 2014. *The Letters of Robert Frost. Volume 1: 1886–1920*, 134, 594–595, 611, 619.

25. Donald Sheehy, Mark Richardson and Robert Faggen eds. 2014. *The Letters of Robert Frost. Volume 1: 1886–1920*, 279, 439, 447.

26. Donald Sheehy, Mark Richardson and Robert Faggen eds. 2014. *The Letters of Robert Frost. Volume 1: 1886–1920* (The Belknap Press of Harvard University Press, Cambridge), 107.

27. Mark Richardson ed. 2007. *The Collected Prose of Robert Frost*, 279, 277; Richard Poirier and Mark Richardson eds. 1995. *Robert Frost: Collected Poems, Prose & Plays*, 757.

28. Donald Sheehy, Mark Richardson and Robert Faggen eds. 2014. *The Letters of Robert Frost. Volume 1: 1886–1920*, 55, 304, 327, 709.

29. Mark Richardson ed. 2007. *The Collected Prose of Robert Frost*, 143.

30. Donald Sheehy, Mark Richardson and Robert Faggen eds. 2014. *The Letters of Robert Frost. Volume 1: 1886–1920*, 330, 583, 594.

31. Mark Richardson ed. 2007. *The Collected Prose of Robert Frost*, 277, 112.

32. Donald Sheehy, Mark Richardson and Robert Faggen eds. 2014. *The Letters of Robert Frost. Volume 1: 1886–1920*, 646, 712, 234.

33. Donald Sheehy, Mark Richardson and Robert Faggen eds. 2014. *The Letters of Robert Frost. Volume 1: 1886–1920*, 265, 394–395; Mark Richardson ed. 2007. *The Collected Prose of Robert Frost*, 112, xxxi.

34. Donald Sheehy, Mark Richardson and Robert Faggen eds. 2014. *The Letters of Robert Frost. Volume 1: 1886–1920*, 456, 370, 695; Mark Richardson ed. 2007. *The Collected Prose of Robert Frost*, 263, 313–314.

35. Richard Poirier and Mark Richardson eds. 1995. *Robert Frost: Collected Poems, Prose & Plays*, 719; Mark Richardson ed. 2007. *The Collected Prose of Robert Frost*, 273, 296.

36. Donald Sheehy, Mark Richardson and Robert Faggen eds. 2014. *The Letters of Robert Frost. Volume 1: 1886–1920*, 421; Mark Richardson ed. 2007. *The Collected Prose of Robert Frost*, 327; Richard Poirier and Mark Richardson eds. 1995. *Robert Frost: Collected Poems, Prose & Plays*, 786.

37. Richard Poirier and Mark Richardson eds. 1995. *Robert Frost: Collected Poems, Prose & Plays*, 719; Mark Richardson ed. 2007. *The Collected Prose of Robert Frost*, 273, 296.

38. Donald Sheehy, Mark Richardson, Robert Bernard Hass and Henry Atmore eds. 2016. *The Letters of Robert Frost. Volume 2: 1920–1928*, 646.

39. George F. Bagby. 1993. *Frost and the Book of Nature* (University of Tennessee Press, Knoxville), 56; Oxford English Dictionary, definition I. 5. for "lodge, v."

40. Jonathan N. Barron. 2015. *How Robert Frost Made Realism Matter* (University of Missouri Press, Columbia).

41. Mark Richardson ed. 2007. *The Collected Prose of Robert Frost*, 79; Richard Poirier and Mark Richardson eds. 1995. *Robert Frost: Collected Poems, Prose & Plays*, 701.

42. Mark Richardson ed. 2007. *The Collected Prose of Robert Frost*, 79; Donald Sheehy, Mark Richardson and Robert Faggen eds. 2014. *The Letters of Robert Frost. Volume 1: 1886–1920*, 70, 210; Richard Poirier and Mark Richardson eds. 1995. *Robert Frost: Collected Poems, Prose & Plays*, 727–728.

43. Robert Faggen. 2006. *The Notebooks of Robert Frost*, 494.

44. Irving Howe. 1963. *The New Republic*. March 23, 26, 27.

45. Nina Baym. 1965. *American Quarterly* 17.4 (Winter), 716.

46. Jay Parini. 1999. *Robert Frost: A Life*, 139, 235.

47. Jay Parini. 1999. *Robert Frost: A Life*, 200.

Subduing the Land

1. Before 1620, the French, Dutch and Spanish had established settlements in North America. Frost's poem "Immigrants" in *West-Running Brook* is the fourth stanza of "The Return of the Pilgrims," published in *The Pilgrim Sprit* by George P. Baker; see Edward Connery Latham ed. 1979. *The Poetry of Robert Frost: The Collected Poems, Complete and Unabridged* (Henry Holt, New York), 555; "The Return of the Pilgrims" is not included in Richard Poirier and Mark Richardson eds. 1995. *Robert Frost: Collected Poems, Prose & Plays* (Library of America, New York).

2. W. Cronon, 2003. *Changes in the Land*. Revised edition (Hill and Wang, New York), chapters 3, 6; G. Whitney, 1994. *From Coastal Wilderness to Fruited Plain* (Cambridge University Press, New York), chapters 5, 7–9; David R. Foster and John D. Aber eds. 2004. *Forests in Time: The Environmental Consequences of 1,000 Years of Change in New England.* (Yale University Press, New Haven), 74–86; Diana Muir. 2000. *Reflections in Bullough's Pond* (University Press of New England, Hanover), 50–54; Jan Albers. 2000. *Hands on the Land: A History of the Vermont Landscape* (MIT Press, Cambridge), 186–190; Christopher McGrory Klyza and Stephen C. Trombulak. 2015. *The Story of Vermont* (University Press of New England, Hanover), 64.

3. William Cronon. 2003. *Changes in the Land: Indians, Colonists and the Ecology of New England*. Revised edition (Hill and Wang, New York), chapter 6; Gordon G. Whitney. 1994. *From Coastal Wilderness to Fruited Plain* (Cambridge University Press, New York), chapters 7–9.

4. Robert Bernard Hass. 2002. *Going by Contraries* (University Press of Virginia, Charlottesville), 90, 93.

5. William A. Sutton, ed. 1976. *Newdick's Season of Frost: An Interrupted Biography of Robert Frost* (State University of New York Press, Albany), 7–8; in her novel "Barkskins" (2016, Scribner, New York, 219–221), Annie Proulx mentions a timber merchant named Frost who lived in Maine ca. 1750.

6. Lesley Lee Francis. 2015. *You Come Too: My Journey with Robert Frost* (University of Virginia Press, Charlottesville), e-book location 3910–3957.

7. A draft of "The Birthplace" in 1923 used less intrusive language: "My father built beside a spring.... Reduced the growth of earth to grass": Donald Sheehy, Mark Richardson, Robert Bernard Hass and Henry Atmore eds. 2016. *The Letters of Robert Frost. Volume 2: 1920–1928* (The Belknap Press of Harvard University Press, Cambridge), 340, note 8.

8. Emily W. B. Russell. 1980. *Bulletin of the Torrey Botanical Club* 107, 442; Donald Sheehy, Mark Richardson and Robert Faggen eds. 2014. *The Letters of Robert Frost. Volume 1: 1886–1920* (The Belknap Press of Harvard University Press, Cambridge), 71–72; Donald Sheehy, Mark Richardson, Robert Bernard Hass and Henry Atmore eds. 2016. *The Letters of Robert Frost. Volume 2: 1920–1928* (The Belknap Press of Harvard University Press, Cambridge), 190.

9. Donald Sheehy, Mark Richardson and Robert Faggen eds. 2014. *The Letters of Robert Frost. Volume 1: 1886–1920*, 644; Richard Poirier and Mark Richardson eds. 1995. *Robert Frost: Collected Poems, Prose & Plays*, 653.

10. Donald Sheehy, Mark Richardson and Robert Faggen eds. 2014. *The Letters of*
Robert Frost. Volume 1: 1886–1920, 704, 625, 581.

11. Robert Faggen. 1997. *Robert Frost and the Challenge of Darwin* (University of Michigan Press, Ann Arbor), 113.

12. Robert Faggen. 2006. *The Notebooks of Robert Frost*, 356, 755.

13. Gregory R. Weaver. 2003. *Journal of the American Chestnut Foundation* 16.2, 14–18; Helen Thompson. 2012. *Nature* 490, 22–23.

14. Ryan W. McEwan, Carolyn H. Keiffer, and Brian C. McCarthy. 2006. *Canadian Journal of Forest Research* 36, 1–11.

15. Donald Sheehy, Mark Richardson and Robert Faggen eds. 2014. *The Letters of Robert Frost. Volume 1: 1886–1920*, 651–652.

16. Michael J. McDowell. 1991. *South Carolina Review* 21.1, 97–98.

17. Ray F. Evert and Susan E. Eichhorn. 2013. *Biology of Plants*. Eighth edition (W.H. Freeman and Company, New York), 626, 628; Tony Rodd and Jennifer Stackhouse. 2008. *Trees* (University of California Press, Berkeley), 77; Frank B. Salisbury and Cleon W. Ross. 1992. *Plant Physiology*. Fourth Edition (Wadsworth, Belmont, CA), 317–318; James H. Speer. 2010. *Fundamentals of Tree-Ring Research*. (University of Arizona Press, Tucson), 55.

18. Robert Faggen. 1997. *Robert Frost and the Challenge of Darwin* (University of Michigan Press, Ann Arbor), 207.

19. Ray F. Evert and Susan E. Eichhorn. 2013. *Biology of Plants*. Eighth Edition, 642–643.

20. David R. Foster. 1999. *Thoreau's Country* (Harvard University Press, Cambridge), 76; William Cronon. 2003. *Changes in the Land: Indians, Colonists and the Ecology of New England*. Revised edition (Hill and Wang, New York), 145; David R. Foster and John D. Aber eds. 2004. *Forests in Time: The Environmental Consequences of 1,000 Years of Change in New England* (Yale University Press, New Haven), 114.

21. Thomas Bailey. 2014. "Reading Robert Frost Environmentally: Contexts Then and Now" in Mark Richardson ed. 2014. *Robert Frost in Context* (Cambridge University Press, Cambridge), 247–248.

22. Frost was familiar with the writings of Henry David Thoreau in which Thoreau noted repeatedly the sprouting of deciduous trees (Frost says that "sprout-lands flourish where the ax has gone" in "The Generations of Men.") Apparently, it did not serve his purpose to acknowledge sprouting in "The Census-Taker."

23. At least some crews in the 1940s used tracked vehicles to clear power line easements, an indication of the destruction wrought for telecommunication: Jan Albers. 2000. *Hands on the Land: A History of the Vermont Landscape*, 272.

24. Virginia Smith (U.S. Naval Academy) wondered whether Frost's correspondence on paper contributed to the demise of trees. I examined twenty of Frost's letters in the archives of the Amherst College Library, all of which he wrote during or before 1920. Nineteen were on heavy paper with a weave pattern, apparently made from linen. The surviving envelopes were embossed: "L. B. Howard, Franconia, NH." The other letter was on light weight paper with darkened gray edges, possibly made from wood pulp. In an August 4, 1917, letter to Otto Mantley-Zorn, Frost noted that a friend's farm was "overrun with barkers or strippers or peelers" that "skin the spruce for pulp" (Sheehy et al., 561). Thus, Frost was aware of the destruction of trees to make paper, but he seems to have rarely, if ever, used such paper around the time he wrote "The Encounter" and "The Line-Gang."

25. Ray F. Evert and Susan E. Eichhorn. 2013. *Biology of Plants*. Eighth Edition, 628.

26. Thomas C. Bailey. 2014. "Reading Frost Environmentally: Contexts Then and Now" in Mark Richardson ed. 2014. *Robert Frost in Context* (Cambridge University Press, Cambridge), 245.

27. Ray F. Evert and Susan E. Eichhorn. 2013. *Biology of Plants*. Eighth Edition, 486–488; Robert I. Bertin. 2002. *Rhodora* 104, 342.

28. Ray F. Evert and Susan E. Eichhorn. 2013. *Biology of Plants*. Eighth Edition, 314; Robert I. Bertin. 2002. *Rhodora* 104: 342.

29. Lawrance Thompson ed. 1964. *Selected Letters of Robert Frost*, 71, 167, 377.

30. Roger Tory Peterson and Margaret McKenny. 1968. *A Field Guide to Wildflowers* (Houghton Mifflin, Boston), 215; Arthur Haines. 2011. *Flora Novae Angliae* (Yale University Press, New Haven), 198–212.

31. But this poem, despite its original title "The Quest of the Orchis," might not have been about orchids at all. Jay Parini concluded that the purple-fringed flower was the fringed gentian, *Gentianopsis crinita*, and that Frost changed the title when he discovered he had misidentified it as an orchid: Jay Parini. 1999. *Robert Frost: A Life*, 57, 334; The habitat and time of blooming in the poem are certainly right for fringed gentians, and gentians do require a search because the seeds may disperse away from the site of the parents and leave no flowers one year where they were abundant the year before. But fringed gentians form single flowers on the tip of each stem, just one or a few per plant. Their inflorescences are not "spires" like those of purple-fringed orchids: Arthur Haines. 2011. *Flora Novae Angliae*, 610; Merritt Lyndon Fernald. 1950. *Gray's Manual of Botany*. 8th edition, 474, 1,159; Roger Tory Peterson and Margaret McKenny. 1968. *A Field Guide to Wildflowers*, 225, 321. So which flowers were they? Would Frost really have confused gentians and orchids? Was he leaving us a mystery he couldn't solve himself?

32. S.L. McKenrick, J.R. Leake and D.J. Read. 2000. *New Phytologist* 145, 539–548.

33. Katherine Kearns. 1994. *Robert Frost and the Poetics of Appetite* (Cambridge University Press, New York), 112.

34. Oxford English Dictionary, "orchis" etymology; "orchidectomy" definition.

35. Robert Bernard Hass. 2002. *Going by Contraries* (University Press of Virginia, Charlottesville), 165–171.

36. Robert Faggen. 1997. *Robert Frost and the Challenge of Darwin*, 155–160.

37. Burell recovered sufficiently to join Frost at the Derry farm for a few years: Richard Poirier and Mark Richardson eds. 1995. *Robert Frost: Collected Poems, Prose & Plays*, 936.

38. Charles G. Willis, et al. 2008. *Proceedings of the National Academy of Sciences* 105, 17029–17030.

39. Robert I. Bertin and Thomas J. Rawinski. 2012. *Vascular Flora of Worcester County, Massachusetts* (Special Publication of the New England Botanical Club), 77–80; Robert I. Bertin. 2002. *Rhodora* 104, 333.

40. Robert Faggen calls this poem "Huttonian" for James Hutton, one of the founders of modern geology, but it is more uniformitarian (which Faggen also notes), in the tradition of Charles Lyell, with evidence of previous cycles still present in later cycles. In Hutton's view, geological cycles erased all traces of earlier cycles in a return to a state of perfection: Robert Faggen. 1997. *Robert Frost and the Challenge of Darwin*, 164; John McPhee. 1998. *Annals of the Former World* (Farrar, Straus and Giroux, New York), 76, 397; Stephan Jay Gould. 1987. *Time's Arrow, Time's Cycle* (Harvard University Press, Cambridge), chapters 3 and 4.

41. Frost read an early version of "Build Soil" at Columbia University in 1921: Donald Sheehy, Mark Richardson, Robert Bernard Hass and Henry Atmore eds. 2016. *The Letters of Robert Frost. Volume 2: 1920–1928*, 162, note 363.

42. Donald Sheehy, Mark Richardson and Robert Faggen eds. 2014. *The Letters of Robert Frost. Volume 1: 1886–1920*, 232.

43. William Cronon 2003. *Changes in the Land*. Revised edition (Hill and Wang, New York), 109–111.

44. Jay Parini. 1999. *Robert Frost: A Life* (Henry Holt, New York), 5.

45. Donald Sheehy, Mark Richardson and Robert Faggen eds. 2014. *The Letters of Robert Frost. Volume 1: 1886–1920* (The Belknap Press of Harvard University Press, Cambridge), 250.

46. Donald Sheehy, Mark Richardson and Robert Faggen eds. 2014. *The Letters of Robert Frost. Volume 1: 1886–1920*, 218, 393, 513, 535, 623, 636.

47. Donald Sheehy, Mark Richardson and Robert Faggen eds. 2014. *The Letters of Robert Frost. Volume 1: 1886–1920*, 227, 240, 553, 635, 690–691.

48. Donald Sheehy, Mark Richardson and Robert Faggen eds. 2014. *The Letters of Robert Frost. Volume 1: 1886–1920*, 217.

49. Donald Sheehy, Mark Richardson and Robert Faggen eds. 2014. *The Letters of Robert Frost. Volume 1: 1886–1920*, 564, 640.

50. Donald Sheehy, Mark Richardson and Robert Faggen eds. 2014. *The Letters of Robert Frost. Volume 1: 1886–1920*, 323, 358, 392.

51. Donald Sheehy, Mark Richardson and Robert Faggen eds. 2014. *The Letters of Robert Frost. Volume 1: 1886–1920*, 581.

52. Lawrance Thompson. 1970. *Robert Frost: Years of Triumph, 1915–1938* (Holt, Rinehart and Winston, New York), 90.

53. Donald Sheehy, Mark Richardson and Robert Faggen eds. 2014. *The Letters of Robert Frost. Volume 1: 1886–1920*, 550–553.

54. Donald Sheehy, Mark Richardson and Robert Faggen eds. 2014. *The Letters of Robert Frost. Volume 1: 1886–1920*, 568; Jay Parini. 1999. *Robert Frost: A Life*, 180–181.

55. Jay Parini. 1999. *Robert Frost: A Life*, 400–401.

56. Edward Connery Latham ed. 1979. *The Poetry of Robert Frost*, 567.

57. Donald Sheehy, Mark Richardson and Robert Faggen eds. 2014. *The Letters of Robert Frost. Volume 1: 1886–1920*, 217, 552.

58. Robert Faggen. 2006. *The Notebooks of Robert Frost* (The Belknap Press of Harvard University Press, Cambridge), 307.

59. This wording is almost certainly a reference to Richard Anthony Proctor's book, *Our Place among the Infinities*.

60. Robert Faggen. 2006. *The Notebooks of Robert Frost*, 585.

61. Donald Sheehy, Mark Richardson and Robert Faggen eds. 2014. *The Letters of Robert Frost. Volume 1: 1886–1920* (The Belknap Press of Harvard University Press, Cambridge), 160; he also bragged that his son Carol had purchased "a new 35-dollar rooster": Donald Sheehy, Mark Richardson, Robert Bernard Hass and Henry Atmore eds. 2016. *The Letters of Robert Frost. Volume 2: 1920–1928* (The Belknap Press of Harvard University Press, Cambridge), 319.

62. Though published in 1934, the concept for this poem might have arisen much earlier and elsewhere. In a 1915 letter, Frost

wrote of a "solitary house-light in a hundred square miles of black mountainside." Donald Sheehy, Mark Richardson and Robert Faggen eds. 2014. *The Letters of Robert Frost. Volume 1: 1886–1920,* 381.

63. Robert Faggen. 2006. *The Notebooks of Robert Frost,* 163.

64. Robert Faggen. 2006. *The Notebooks of Robert Frost,* 266, 318, 672.

65. Robert Faggen. 1997. *Robert Frost and the Challenge of Darwin,* 250–251.

66. Mark Richardson ed. 2007. *The Collected Prose of Robert Frost,* 100, 209, 212, 351.

Farming

1. Mark Richardson ed. 2007. *The Collected Prose of Robert Frost* (The Belknap Press of Harvard University Press, Cambridge), 112, 314; Donald Sheehy, Mark Richardson and Robert Faggen eds. 2014. *The Letters of Robert Frost. Volume 1: 1886–1920,* 265, 586, 594, 177, 541, 614, 730.

2. Robert Bernard Hass. 2014. "'Measuring Myself against all Creation': Robert Frost and Pastoral" in Mark Richardson ed. 2014. *Robert Frost in Context* (Cambridge University Press, Cambridge), 115.

3. Donald Sheehy, Mark Richardson and Robert Faggen eds. 2014. *The Letters of Robert Frost. Volume 1: 1886–1920,* 131; Mark Richardson ed. 2007. *The Collected Prose of Robert Frost,* 112, xxxi.

4. Robert Bernard Hass. 2014. "'Measuring Myself against all Creation': Robert Frost and Pastoral" in Mark Richardson ed. 2014. *Robert Frost in Context* (Cambridge University Press, Cambridge), 116.

5. Robert Faggen. 2006. *The Notebooks of Robert Frost* (The Belknap Press of Harvard University Press, Cambridge), 332.

6. Frost included an early version of "Plowmen" in a letter to his daughter in 1920: Donald Sheehy, Mark Richardson and Robert Faggen eds. 2014. *The Letters of Robert Frost. Volume 1: 1886–1920,* 729.

7. Robert Faggen. 1997. *Robert Frost and the Challenge of Darwin* (University of Michigan Press, Ann Arbor), 136.

8. Lawrance Thompson. 1970. *Robert*

Frost: The Years of Triumph (Holt, Rinehart and Winston, New York), 346; Donald Sheehy, Mark Richardson, Robert Bernard Hass and Henry Atmore eds. 2016. *The Letters of Robert Frost. Volume 2: 1920–1928* (The Belknap Press of Harvard University Press, Cambridge), 227; Thomas Lask. 1963. "A poet of rural spirit." *The New York Times* (January 30).

9. Robert Faggen. 2006. *The Notebooks of Robert Frost,* 77, 585.

10. Donald Sheehy, Mark Richardson, Robert Bernard Hass and Henry Atmore eds. 2016. *The Letters of Robert Frost. Volume 2: 1920–1928* (The Belknap Press of Harvard University Press, Cambridge), 457.

11. Donald Sheehy, Mark Richardson, Robert Bernard Hass and Henry Atmore eds. 2016. *The Letters of Robert Frost. Volume 2: 1920–1928,* 393; Mark Richardson ed. 2007. *The Collected Prose of Robert Frost,* 252; Lesley Lee Francis. 2014. "The Derry Years of Robert Frost" in Mark Richardson ed. 2014. *Robert Frost in Context* (Cambridge University Press, Cambridge), 266–267.

12. Donald Sheehy, Mark Richardson and Robert Faggen eds. 2014. *The Letters of Robert Frost. Volume 1: 1886–1920,* 361, 438, 439, 504, 638, 661, 667, 679–680, 684, 687, 418, 670.

13. Donald Sheehy, Mark Richardson and Robert Faggen eds. 2014. *The Letters of Robert Frost. Volume 1: 1886–1920,* 55.

14. Robert Faggen. 2006. *The Notebooks of Robert Frost,* 386.

15. Virginia F. Smith discusses several aspects of apples as they appear in Frost's poetry. 2016. "Frost on the Apple." *Interdisciplinary Studies in Literature and Environment.* DOI: https://doi.org/10.1093/isle/isw 074.

16. Virginia F. Smith. 2016. "Frost on the Apple." *Interdisciplinary Studies in Literature and Environment.* DOI: https://doi.org/ 10.1093/isle/isw074; Donald Sheehy, Mark Richardson and Robert Faggen eds. 2014. *The Letters of Robert Frost. Volume 1: 1886–1920,* 313, 661, see also 668; Donald Sheehy, Mark Richardson, Robert Bernard Hass and

Henry Atmore eds. 2016. *The Letters of Robert Frost. Volume 2: 1920–1928*, 562.

17. Robert Faggen. 2006. *The Notebooks of Robert Frost*, 410.

18. William Cronon. 2003. *Changes in the Land. Indians, Colonists and the Ecology of New England*. Revised edition (Hill and Wang, New York), chapter 3.

19. Mark Richardson ed. 2007. *The Collected Prose of Robert Frost*, 26.

20. One lesson might have been from "the lonely cow" that "was as dissatisfied with America as Sinclair Lewis": Robert Faggen. 2006. *The Notebooks of Robert Frost*, 255.

21. Mark Richardson ed. 2007. *The Collected Prose of Robert Frost*, 92.

22. Richard Poirier and Mark Richardson eds. 1995. *Robert Frost: Collected Poems, Prose & Plays* (Library of America, New York), 786.

23. Jay Parini. 1999. *Robert Frost: A Life* (Henry Holt, New York), 110.

24. Donald Sheehy, Mark Richardson and Robert Faggen eds. 2014. *The Letters of Robert Frost. Volume 1: 1886–1920*, 482.

25. Donald Sheehy, Mark Richardson and Robert Faggen eds. 2014. *The Letters of Robert Frost. Volume 1: 1886–1920*, 308.

26. Frost pointed out to Louis ("Looiss") Untermeyer that he (Frost) was not "altogether of old stock" himself: Donald Sheehy, Mark Richardson and Robert Faggen eds. 2014. *The Letters of Robert Frost. Volume 1: 1886–1920*, 696.

27. A cautionary note: in a 1917 letter to Amy Lowell, Frost denied using "dialect" in *North of Boston*: Donald Sheehy, Mark Richardson and Robert Faggen eds. 2014. *The Letters of Robert Frost. Volume 1: 1886–1920*, 580–581; in 1894, however, he wrote to Susan Hayes Ward: "I justify the use to dialect" (*Letters*, 35). He also used seemingly phonetic spellings of mispronunciations in at least two prose pieces (Mark Richardson ed. 2007. *The Collected Prose of Robert Frost*, 53; Richard Poirier and Mark Richardson eds. 1995. *Robert Frost: Collected Poems, Prose & Plays*, 650. Finally, two friends of mine from Georgia noted, after the election of Jimmy Carter in 1976, that we now had a president without an accent. Dialect, for one who speaks it, is not dialect.

28. Mark Richardson. 1997. *The Ordeal of Robert Frost* (University of Illinois Press, Urbana), 239–240.

29. Robert Faggen. 2006. *The Notebooks of Robert Frost*, 332.

30. Robert Faggen claimed that the couple was lost in the woods because Fred replied to his wife with a question (1997. *Robert Frost and the Challenge of Darwin*, 288). But a question does not mean they were lost. The wording is similar to that in "The Mountain" when the visitor halted the driver of the ox-cart to ask him a question: "'What town is this?' I asked. 'This? Lunenburg.'" The driver needed just a moment to focus on the question, but he wasn't lost. Neither was Fred. He just needed a moment to refocus from his own thoughts to his wife's question. Each man uses his own brief question to get his bearings on the larger question being asked, but each is in full command of his bearings in the countryside.

31. George Bagby discusses the personification of nature, including nature's ability to love humans, in "Two Look at Two." 1993. *Frost and the Book of Nature* (University of Tennessee Press, Knoxville), 169–175.

32. Jack Larkin. 1988. *The Reshaping of Everyday Life 1790–1840*. (Harper Perennial, New York), 19.

33. Tim Kendall. 2012. *The Art of Robert Frost* (Yale University Press, New Haven), 27–28.

34. Richard Poirier and Mark Richardson eds. 1995. *Robert Frost: Collected Poems, Prose & Plays*, 784.

35. Robert Faggen. 2006. *The Notebooks of Robert Frost*, 124.

36. Robert Faggen. 2006. *The Notebooks of Robert Frost*, 374.

37. The curve of the scythe might have been the source of Frost's description of one of the subtleties of poetry. In "Conversations on the Craft of Poetry" with Cleanth Brooks, Robert Penn Warren and Kenny Withers, Frost described the nuance that is often lost in translation as "the way the

words are curved": Richard Poirier and Mark Richardson eds. 1995. *Robert Frost: Collected Poems, Prose & Plays*, 856.

38. H.M. Cottrell. 1902. Bulletin 109, Farm Department, Experiment Station of the Kansas State Agricultural College, Manhattan, 217–222.

39. Thomas Lask. 1963. "A poet of rural spirit." *The New York Times* (January 30).

40. Donald Sheehy, Mark Richardson and Robert Faggen eds. 2014. *The Letters of Robert Frost. Volume 1: 1886–1920*, 294; the editors of "Letters" identify "butterfly weed" as the common name of *Asclepias tuberosa*. Frost, however, was almost certainly using "butterfly weed" as a general reference to flowering weeds frequented by butterflies. *Asclepias tuberosa* is a milkweed that is rare in southern New Hampshire, that lives in dry, upland sites, not by brooks, and that is rarely, if ever, eaten by cows: Merritt Lyndon Fernald. 1950. *Gray's Manual of Botany*. 8th edition (D. Van Nostrand, New York), 1,172; Natural Resources Conservation Service. 2014. Plants Database. http://plants.usda.gov/java/county?state_name=New%20Hampshire&statefips=33&symbol=ASTU.

41. Donald Sheehy, Mark Richardson and Robert Faggen eds. 2014. *The Letters of Robert Frost. Volume 1: 1886–1920*, 318; Robert Faggen. 1997. *Robert Frost and the Challenge of Darwin*, 46–47.

42. Kathleen Morrison. 1974. *Robert Frost: A Pictorial Chronicle* (Holt, Rinehart & Winston, New York), 46.

43. Donald Sheehy, Mark Richardson and Robert Faggen eds. 2014. *The Letters of Robert Frost. Volume 1: 1886–1920*, 359.

44. The Frost Place, 158 Ridge Road, Franconia, NH. www.frostplace.org.

45. Donald Sheehy, Mark Richardson and Robert Faggen eds. 2014. *The Letters of Robert Frost. Volume 1: 1886–1920*, 63, 321, 336–337.

46. Robert Bernard Hass. 2002. *Going by Contraries*, 64–66.

47. Donald Sheehy, Mark Richardson and Robert Faggen eds. 2014. *The Letters of Robert Frost. Volume 1: 1886–1920*, 332–333.

48. Robert Faggen. 2006. *The Notebooks of Robert Frost*, 113, 372.

49. Donald Sheehy, Mark Richardson and Robert Faggen eds. 2014. *The Letters of Robert Frost. Volume 1: 1886–1920*, 336–337.

50. Mark Richardson ed. 2007. *The Collected Prose of Robert Frost*, 247; Donald Sheehy, Mark Richardson and Robert Faggen eds. 2014. *The Letters of Robert Frost. Volume 1: 1886–1920*, 135, 385, 587, 603.

51. Richard Poirier and Mark Richardson eds. 1995. *Robert Frost: Collected Poems, Prose & Plays*, 784.

52. David Orr. 2015. *The Road Not Taken* (Penguin Press, New York).

Seasons

1. Nina Baym. 1965. *American Quarterly* 17.4 (Winter), 714; George F. Bagby. 1993. *Frost and the Book of Nature* (University of Tennessee Press, Knoxville), 139.

2. In 2012, there was a mature, thriving peach tree on the grounds of the Frost Farm in Derry, NH, but I saw no peach trees near the Frost Place in Franconia, NH. "There Are Roughly Zones," published in 1939, could be a story of a failed attempt to grow peaches too far north.

3. Robert Faggen. 2006. *The Notebooks of Robert Frost*, 74.

4. Robert Faggen. 2006. *The Notebooks of Robert Frost* (The Belknap Press of Harvard University Press, Cambridge), 659.

5. A. J. Herbertson. 1901? *Outlines of Physiography: An Introduction to the Study of the Earth*. Third edition (Edward Arnold, London), 118.

6. Donald Sheehy, Mark Richardson and Robert Faggen eds. 2014. *The Letters of Robert Frost. Volume 1: 1886–1920* (The Belknap Press of Harvard University Press, Cambridge), 614, 326.

7. Virginia F. Smith. 2016. *Interdisciplinary Studies in Literature and Environment*, https://doi.org/10.1093/isle/isw074, 9–10.

8. Robert Faggen. 1997. *Robert Frost and the Challenge of Darwin* (University of Michigan Press, Ann Arbor), 139; to test this yourself, put one hand in hot water for a minute, the other in ice water at the same time, then put both hands in room-

temperature water. Do your two hands feel the same?

9. Robert Faggen. 2006. *The Notebooks of Robert Frost*, 644.

10. Mark Richardson ed. 2007. *The Collected Prose of Robert Frost* (The Belknap Press of Harvard University Press, Cambridge), 61.

11. Natalie S. Bober. 1991. *A Restless Spirit: The Story of Robert Frost* (Henry Holt, New York), 27; Richard Poirier and Mark Richardson eds. 1995. *Robert Frost: Collected Poems, Prose & Plays* (Library of America, New York), 778.

12. Robert Faggen. 1997. *Robert Frost and the Challenge of Darwin*, 264; Roger Tory Peterson. 1980. *A Field Guide to the Birds East of the Rockies* (Houghton Mifflin, Boston), 267.

13. Edward O. Wilson. 1970. pp. 133–155 in Ernest Sondheimer and John B. Simeone. 1970. *Chemical Ecology* (Academic Press, New York), 138; moth species that might fit Frost's description ("bright-black-eyed silvery creature, brushed with brown") and that are known to become active in winter in New England include *Ufeus satyricus, Lithophane thaxteri, Paleacrita vernata* and *Lycia ursaria* (information on winter activity provided by John E. Rawlins, Director, Center of Biodiversity and Ecosystems and Curator of Invertebrate Zoology, Carnegie Museum of Natural History, Pittsburgh).

14. Earl E. Berkley. 1931. *Botanical Gazette* 92.1, 85–93; Jay Parini. 1999. *Robert Frost: A Life.* (Henry Holt, New York), 121.

15. Richard Poirier and Mark Richardson eds. 1995. *Robert Frost: Collected Poems, Prose & Plays*, 777.

16. Thomas Eisner. 2003. *For the Love of Insects* (The Belknap Press of Harvard University Press, Cambridge), 389–393; Carol L. Boggs and Birgitt Dau. 2004. *Environmental Entomology* 33, 1020–1024; Robert Faggen. 1997. *Robert Frost and the Challenge of Darwin*, 72; Owen D.V. Sholes. 2017. *The Explicator* 75.1, 1–3.

17. Susan W. Beatty. 1984. *Ecology* 65, 1406–1419.

18. Glenn Adelson and John Elder. 2006. *Interdisciplinary Studies in Literature and Environment* 13.2, 8–13.

19. Frank B. Salisbury and Cleon W. Ross. 1992. *Plant Physiology.* Fourth Edition (Wadsworth, Belmont, CA), 103–104; much of the water evaporates directly from the pool itself, but the reader can easily ignore that fact.

20. Nina Baym 1965. *American Quarterly* 17.4 (Winter), 717.

21. Tim Kendall. 2012. *The Art of Robert Frost* (Yale University Press, New Haven), 217; Frost was fully explicit elsewhere that gardens were "the ruling passion with me": Donald Sheehy, Mark Richardson and Robert Faggen eds. 2014. *The Letters of Robert Frost. Volume 1: 1886–1920*, 702.

22. Mark Richardson. 1997. *The Ordeal of Robert Frost* (University of Illinois Press, Urbana), 46.

23. Frost wrote to his daughter Lesley, "First bluebirds for us this morning" and mentioned the impending arrival of bluebirds in a letter to Amy Lowell: Donald Sheehy, Mark Richardson and Robert Faggen eds. 2014. *The Letters of Robert Frost. Volume 1: 1886–1920*, 607, 541.

24. Richard Poirier and Mark Richardson eds. 1995. *Robert Frost: Collected Poems, Prose & Plays*, 812.

25. Robert Bernard Hass. 2002. *Going by Contraries* (University Press of Virginia, Charlottesville), 66.

26. Donald Sheehy, Mark Richardson and Robert Faggen eds. 2014. *The Letters of Robert Frost. Volume 1: 1886–1920*, 387.

27. Jay Parini. 1999. *Robert Frost: A Life*, 56–58; Richard Poirier and Mark Richardson eds. 1995. *Robert Frost: Collected Poems, Prose & Plays*, 935.

28. The final note appears in Richard Poirier and Mark Richardson eds. 1995. *Robert Frost: Collected Poems, Prose & Plays*, 426, but not in Edward Connery Latham ed. 1979. *The Poetry of Robert Frost: The Collected Poems, Complete and Unabridged* (Henry Holt, New York), 412; see also lines 370–371 of "Kitty Hawk."

29. Robert Faggen. 2006. *The Notebooks of Robert Frost*, 4; see also George F. Bagby. 1993. *Frost and the Book of Nature*, 81.

30. Stephan Jay Gould. 1989. *Wonderful Life* (W.W. Norton, New York), 291.

31. Merritt Lyndon Fernald. 1950. *Gray's Manual of Botany*. 8th edition (D. Van Nostrand, New York), 1,225; Paul Muldoon supposes that the white flower was actually *Prunella laciniata*, the self-heal, whose blooms are often white ("Robert Frost's Design," in Mark Richardson ed. 2014. *Frost in Context* [Cambridge University Press, Cambridge], 54); Muldoon is almost certainly incorrect because, first, Frost was a skilled botanist, and, second, *P. laciniata* is not found in New Hampshire (http://plants.usda.gov/core/profile?symbol=Prla7).

32. Ray F. Evert and Susan E. Eichhorn. 2013. *Biology of Plants*. Eighth Edition (W.H. Freeman, New York), chapter 20: Evolution of the Angiosperms, 477–500.

33. P.J. Gullan and P.S. Cranston. 1994. *The Insects: An Outline of Entomology* (Chapman and Hall, New York), 174–176.

34. Richard Poirier and Mark Richardson eds. 1995. *Robert Frost: Collected Poems, Prose & Plays*, 800.

35. Robert Faggen. 2006. *The Notebooks of Robert Frost*, 497; Donald Sheehy, Mark Richardson and Robert Faggen eds. 2014. *The Letters of Robert Frost. Volume 1: 1886–1920*, 333, 497.

36. Donald Sheehy, Mark Richardson and Robert Faggen eds. 2014. *The Letters of Robert Frost. Volume 1: 1886–1920*, 704; Marc D. Abrams and Gregory J. Nowacki. 1992. *Bulletin of the Torrey Botanical Club* 119, 19–28; Marc D. Abrams. 1998. *Bioscience* 48, 355–364; David R. Foster and John D. Aber eds. 2004. *Forests in Time: The Environmental Consequences of 1,000 Years of Change in New England* (Yale University Press, New Haven), 69.

37. Donald Sheehy, Mark Richardson and Robert Faggen eds. 2014. *The Letters of Robert Frost. Volume 1: 1886–1920*, 55.

38. Donald Sheehy, Mark Richardson and Robert Faggen eds. 2014. *The Letters of Robert Frost. Volume 1: 1886–1920*, 496; Robert Faggen. 2006. *The Notebooks of Robert Frost*, 659.

Agrarian Diaspora

1. Jay Parini. 1999. *Robert Frost: A Life* (Henry Holt, New York), 3.

2. Richard W. Wilkie and Jack Tager eds. 1991. *Historical Atlas of Massachusetts* (University of Massachusetts Press, Amherst), 140–144; Christopher McGrory Klyza and Stephen C. Trombulak. 2015. *The Story of Vermont*. Second edition (University Press of New England, Hanover), 91, 104, 129; Tom Wessels. 1997. *Reading the Forested Landscape: A Natural History of New England* (The Countryman Press, Woodstock, VT), 169.

3. Mark Richardson ed. 2007. *The Collected Prose of Robert Frost* (The Belknap Press of Harvard University Press, Cambridge), 9; Frost imagines another ruined ancient city (Ctesiphon) in "The Ingenuities of Debt."

4. Lawrance Thompson ed. 1964. Selected Letters of Robert Frost. (Holt, Rinehart and Winston, New York), 89, 627.

5. Paul Muldoon. 2014. "Robert Frost's Design" in Mark Richardson ed. 2014. *Frost in Context* (Cambridge University Press, Cambridge), 51; Henry David Thoreau used the word "dent" four times in Walden (e.g., "Now only a dent in the earth marks the site of these dwellings").

6. Robert Bernard Hass. 2002. *Going by Contraries* (University Press of Virginia, Charlottesville), 188, 195.

7. Irving Howe. 1963. *The New Republic*. March 23, 28; Nina Baym. 1965. *American Quarterly* 17.4 (Winter), 719.

8. Nina Baym. 1965. *American Quarterly* 17.4 (Winter), 718–719; Robert Bernard Hass. 2002. *Going by Contraries*, 83, 97.

9. P.G. Wright. 1970. *Contemporary Physics* 11.6, 581.

10. Robert Faggen. 2006. *The Notebooks of Robert Frost*, 19; Mark Richardson ed. 2007. *The Collected Prose of Robert Frost*, 151; Donald Sheehy, Mark Richardson and Robert Faggen eds. 2014. *The Letters of Robert Frost. Volume 1: 1886–1920* (The Belknap Press of Harvard University Press, Cambridge), 581.

11. Robert Faggen. 1997. *Robert Frost and the Challenge of Darwin* (University of Michigan Press, Ann Arbor), 111; Irving Howe. 1963. *The New Republic*, March 23, 23.

12. Robert Faggen. 1997. *Robert Frost and the Challenge of Darwin*, 275.

13. Robert Faggen. 1997. *Robert Frost and the Challenge of Darwin*, 70.

Ecological Succession

1. Catherine Keever. 1950. *Ecological Monographs* 20: 229–250; Fakhri A. Bazzaz. 1968. *Ecology* 49: 924–936; Robert H. Whittaker. 1975. *Communities and Ecosystems.* 2nd edition (Macmillan, New York), 173–179; Charles J. Krebs. 2001. *Ecology* (Benjamin Cummings, Boston), 406–409.

2. Oxford English Dictionary "succession" entry IV.14.f.: "The sequence of ecological changes in which one group of plant or animal species is replaced by another." 1860. H. D. Thoreau. David R. Foster. 1999. *Thoreau's Country* (Harvard University Press, Cambridge), 134.

3. William S. Cooper. 1922. *Ecology* 3, 9–10.

4. John G. Torrey. 1978. *Bioscience* 28, 586.

5. David R. Foster and John D. Aber eds. 2004. *Forests in Time*, 25, 85, 125; David R. Foster. 1999. *Thoreau's Country*, 136; James R. Runkle and Todd C. Yetter. 1987. *Ecology* 68, 417–424.

6. Frederic E. Clements. 1916. *Plant Succession: An Analysis of the Development of Vegetation.* Carnegie Institution of Washington, Publication 242, iii; William S. Cooper. 1922. *Ecology* 3, 7–10.

7. David R. Foster and John D. Aber eds. 2004. *Forests in Time*, 48–62; Robert H. Whittaker. 1975. *Communities and Ecosystems*, 179–183.

8. Marc D. Abrams. 1998. *Bioscience* 48: 355–364; Marc D. Abrams and Gregory J. Nowacki. 1992. *Bulletin of the Torrey Botanical Club* 119: 19–28; F. Herbert Bormann and Gene E. Likens. 1979. *American Scientist* 67.6, 660–669.

9. Eugene P. Odum 1950. *Ecology* 31,

587–605; David W. Johnston and Eugene P. Odum. 1956. *Ecology* 37, 50–62.

10. Colin Nickerson. 2013. *Boston Globe*, August 31, A1.

11. John Kricher. 1997. *Northeastern Naturalist* 5, 165–174; David R. Foster, Glenn Motzkin and Benjamin Slater. 1998. *Ecosystems* 1, 96–119; Brian Beckage et al. 2008. *Proceedings of the National Academy of Sciences* 105, 4197–4202; Gregory J. Nowacki and Marc D. Abrams. 2015. *Global Change Biology* 21, 314–334; Neil Pederson et al. 2015. *Global Change Biology* 21, 2105–2110; Matthais Bürgi et al. 2017. *Ecosystems* 20, 94–103.

12. John Elder. 1998. *Reading the Mountains of Home* (Harvard University Press, Cambridge), 1–2, 14, 20, 107; Michael J. McDowell. 1991. *South Carolina Review* 21.1, 93.

13. Donald Sheehy, Mark Richardson and Robert Faggen eds. 2014. *The Letters of Robert Frost. Volume 1: 1886–1920*, 688.

14. While there is no doubt that meadow sweet, steeple bush and hardhack are shrubs, there may be confusion about which species Frost was describing. Though the names "meadow sweet" and "hardhack" are now applied to different species, in the early twentieth century, meadow sweet referred to *S. latifolia* and hardhack referred to *S. tomentosa*. Steeple bush, then and now, refers to *S. tomentosa*. All of these common names gave Frost synonyms with different sounds or syllables, a useful set of options for a poet. Arthur Haines. 2011. *Flora Novae Angliae* (Yale University Press, New Haven), 819–820; William S. Cooper. 1922. *Ecology* 3, 7–16.

15. Robert Faggen. 2006. *The Notebooks of Robert Frost*, 584, 420.

16. Oxford English Dictionary, entry 1. a. for "copse, *n.*"

17. Edward Connery Latham ed. 1979. *The Poetry of Robert Frost: The Collected Poems, Complete and Unabridge* (Henry Holt, New York), 548.

18. Tom Wessels. 1997. *Reading the Forested Landscape*, 42, David R. Foster. 1999. *Thoreau's Country*, 189.

19. Massachusetts Audubon Society.

2015. State of the Birds: Wood Thrush *Hylocichla mustelina*. Breeding bird survey. http://www.massaudubon.org/our-conservation-work/wildlife-research-conservation/statewide-bird-monitoring/state-of-the-birds/find-a-bird/(id)/WOTH.

20. Hal H. Harrison. 1975. *A Field Guide to Birds' Nests in the United States east of the Mississippi River* (Houghton Mifflin Company, Boston), 104, 105.

21. Calls of both species became rare after 1979 as trees filled in the field behind my house, but have recovered somewhat since houses were built nearby and our neighbor had some trees cut as part of his timber management plan.

22. Donald Sheehy, Mark Richardson and Robert Faggen eds. 2014. *The Letters of Robert Frost. Volume 1: 1886–1920*, 53.

23. Tom Wessels. 1997. *Reading the Forested Landscape*, 45; Robert I. Bertin and Thomas J. Rawinski. 2012. *Vascular Flora of Worcester County, Massachusetts* (Special Publication of the New England Botanical Club), 45.

24. Chiang Yee. 1936. *The Chinese Eye.* Second edition (Indiana University Press, Bloomington), 89–90.

25. Donald Sheehy, Mark Richardson and Robert Faggen eds. 2014. *The Letters of Robert Frost. Volume 1: 1886–1920*, 661.

26. George F. Bagby. 1993. *Frost and the Book of Nature* (University of Tennessee Press, Knoxville), 131–132.

27. John Elder. 1998. *Reading the Mountains of Home*, 93–94; George F. Bagby. 1993. *Frost and the Book of Nature*, 84–85.

28. Robert Faggen. 1997. *Robert Frost and the Challenge of Darwin*, 139.

29. Robert Faggen concluded that the word "ebony" connoted "a darkness that comes from common human roots in soot." This is almost certainly not the case in "Blueberries." Blueberry shrubs (in the genus *Vaccinium*) sometimes have fruit that is "blue-black" with a waxy glaucous coating on the epidermis, the bluish "mist" in line 25. Frost used "ebony" as a description of the fruit, not as a reference to humans: Robert Faggen. 1997. *Robert Frost and the Chal-*

lenge *of Darwin*, 139–40; Arthur Haines. 2011. *Flora Novae Angliae*, 561.

30. Robert Faggen. 2006. *The Notebooks of Robert Frost*, 186.

31. When asked why he didn't plant a flower garden while in England, Frost wrote, "I like flowers you know but I like em wild." Donald Sheehy, Mark Richardson and Robert Faggen eds. 2014. *The Letters of Robert Frost. Volume 1: 1886–1920*, 102.

32. Robert Faggen. 2006. *The Notebooks of Robert Frost*, 186.

Life Cycles

1. Matisse in the Studio. 2017. Museum of Fine Arts, Boston. http://www.mfa.org/exhibitions/matisse-in-the-studio.

2. George F. Bagby. 1993. *Frost and the Book of Nature* (University of Tennessee Press, Knoxville), 165.

3. Fiona Stafford. 2016. *The Long, Long Life of Trees* (Yale University Press, New Haven), e-book location 1930.

4. Richard Poirier and Mark Richardson eds. 1995. *Robert Frost: Collected Poems, Prose & Plays* (Library of America, New York), 714.

5. Jay Parini. 1999. *Robert Frost: A Life* (Henry Holt, New York), 111; Merritt Lyndon Fernald. 1950. *Gray's Manual of Botany.* 8th edition (D. Van Nostrand, New York), 1225.

6. Integrated Taxonomic Information System (ITIS) Report: *Pseudacris crucifer* (Wied-Neuwied, 1838). http://www.itis.gov/servlet/SingleRpt/SingleRpt?search_topic=TSN&search_value=207303.

7. International Commission on Zoological Nomenclature. 2000. *International Codes of Zoological Nomenclature.* Fourth edition. http://www.nhm.ac.uk/hosted-sites/iczn/code/.

8. G. Ledyard Stebbins. 1974. *Flowering Plants: Evolution Above the Species Level* (The Belknap Press of Harvard University Press, Cambridge), 352; The Global Biodiversity Information Facility: GBIF Backbone Taxonomy, 2013-07-01. http://www.gbif.org/species/5015; L. Watson and M.J. Dallwitz. 1992 onward. The families of flowering

plants: Descriptions, illustrations, identification, and information retrieval. Version: 30 June 2014. http://delta-intkey.com.

9. R. H. Marrs, M. G. Le Duc, R. J. Mitchell, D. Goddardt, S. Patersons and R. J. Pakeman. 2000. *Annals of Botany* 85 (Supplement B): 3–15.

10. Jennifer Buron, Danielle Lavigne, Kristine Grote, Rebecca Takis, Owen Sholes. 1998. *Northeastern Naturalist* 5, 359–362; David R. Foster and John D. Aber eds. 2004. *Forests in Time*, 111, 114, 125.

11. Owen D.V. Sholes. 2013. *Journal of the Torrey Botanical Society* 140, 364–368.

12. May R. Berenbaum. 1995. *Bugs in the System* (Addison Wesley, Reading, MA), 131.

13. Sanborn C. Brown. 1978. *Wines & Beers of Old New England* (University Press of New England. Hanover), 3.

14. R. H. Marrs, M. G. Le Duc, R. J. Mitchell, D. Goddardt, S. Patersons and R. J. Pakeman. 2000. *Annals of Botany* 85 (Supplement B): 3–15.

15. Robert Faggen. 2006. *The Notebooks of Robert Frost*, xiv.

16. The Robert Frost Farm, Derry, NH. http://robertfrostfarm.org/index.html.

17. Donald Sheehy, Mark Richardson and Robert Faggen eds. 2014. *The Letters of Robert Frost. Volume 1: 1886–1920*, 627.

18. Reginald L. Cook. 1955. "A Walk with Robert Frost." *Yankee Magazine* 19.11, http://www.frostfriends.org/cookpage.html (accessed 8/3/2013); hay-scented fern (*Dennstaedtia punctilobula*) and lady fern (*Athyrium angustum*) are still widespread: Robert I. Bertin and Thomas J. Rawinski. 2012. *Vascular Flora of Worcester County, Massachusetts* (Special Publication of the New England Botanical Club), 40, 44.

19. In a letter to Harold Rugg, Frost refers to a "mountain for the ferns" near Lake Willoughby in NH: Donald Sheehy, Mark Richardson and Robert Faggen eds. 2014. *The Letters of Robert Frost. Volume 1: 1886–1920*, 284–285; see also pages 487, 645.

20. Tim Kendall. 2012. *The Art of Robert Frost*, 109–112.

21. Mark Richardson ed. 2007. *The Collected Prose of Robert Frost* (The Belknap Press of Harvard University Press, Cambridge), 30; Frost's daughter Marjorie was born in 1905: Richard Poirier and Mark Richardson eds. 1995. *Robert Frost: Collected Poems, Prose & Plays*, 937.

22. Donald Sheehy, Mark Richardson and Robert Faggen eds. 2014. *The Letters of Robert Frost. Volume 1: 1886–1920*, 627.

23. Lesley Lee Francis is sure that these characters are "the poet and his daughter" (*You Come Too: My Journey with Robert Frost*. University of Virginia Press, Charlottesville, location 437).

24. Turning to other things also appears in "Something for Hope," where the reader is asked to keep busy with other things, and in "In the Home Stretch" where the "woods" are "waiting to steal a step on us whenever / we drop our eyes or turn to other things."

25. Jay Parini. 1999. *Robert Frost: A Life*, 182.

26. Ray F. Evert and Susan E. Eichhorn. 2013. *Biology of Plants*. Eighth Edition (W.H. Freeman, New York), 401, 409.

27. Richard Poirier and Mark Richardson eds. 1995. *Robert Frost: Collected Poems, Prose & Plays*, 802; the same encounter is mentioned in a letter to Jack Haines in 1916: Donald Sheehy, Mark Richardson and Robert Faggen eds. 2014. *The Letters of Robert Frost. Volume 1: 1886–1920*, 465.

28. Ray F. Evert and Susan E. Eichhorn. 2013. *Biology of Plants*. Eighth Edition (W.H. Freeman, New York), 698.

29. Robert I. Bertin and Thomas J. Rawinski. 2012. *Vascular Flora of Worcester County, Massachusetts*. (Special Publication of the New England Botanical Club. Cambridge), 138–139.

30. Flora of North America. FNA Vol. 3: Betulaceae: *Alnus: Alnus glutinosa*. http://www.efloras.org/florataxon.aspx?flora_id=1&taxon_id=233500032; Robert I. Bertin and Thomas J. Rawinski. 2012. Vascular Flora of Worcester County, Massachusetts, 115.

31. Nathaniel Lord Britton and Addison Brown. 1970. *An Illustrated Flora of the Northern United States and Canada*. 2nd edition (Dover, New York), volume 2, 489;

X.P. Fang and J.L. McLaughlin. 1990. *Fitoterapia* 61, 176–177.

32. Merritt Lyndon Fernald. 1950. *Gray's Manual of Botany*, 1,150; according to his daughter's journal, Frost transplanted lilacs in 1907 from a house that burned down in 1867: George Monteiro. 2015. *Robert Frost's Poetry of Rural Life* (McFarland, Jefferson, NC), 35.

33. Robert Faggen. 2006. *The Notebooks of Robert Frost*, 332.

34. Robert Faggen. 1997. *Robert Frost and the Challenge of Darwin*, 275.

35. Edward Connery Latham ed. 1979. *The Poetry of Robert Frost: The Collected Poems, Complete and Unabridged* (Henry Holt, New York), 552.

36. Tim Kendall. 2012. *The Art of Robert Frost*, 9.

37. Jay Parini. 1999. *Robert Frost: A Life*, 79–80.

38. George Monteiro. 2015. *Robert Frost's Poetry of Rural Life* (McFarland, Jefferson, NC), 37.

39. Jay Parini. 1999. *Robert Frost: A Life*, 228–229; Mark Richardson ed. 2007. *The Collected Prose of Robert Frost*, 88, 264.

40. Mark Richardson ed. 2007. *The Collected Prose of Robert Frost* (The Belknap Press of Harvard University Press, Cambridge), 275.

41. Lawrence K. Forcier. 1975. *Science* 189, 808–810; Tim Kendall. 2012. *The Art of Robert Frost* (Yale University Press, New Haven), 247.

42. Robert Faggen. 1997. *Robert Frost and the Challenge of Darwin* (University of Michigan Press, Ann Arbor), 203–208.

43. James R. Runkle and Todd C. Yetter. 1987. *Ecology* 68, 417–424.

44. Tim Kendall. 2012. *The Art of Robert Frost*, 265–269.

45. Robert Faggen. 1997. *Robert Frost and the Challenge of Darwin*, 207–208.

46. Mark Richardson ed. 2007. *The Collected Prose of Robert Frost*, 107, 274; Robert Faggen. 1997. *Robert Frost and the Challenge of Darwin*, 207, 208.

47. Robert Faggen. 1997. *Robert Frost and the Challenge of Darwin*, 208.

48. Frost was familiar with sugaring:

Donald Sheehy, Mark Richardson and Robert Faggen eds. 2014. *The Letters of Robert Frost. Volume 1: 1886–1920* (The Belknap Press of Harvard University Press, Cambridge), 274, 486, 662, 707; see also lines 136–138 in "Maple."

49. Donald Sheehy, Mark Richardson and Robert Faggen eds. 2014. *The Letters of Robert Frost. Volume 1: 1886–1920*, 497; Robert Faggen. 2006. *The Notebooks of Robert Frost* (The Belknap Press of Harvard University Press, Cambridge), 497.

50. Robert Faggen. 2006. *The Notebooks of Robert Frost*, 524.

51. Hal H. Harrison. 1975. *A Field Guide to Birds' Nests in the United States East of the Mississippi River* (Houghton Mifflin, Boston), 120; Barns are interesting nest sites for phoebes because the birds sometimes seem confused by all the rafters and build multiple nests (one year, there were two phoebe nests less than a meter apart in my woodshed). This behavior might be a waste of energy, or it might provide some defense by inducing cowbirds to lay their parasitic eggs in an untended nest.

52. Kathleen Morrison. 1974. *Robert Frost: A Pictorial Chronicle* (Holt, Rinehart & Winston, New York), 46.

53. Joseph Brodsky. 1994. *The New Yorker*, Sept. 26, 73.

54. The thrush is central to "Come In": "As I came to the edge of the woods, / Thrush music—hark!" But which species of thrush is it? The robin is too common, the hermit thrush only moderately interesting, and the olive-backed, gray-cheeked and Bicknell's thrushes too rare (and the last lives only at high elevations). The veery's song rises and falls repeatedly, and has a quality that fits the song in "An Unhistoric Spot" ("The lone thrush gurgles nectar in his throat"). In contrast, the song of the wood thrush is sweet and bubbling but also varied, distinctive and almost electronic in quality, not quite a "gurgle" like that of the veery. But either species, veery or wood thrush, would induce most people to exclaim, "Hark!" (or some present day equivalent) when they heard it. They would stop and draw closer to hear this distinctive tune

from high in a tree, even if they were in the middle of doing something else.

55. Joseph Brodsky. 1994. *The New Yorker.* Sept. 26, 74.

56. The thatched house was almost certainly The Gallows, a house in which the Frosts lived while in England in 1914 (Jay Parini. 1999. *Robert Frost: A Life,* 153). Frost observed the ruined house first-hand in 1957 (Parini, 400), but "The Thatch" was published in 1930 (Edward Connery Latham ed. 1979. *The Poetry of Robert Frost* [Henry Holt, NY], 554), so news of the "unmended" state of the house must have come from friends ("They tell me..." line 31); George Bagby discusses "The Thatch" at some length: George F. Bagby. 1993. *Frost and the Book of Nature* (University of Tennessee Press, Knoxville), 157.

57. George F. Bagby. 1993. *Frost and the Book of Nature,* 193, 91.

58. Michael Begon, Colin R. Townsend and John L. Harper. 2006. *Ecology* (Blackwell, Malden, MA), 327–329.

59. Jacob Kalff. 2002. *Limnology* (Prentice Hall, Upper Saddle River, NJ), 438.

60. John F. Lynen. 1960. *The Pastoral Art of Robert Frost* (Yale University Press, New Haven), 145.

61. There was a wood-related death in "Out, Out—," written at about the same time as "The Wood-Pile," and turning to other things was also part of that story. After the boy was killed by the saw while cutting wood, the surviving family members went about other business: "And they, since they / Were not the one dead, turned to their affairs."

Conclusion

1. Richard Poirier and Mark Richardson eds. 1995. *Robert Frost: Collected Poems, Prose & Plays,* 696.

2. John F. Lynen. 1960. *The Pastoral Art of Robert Frost* (Yale University Press, New Haven), 2; Robert Bernard Hass. 2002. *Going by Contraries* (University Press of Virginia, Charlottesville), 138; in 1915, Frost wrote, "You are not going to make the mistake that Pound makes of assuming that my simplicity is that of an untutored child. I am not undesigning." Donald Sheehy, Mark Richardson and Robert Faggen eds. 2014. *The Letters of Robert Frost. Volume 1: 1886–1920* (The Belknap Press of Harvard University Press, Cambridge), 132.

3. Richard Poirier and Mark Richardson eds. 1995. *Robert Frost: Collected Poems, Prose & Plays,* 804.

4. Irving Howe. 1963. *The New Republic.* March 23, 26, 27.

5. John F. Lynen. 1960. *The Pastoral Art of Robert Frost,* 48; Jay Parini. 1999. *Robert Frost: A Life,* 69.

6. Robert Faggen. 2006. *The Notebooks of Robert Frost,* 494.

7. Richard Poirier and Mark Richardson eds. 1995. *Robert Frost: Collected Poems, Prose & Plays,* 777.

8. Robert P. Sharp. 1988. *Living Ice* (Cambridge University Press, Cambridge), 143–144.

9. Wayne Petersen. 2012. *Sanctuary* 51 (1): 18–19.

10. J. Hall Cushman and Dennis D. Murphy. 1993. pp. 37–44 in T. R. New. Conservation of Lycaenidae (Butterflies). Occasional Paper of the IUCN Species Survival Commission No. 8. https://portals.iucn.org/library/efiles/edocs/ssc-op-008.pdf.

Further Reading
and Sources

Frost's Life and Poetry

Bagby, George F. *Frost and the Book of Nature*. Knoxville: University of Tennessee Press, 1993.

Barron, Jonathan N. *How Robert Frost Made Realism Matter*. Columbia: University of Missouri Press, 2015.

Baym, Nina "An Approach to Robert Frost's Nature Poetry." *American Quarterly* 17, no. 4 (Winter 1965): 713–723.

Elder, John. *Reading the Mountains of Home*. Cambridge, MA: Harvard University Press, 1998.

Kemp, John C. *Robert Frost and New England*. Princeton: Princeton University Press, 1979.

Kendall, Tim. *The Art of Robert Frost*. New Haven, CT: Yale University Press, 2012.

Lynen, John F. *The Pastoral Art of Robert Frost*. New Haven, CT: Yale University Press, 1960.

Melvin, Betsy, and Tom Melvin. *Robert Frost's New England*. Hanover, NH: University Press of New England, 2000.

Monteiro, George. *Robert Frost's Poetry of Rural Life*. Jefferson, NC: McFarland, 2015.

Morrison, Kathleen. *Robert Frost: A Pictorial Chronicle*. New York: Holt, Rinehart & Winston, 1974.

Orr, David. *The Road Not Taken*. New York: Penguin Press, 2015.

Parini, Jay. *Robert Frost: A Life*. New York: Henry Holt, 1999.

Richardson, Mark, ed. *Robert Frost in Context*. Cambridge: Cambridge University Press, 2014.

Rothman, Joshua. "Robert Frost: Darkness or Light?" Page-Turner (blog), *The New Yorker*, January 29, 2013, http://www.newyorker.com/online/blogs/books/2013/01/robert-frost-darkness-or-light.html.

Environmental History

Albers, Jan. *Hands on the Land: A History of the Vermont Landscape*. Cambridge, MA: MIT Press, 2000.

Connell, Joseph H., and Ralph O. Slatyer. "Mechanisms of Succession in Natural Communities and Their Role in Community Stability and Organization." *The American Naturalist* 111, no. 982 (Winter 1977): 1119–1144.

Further Reading and Sources

Cornell Laboratory of Ornithology. http://www.birds.cornell.edu/Page.aspx?pid=1478.

Cronon, William. *Changes in the Land: Indians, Colonists and the Ecology of New England*. Rev. ed. New York: Hill and Wang, 2003.

Foster, Charles H. W., ed. *Stepping Back to Look Forward*. Petersham, MA: Harvard Forest, 1998.

Foster, David R. *Thoreau's Country*. Cambridge: Harvard University Press, 1999.

Foster, David R., and John D. Aber, eds. *Forests in Time: The Environmental Consequences of 1,000 Years of Change in New England*. New Haven, CT: Yale University Press, 2004.

Hawke, David Freeman. *Everyday Life in Early America*. New York: Harper, 1988.

Klyza, Christopher McGrory, and Stephen C. Trombulak. *The Story of Vermont*. 2nd ed. Hanover, NH: University Press of New England, 2015.

Larkin, Jack. *The Reshaping of Everyday Life 1790–1840*. New York: Harper Perennial, 1988.

Muir, Diana. *Reflections in Bullough's Pond*. Hanover, NH: University Press of New England, 2000.

Nickerson, Colin. "New England Sees a Return of Forests, Wildlife: The Woods Are Lovely, Dark, and Back." *Boston Globe*, 31 August 2013. http://www.bostonglobe.com/metro/2013/08/31/new-england-sees-return-forests-and-wildlife/lJRxacvGcHeQDmtZt09WvN/story.html.

Petersen, Wayne. "Old Barns and Their Birds." *Sanctuary: The Journal of the Massachusetts Audubon Society* 51, no. 1 (Winter 2012): 18–19.

Primack, Richard B. *Walden Warming: Climate Changes Comes to Thoreau's Woods*. Chicago: University of Chicago Press, 2014.

Proulx, Annie. *Barkskins, a Novel*. New York: Scribner's, 2016.

Russell, Emily, W. B. *People and the Land Through Time*. New Haven, CT: Yale University Press, 1997.

Thoreau, Henry David. *Walden*. Boston: Ticknor and Fields, 1854

Wessels, Tom. *Reading the Forested Landscape: A Natural History of New England*. Woodstock, VT: The Countryman Press, 1997.

Whitney, Gordon G. *From Coastal Wilderness to Fruited Plain*. New York: Cambridge University Press, 1994.

Frost's Writings: Poems, Prose, Plays, Notebooks and Letters

Faggen, Robert. *The Notebooks of Robert Frost*. Cambridge, MA: Belknap Press of Harvard University Press, 2006.

Latham, Edward Connery, ed. *The Poetry of Robert Frost: The Collected Poems, Complete and Unabridged*. New York: Henry Holt, 1979.

Poirier, Richard, and Mark Richardson, eds. *Robert Frost: Collected Poems, Prose & Plays*. New York: Library of America, 1995.

Richardson, Mark, ed. *The Collected Prose of Robert Frost*. Cambridge, MA: Belknap Press of Harvard University Press, 2007.

Sheehy, Donald, Mark Richardson, and Robert Faggen, eds. *The Letters of Robert Frost: Volume 1: 1886–1920*. Cambridge, MA: Belknap Press of Harvard University Press, 2014.

Sheehy, Donald, Mark Richardson, Robert Bernard Hass, and Henry Atmore, eds. *The Letters of Robert Frost. Volume 2: 1920–1928.* Cambridge, MA: Belknap Press of Harvard University Press, 2016.

Thompson, Lawrance, ed. *Selected Letters of Robert Frost.* New York: Holt, Rinehart and Winston, 1964.

Biographies and Literary Analysis

Adelson, Glenn, and John Elder. "Robert Frost's Ecosystem of Meanings in 'Spring Pools.'" *Interdisciplinary Studies in Literature and Environment* 13, no. 2 (Summer 2006): 1–17.

Bagby, George F. *Frost and the Book of Nature.* Knoxville: University of Tennessee Press, 1993.

Bailey, Thomas C. "Robert Frost as Nature Poet and Naturalist." In *The Robert Frost Encyclopedia*, edited by Nancy Lewis Tuten and John Zubizarreta. Greenwood Press, 2001.

Barron, Jonathan N. *How Robert Frost Made Realism Matter.* Columbia: University of Missouri Press, 2015.

Baym, Nina. "An Approach to Robert Frost's Nature Poetry." *American Quarterly* 17, no. 4 (Winter 1965): 713–723.

Bober, Natalie S. *A Restless Spirit: The Story of Robert Frost.* New York: Henry Holt, 1991.

Brodsky, Joseph. "On Grief and Reason." *The New Yorker*, September 1994.

Brower, Reuben. *The Poetry of Robert Frost: Constellations of Intention.* New York: Oxford University Press, 1963.

Elder, John. *Reading the Mountains of Home.* Cambridge, MA: Harvard University Press, 1998.

Faggen, Robert. *Robert Frost and the Challenge of Darwin.* Ann Arbor: University of Michigan Press, 1997.

Francis, Lesley Lee. *You Come Too: My Journey with Robert Frost.* Charlottesville: University of Virginia Press, 2015.

Hass, Robert Bernard. *Going by Contraries.* Charlottesville: University of Virginia Press, 2002.

Howe, Irving. "Robert Frost: A Momentary Stay." *The New Republic*, March 1963.

Kearns, Katherine. *Robert Frost and the Poetics of Appetite.* New York: Cambridge University Press, 1994.

Kendall, Tim. *The Art of Robert Frost.* New Haven, CT: Yale University Press, 2012.

Lask, Thomas. "A Poet of Rural Spirit." *The New York Times*, January 30, 1963. http://www.nytimes.com/books/99/04/25/specials/frost-obit2.html.

Lynen, John F. *The Pastoral Art of Robert Frost.* New Haven, CT: Yale University Press, 1960.

McDowell, Michael J. "Since Earth is Earth: An Ecological Approach to Robert Frost's Poetry." *South Carolina Review* 24, no.1 (Fall 1991): 92–100.

Meyers, Jeffrey. *Robert Frost: A Biography.* Boston: Houghton Mifflin Company, 1996.

Monteiro, George. *Robert Frost's Poetry of Rural Life.* Jefferson, NC: McFarland, 2015.

Morrison, Kathleen. *Robert Frost: A Pictorial Chronicle.* New York: Holt, Rinehart & Winston, 1974.

Further Reading and Sources

Museum of Fine Arts. 2017. Matisse in the Studio: exhibition, Boston. http://www. mfa.org/exhibitions/matisse-in-the-studio (retrieved 7/30/17).

Orr, David. *The Road Not Taken.* New York: Penguin Press, 2015.

Parini, Jay. *Robert Frost: A Life.* New York: Henry Holt, 1999.

Richardson, Mark. *The Ordeal of Robert Frost.* Urabana: University of Illinois Press, 1997.

Richardson, Mark, ed. *Robert Frost in Context.* New York: Cambridge University Press, 2014.

Rothman, Joshua. "Robert Frost: Darkness or Light?" Page-Turner (blog), *The New Yorker,* January 29, 2013, http://www.newyorker.com/online/blogs/books/2013/ 01/robert-frost-darkness-or-light.html.

Sholes, Owen D.V. "Bleeding Trees in the Poetry of Robert Frost." *The Robert Frost Review,* No. 26 (2016): 31–39.

Sholes, Owen D.V. "Death or Nourishment in Robert Frost's 'Blue-Butterfly Day'?" *The Explicator* 75, no. 1 (Spring 2017): 1–3.

Smith, Virginia F. "Frost on the Apple." *Interdisciplinary Studies in Literature and Environment* 23, no. 4 (Fall 2016): 677–693, DOI: https://doi.org/10.1093/isle/isw074.

Sutton, William A., ed. *Newdick's Season of Frost: An Interrupted Biography of Robert Frost.* Albany: State University of New York Press, 1976.

Thompson, Lawrance. *Robert Frost: Years of Triumph, 1915–1938.* New York: Holt, Rinehart and Winston, 1970.

Untermeyer, Louis. *The Complete Poetical Works of Amy Lowell.* Cambridge, MA: Riverside Press, 1955.

Yee, Chiang. *The Chinese Eye,* 2nd ed. Bloomington: Indiana University Press, 1936.

Science, Natural History and New England

Abrams, Marc D. "The Red Maple Paradox." *Bioscience* 48, no. 5 (May 1998): 355–364.

Abrams, Marc D., and Gregory J. Nowacki. "Historical Variation in Fire, Oak Recruitment, and Post-Logging Accelerated Succession in Central Pennsylvania." *Bulletin of the Torrey Botanical Club* 119, no.1 (January 1992): 19–28.

Albers, Jan. *Hands on the Land: A History of the Vermont Landscape.* Cambridge, MA: MIT Press, 2000.

Arms, Karen, Paul Feeny and Robert C. Lederhouse. "Sodium: Stimulus for Puddling Behavior by Tiger Swallowtail Butterflies, *Papilio glaucus."* *Science* 185, no. 4148 (July 1974): 372–374.

Askins, Robert A. "Recovery and Future of the Northeastern Forest." *Northeastern Naturalist* 5, no. 2 (April 1998): 97–98.

Bazzaz, Fakhri A. "Succession on Abandoned Fields in the Shawnee Hills of Southern Illinois." *Ecology* 49, no. 5 (Summer 1968): 924–936.

Beatty, Susan W. "Influence of Microtopography and Canopy Species on Spatial Patterns of Forest Understory Plants." *Ecology* 65, no. 5 (October 1984): 1406–1419

Beckage, Brian, Ben Osborne, Daniel G. Gavin, Carolyn Pucko, Thomas Siccama and Timothy Perkins. "A Rapid Upward Shift of a Forest Ecotone During 40 Years of Warming in the Green Mountains of Vermont." *Proceedings of the National Academy of Sciences* 105, no. 11 (April 2008): 4197–4202.

Further Reading and Sources

Begon, Michael, Colin R. Townsend and John L. Harper. *Ecology: From Individuals to Ecosystems*. Malden, MA: Blackwell, 2006.

Berenbaum, May R. *Bugs in the System*. Reading, MA: Addison Wesley, 1995.

Berkley, Earl E. "Marcescent Leaves of Certain Species of *Quercus*." *Botanical Gazette* 92, no. 1 (September 1931): 85–93.

Bertin, Robert I. "Losses of Native Plant Species from Worcester, Massachusetts." *Rhodora* 104, no. 920 (Fall 2002): 325–349.

Bertin, Robert I. *Vascular Flora of Worcester, Massachusetts*. Cambridge, MA: New England Botanical Club, 2000.

Bertin, Robert I., and Thomas J. Rawinski. *Vascular Flora of Worcester County, Massachusetts*. Cambridge, MA: New England Botanical Club, 2012.

Boggs, Carol L., and Birgitt Dau. "Resource Specialization in Puddling Lepidoptera." *Environmental Entomology* 33, no. 4 (August 2004): 1020–1024.

Bormann, F. Herbert and Gene E. Likens. "Catastrophic Disturbance and the Steady State in Northern Hardwood Forests: A New Look at the Role of Disturbance in the Development of Forest Ecosystems Suggests Important Implications for Land-Use Policies." *American Scientist* 67, no. 6 (Winter 1979): 660–669.

Britton, Nathaniel Lord, and Addison Brown. *An Illustrated Flora of the Northern United States and Canada*. 2nd ed. New York: Dover Publications, 1970.

Brown, Sanborn C. *Wines & Beers of Old New England*. Hanover, NH: University Press of New England, 1978.

Bürgi, Matthais, Lars Östlund and David J. Mladenoff. "Legacy Effects of Human Land Use: Ecosystems as Time-Lagged Systems." *Ecosystems* 20, no. 1 (January 2017): 94–103.

Buron, Jennifer, Danielle Lavigne, Kristine Grote, Rebecca Takis and Owen D.V. Sholes. "Association of Vines and Trees in Second-Growth Forest." *Northeastern Naturalist* 5, no. 4 (Winter 1998): 359–362.

Clements, Frederic E. *Plant Succession: An Analysis of the Development of Vegetation*. Washington, D.C.: Carnegie Institution of Washington, 1916.

Cooper, William S. "The Ecological Life History of Certain Species of *Ribes* and Its Application to the Control of the White Pine Blister Rust." *Ecology* 3, no. 1 (January 1922): 7–16

Cormier, Robert J. *The New Book of the Proprietors of Common and Undivided Lands in Shrewsbury* (transcript). Worcester, MA: American Antiquarian Society, 1977.

Cottrell, H.M. 1902. Spontaneous Combustion of Alfalfa. Bulletin 109, Farm Department, Experiment Station of the Kansas State Agricultural College, Manhattan. pp. 217–222 (accessed 8/11/13). http://books.google.com/books?id=QhQnAQAA MAAJ&printsec=frontcover&source=gbs_ge_summary_r&cad=0#v=onepage&q &f=false.

Cronon, William. *Changes in the Land: Indians, Colonists and the Ecology of New England*. Rev. ed. New York: Hill and Wang, 2003.

Darwin, Charles. *On the Origin of Species by Means of Natural Selection*. London: Penguin Books, 1859.

Eisner, Thomas. *For the Love of Insects*. Cambridge, MA: Belknap Press of Harvard University Press, 2003.

Evert, Ray F., and Susan E. Eichhorn. *Biology of Plants*. 8th ed. New York: W.H. Freeman and Company, 2013.

Further Reading and Sources

Fang, X.P., and J.L. McLaughlin. "Ursolic Acid, a Cytotoxic Component of the Berries of *Ilex verticillata.*" *Fitoterapia* 61, no. 2 (April 1990): 176–177.

Fernald, Merritt Lyndon. *Gray's Manual of Botany.* 8th edition. New York: D. Van Nostrand, 1950.

Flora of North America. FNA Vol. 3: Betulaceae: *Alnus: Alnus glutinosa.* http://www.efloras.org/florataxon.aspx?flora_id=1&taxon_id=233500032 (retrieved 7/17/2017).

Forcier, Lawrence K. "Reproductive Strategies and the Co-occurrence of Climax Tree Species." *Science* 189, no. 4205 (September 1975): 808–810.

Foster, David R. *Thoreau's Country.* Cambridge: Harvard University Press, 1999.

Foster, David R., and John D. Aber, eds. *Forests in Time: The Environmental Consequences of 1,000 Years of Change in New England.* New Haven, CT: Yale University Press, 2004.

Foster, David R., Glenn Motzkin and Benjamin Slater. "Land-Use History as Long-Term Broad-Scale Disturbance: Regional Forest Dynamics in Central New England." *Ecosystems* 1, no. 1 (January 1998): 96–119.

Futuyma, Douglas. *Evolution.* 2nd ed. Sunderland, MA: Sinauer Associates, 2009.

Garrison, Elina, and Jay Gedir. 2006. *Ecology and Management of White-Tailed Deer in Florida.* Florida Fish and Wildlife Conservation Commission. 49 p (accessed 11/28/12). http://myfwc.com/media/544905/ecology_and_management_of_white-tailed_deer_in_florida.pdf.

The Global Biodiversity Information Facility: GBIF Backbone Taxonomy, 2013-07-01. Accessed via http://www.gbif.org/species/5015 (7/2/2014).

Gould, Stephen Jay. *Time's Arrow, Time's Cycle.* Cambridge, MA: Harvard University Press, 1987.

Gould, Stephen Jay. *Wonderful Life.* New York: W.W. Norton, 1989.

Gullan, P.J. and P.S. Cranston. *The Insects: An Outline of Entomology.* New York: Chapman and Hall, 1994.

Haines, Arthur. *Flora Novae Angliae.* New Haven, CT: Yale University Press, 2011.

Harborne, J. B. *Introduction to Ecological Biochemistry.* New York: Academic Press, 1982.

Harrison, Hal H. *A Field Guide to Birds' Nests in the United States East of the Mississippi River.* Boston: Houghton Mifflin Company, 1975.

Herbertson, A. J. *Outlines of Physiography: An Introduction to the Study of the Earth.* 3rd ed. London: Edward Arnold, 1901 http://archive.org/details/outlinesofphysio00herb (accessed 12/3/12).

International Commission on Zoological Nomenclature. 2000. *International Codes of Zoological Nomenclature.* 4th edition. http://www.nhm.ac.uk/hosted-sites/iczn/code/ (accessed 11/29/12).

Integrated Taxonomic Information System (ITIS) Report: *Pseudacris crucifer* (Wied-Neuwied, 1838). http://www.itis.gov/servlet/SingleRpt/SingleRpt?search_topic=TSN&search_value=207303 (accessed 11/29/12).

Johnston, David W., and Eugene P. Odum "Breeding Bird Populations in Relation to Plant Succession on the Piedmont of Georgia." *Ecology* 37, no. 1 (January 1956): 50–62.

Kalff, Jacob. *Limnology.* Upper Saddle River, NJ: Prentice Hall, 2002.

Kaston, Benjamin J. "Spiders of Connecticut." *State Geological and Natural History Survey Bulletin No. 70.* Hartford, CT. 1948.

Further Reading and Sources

Keever, Catherine. "Causes of Succession on Old Fields of the Piedmont, North Carolina." *Ecological Monographs* 20, no. 3 (July 1950): 229–250.

Klyza, Christopher McGrory, and Stephen C. Trombulak. *The Story of Vermont*. 2nd ed. Hanover, NH: University Press of New England, 2015.

Krebs, Charles J. *Ecology*. Boston: Benjamin Cummings, 2001.

Kricher, John. "Nothing Endures but Change: Ecology's Newly Emerging Paradigm." *Northeastern Naturalist* 5, no. 2 (April 1998): 165–174.

Marrs, R. H., M. G. Le Duc, R. J. Mitchell, D. Goddardt, S. Patersons and R. J. Pakeman. "The Ecology of Bracken: Its Role in Succession and Implications for Control." *Annals of Botany* 85, no. 2 (April 2000): 3–15.

Massachusetts Audubon Society. 2015. State of the Birds: Wood Thrush *Hylocichla mustelina*. Breeding bird survey. http://www.massaudubon.org/our-conservation-work/wildlife-research-conservation/statewide-bird-monitoring/state-of-the-birds/find-a-bird/(id)/WOTH.

McEwan, Ryan W., Carolyn H. Keiffer, and Brian C. McCarthy "Dendroecology of American Chestnut in a Disjunct Stand of Oak-Chestnut Forest." *Canadian Journal of Forest Research* 36, no. 1 (2006): 1–11.

McKenrick, S.L., J.R. Leake and D.J. Read. "Symbiotic Germination and Development of Myco-heterotrophic Plants in Nature: Transfer of Carbon from Ectomycorrhizal *Salix repens* and *Betula pendula* to the Orchid *Corallorhiza trifida* Through Shared Hyphal Connections." *New Phytologist* 145, no. 3 (March 2000): 539–548.

McPhee, John. *Annals of the Former World*. New York: Farrar Straus and Giroux, 1998.

Molles, Manuel C., Jr. *Ecology*. 6th edition. New York: McGraw-Hill, 2013.

Muir, Diana. *Reflections in Bullough's Pond*. Hanover, NH: University Press of New England, 2000.

Natural Resources Conservation Service. 2014. Plants Database. http://plants.usda.gov/java/. United States Department of Agriculture. Accessed 5/23/14.

New, T. R., ed. Conservation Biology of Lycaenidae (Butterflies). Occasional Paper of the IUCN Species Survival Commission No. 8. 1993. https://portals.iucn.org/library/efiles/edocs/ssc-op-008.pdf (accessed 2/7/14).

Nickerson, Colin. "New England Sees a Return of Forests, Wildlife: The Woods Are Lovely, Dark, and Back." *Boston Globe*, 31 August 2013. http://www.bostonglobe.com/metro/2013/08/31/new-england-sees-return-forests-and-wildlife/lJRxacvGcHeQDmtZt09WvN/story.html.

Nowacki, Gregory J., and Marc D. Abrams. "Is Climate an Important Driver of Post–European Vegetation Change in the Eastern United States?" *Global Change Biology* 21, no. 1 (June 2014): 314–334.

Odum, Eugene P. "Bird Populations of the Highlands (North Carolina) Plateau in Relation to Plant Succession and Avian Invasion." *Ecology* 31, no. 4 (October 1950): 587–605.

Parsons, Frances Theodora. *How to Know the Wildflowers*. New York: Charles Scribner's Sons, 1989. 498 p.; Gerstein Science Information Centre, University of Toronto, Internet Archive: https://archive.org/details/howtoknowwildflo00star uoft (accessed 5/27/2014).

Pederson, Neil, et al. "Climate Remains an Important Driver of Post–European Vegetation Change in the Eastern United States." *Global Change Biology* 21, no. 6 (December 2014): 2105–2110.

Further Reading and Sources

Peterson, Roger Tory. *A Field Guide to the Birds East of the Rockies*. Boston: Houghton Mifflin Company, 1980.

Peterson, Roger Tory, and Margaret McKenny. *A Field Guide to Wildflowers*. Boston: Houghton Mifflin Company, 1968.

Petersen, Wayne. "Old Barns and Their Birds." *Sanctuary: The Journal of the Massachusetts Audubon Society* 51, no. 1 (Winter 2012): 18–19.

Primack, Richard B. *Walden Warming: Climate Changes Comes to Thoreau's Woods*. Chicago: University of Chicago Press, 2014.

Proulx, Annie. *Barkskins: A Novel*. New York: Scribner's, 2016.

Rodd, Tony, and Jennifer Stackhouse. *Trees*. Berkely: University of California Press, 2008.

Runkle, James R., and Todd C. Yetter "Treefalls Revisited: Gap Dynamics in the Southern Appalachians." *Ecology* 68, no. 2 (April 1987): 417–424.

Russell, Emily W. B. *People and the Land Through Time*. New Haven, CT: Yale University Press, 1997.

Russell, Emily W. B. "Vegetational Change in Northern New Jersey from Precolonization to Present: A Palynological Interpretation." *Bulletin of the Torrey Botanical Club* 107, no. 3 (July 1980): 432–446.

Salisbury, Frank B., and Cleon W. Ross. *Plant Physiology*. 4th ed. Belmont, CA: Wadsworth, 1992.

Sharp, Robert P. *Living Ice*. New York: Cambridge University Press, 1988.

Sholes, Owen D.V. "Effects of Ice Storm Damage on Radial Growth of *Quercus* spp." *Journal of the Torrey Botanical Society* 140, no. 3 (July 2013): 364–368.

Speer, James H. *Fundamentals of Tree-Ring Research*. Tucson: University of Arizona Press, 2010.

Stafford, Fiona. *The Long, Long Life of Trees*. New Haven, CT: Yale University Press, 2016.

Stebbins, G. Ledyard. *Flowering Plants: Evolution Above the Species Level*. Cambridge, MA: Belknap Press of Harvard University Press, 1974.

Thompson, Helen. "The Chestnut Resurrection." *Nature* 490, no. 7418 (October 2012): 22–23

Thoreau, Henry David. *Walden, and On the Duty of Civil Disobedience*. New York: New American Library, 1964. Kindle.

Torrey, John G. "Nitrogen Fixation by Actinomycete-Nodulated Angiosperms." *Bioscience* 28, no. 9 (September 1978): 586–592.

Vallery-Radot, René. *La Vie de Pasteur*. Translated by R. L. Devonshire. New York: Garden City Publishing, 1924.

Watson, L., and M.J. Dallwitz. 1992 onward. The families of flowering plants: descriptions, illustrations, identification, and information retrieval. Version: 30 June 2014. http://delta-intkey.com.

Weaver, Gregory R. "Chestnut Ghosts: Remnants of the Primeval American Chestnut Forest of the Southern Appalachians." *Journal of the American Chestnut Foundation* 16, no. 2 (Spring 2003): 14–18.

Wessels, Tom. *Reading the Forested Landscape: A Natural History of New England*. Woodstock, VT: Countryman Press of W.W. Norton, 1997.

Whitney, Gordon G. *From Coastal Wilderness to Fruited Plain*. New York: Cambridge University Press, 1994.

Whittaker, Robert H. *Communities and Ecosystems*. 2nd edition. New York: Macmillan, New York. 1975.

Further Reading and Sources

Wilkie, Richard W., and Jack Tager, eds. *Historical Atlas of Massachusetts*. Amherst: University of Massachusetts Press, 1991.

Willis, Charles G., Brad Ruhfel, Richard B. Primack, Abraham J. Miller-Rushing and Charles C. Davis. "Phylogenetic Patterns of Species Loss in Thoreau's Woods Are Driven by Climate Change." *Proceedings of the National Academy of Sciences* 105, no. 44 (November 2008): 17,029–17,033.

Wilson, Edward O. "Chemical Communication Within Animal Species." In *Chemical Ecology*, edited by Ernest Sondheimer and John B. Simeone, 133–155. New York: Academic Press, 1970.

Wright, P.G. "Entropy and Disorder." *Contemporary Physics* 11, no. 6 (1970): 581–588.

Index

abandonment of property 4, 7, 9, 17, 22, 27, 55, 58–61, 95–96, 98–100, 102, 106–108, 110–111, 116, 124, 129, 132, 134, 137, 139, 141, 142, 144
Abercrombie, Lascelles 42
"Acceptance" 83, 133
Acer 127; *see also* maple
"After Apple Picking" 51, 53, 77
alder 34, 48, 60, 72, 113, 122–124
Allen, Grant 64
Alnus 122–123; *see also* alder
Ambrosia 24; *see also* ragweed
"America Is Hard to See" 24, 50
Amherst (MA) 18, 49, 90, 99, 120
apple 15, 44, 47–49, 51–55, 66, 77, 94, 96, 105–106, 116, 127–128, 143
ash (mineral) 101, 104, 110, 137
ash (tree) 16
"Asking for Roses" 87
Asplenium 122
aster 78, 92
astronomy 13, 83, 115
"At Woodward's Gardens" 17
"Auspex" 17
autumn 30, 44, 52, 56, 68–69, 77–79, 83, 89, 91–94, 114, 117, 129–130, 135–136
"The Ax-Helve" 44, 143

bacteria 45, 102, 122, 134, 136
"The Bad Island—Easter" 46
Bailey, Loren 13
balsam fir 103
bark (tree) 7, 15, 27, 31–32, 34, 37, 72, 91, 111, 117, 132, 136
barn 2–3, 8–10, 22–23, 26, 49, 53, 60, 62, 65, 68, 73, 94–97, 101, 124, 132, 134, 142–143
Bartlett, John 64
"The Bear" 15, 96, 130
beech 16, 78–79

"Beech" 15
beetle 2, 32
"Bereft" 93
berry 2, 15, 102, 104, 110–111, 113, 116, 118, 123, 131–132; *see also* blueberry; raspberry; winterberry
Bethlehem (NH) 18
"Beyond Words" 76
birch 15, 25–26, 29–30, 70, 76, 92, 103, 105, 111, 113–114, 116–119, 138, 143–144
"Birches" 15, 29, 76, 111, 116–117, 122, 138
"The Birthplace" 24, 27, 105, 141–142
black alder 123–124
"The Black Cottage" 99, 141
bloom, blossom 2, 25, 30, 34, 42, 52–53, 55, 63–64, 69, 72, 78–79, 82, 86–89, 91, 98, 104–105, 110–111, 116, 125; *see also* flower
"Blue-Butterfly Day" 81, 143
"A Blue Ribbon at Amesbury" 51, 75
"Blueberries" 50, 104, 110–111, 114, 118, 131
blueberry 2, 15, 25, 104, 110–111, 118, 131
bluebird 69, 77, 84, 107, 144
"The Bonfire" 25, 28, 32, 41, 50, 54, 58, 84, 90, 115, 119, 122–123
botanizing 14, 96, 111, 122, 138
bough 25, 30, 79, 106, 109, 123–124, 130, 133, 142
"A Boundless Moment" 79, 130
A Boy's Will 51, 61, 67, 87, 93, 96, 108
bracken fern (brake) 57, 116, 120, 122, 144
Bread Loaf School 18
brook 8, 16, 48–49, 55–60, 63, 80–82, 85, 87, 92, 98, 100, 136; *see also* stream
"A Brook in the City" 55–56
"Brown's Descent" 74–75
brush (plants) 23, 25–26, 28–32, 50, 81, 90, 92, 103, 107, 115, 117
Buckley, Christopher "Blind Boss" 17
bud 2, 30, 82, 130, 133

173

Index

"Build Soil" 38, 50
Burell, Carl 13–14, 35, 86
bush 2, 25, 76, 102, 104, 110–111, 123, 131, 143

"A Cabin in the Clearing" 24, 45
California 13, 17, 51, 75, 96
Calypso 34, 115
Carleton, Lucinda 125
carrot 20
cedar 34, 143–144
cellar 7, 10, 53–54, 56–57, 59, 94, 96, 100–101, 104, 124–125, 128, 136, 139, 142–143
"The Cellar Hole" 96
"The Census-Taker" 10, 30, 32, 100, 141
cherry 15, 48
chestnut 26
chimney 8–9, 21–22, 68, 97, 130, 145
"Choice of Society" 109
Christmas 28, 42, 79–80, 126
"Christmas Trees" 126
"Class Hymn" 57
"Clear and Colder" 93
Clematis 115
"A Cliff Dwelling" 24
climax (succession) 103
"Closed for Good" 135
"A Cloud Shadow" 80
"The Cocoon" 45
"The Code" 60, 62–64
"Come In" 16, 86, 106–107, 133–134, 144
Comptonia 102; see also sweetfern
continuity 144
Corallorhiza 35
coralroot 35, 87
corn 53, 143
countryside 3, 5, 9, 11, 14, 16–17, 19, 34, 37, 55, 60, 66–67, 95–97, 99, 107, 116, 120, 124, 138, 140–141, 143–144
cow 2, 13, 15, 45, 54, 64–67, 96, 143
"The Cow in Apple Time" 54, 66, 96
Cox, Sydney 42, 115
crop 20, 23, 25–26, 48, 53–54, 62, 64, 93, 135, 141
Cypripedium (Cyprepedium) 36–37, 115

Dalkins' Little Indulgence 24
Dana, Mrs. William Starr 14
Darwin, Charles 36, 46
Davies, W.H. 14
dead, death 10, 14, 15, 24, 26, 28–32, 41, 43–44, 55, 57, 62, 69, 77, 73, 77–79, 81, 83, 86, 89, 92, 96–97, 99–101, 103, 105, 110, 122, 124–126, 128, 130, 134–137, 139, 141–143
"The Death of the Hired Man" 58, 132
decay, decomposition 3, 7, 79, 91–92, 94, 96–98, 108, 113, 134–138, 145; see also molder
Derry (NH) 13–14, 48–49, 52, 92, 96, 119–120
description 4–6, 14–17, 21, 26, 41–42, 55, 69, 81, 83, 85, 97, 105, 117, 133, 137–140
"Desert Places" 64–65, 70, 77–78
desertion 59, 96, 99, 111, 118, 125, 132
"Design" 2, 15–16, 88–89, 115, 129, 138
destruction 23, 25–27, 30, 38–39, 87, 100, 123, 125, 144
"Devotion" 38
"Directive" 10, 55, 58–59, 96, 100–101, 106, 124–126, 139, 141–142
disease 23, 26, 45–46, 52, 55
disturbance 37, 75, 102, 136, 144
"Does No One at All Ever Feel This Way in the Least?" 39
"The Door in the Dark" 20
dooryard 68, 125
"Down the Brook ... and Back" 56
"A Dream Pang" 106, 142
drink 10, 56, 58–59, 66, 77, 81, 83, 101, 118
"A Drumlin Woodchuck" 141
"Dust of Snow" 74

ecological succession 7, 48, 68, 102–113, 116, 118–119, 124, 126, 130–131, 144
"The Egg and the Machine" 51
Einstein, Albert 46
Eliot, Thomas Stearns (T. S.) 125
elm 8, 10, 101
Emerson, Ralph Waldo 21, 139
"An Encounter" 31, 34, 143
England 18, 24, 40–43, 45, 49, 134
entropy 97–98
environmental history 6, 10–11, 15, 19, 138, 141, 143
erosion 37–39
"Evening in a Sugar Orchard" 83, 130
"Evil Tendencies Cancel" 26
evolution 36
excess 30, 33, 44–45, 55, 71, 119
"The Exposed Nest" 25, 64, 121, 131
extravagance 23, 44–45, 98

"The Falls" 119
fear 41–42, 44, 57, 66, 74, 82, 90, 110, 118, 141
fence 3, 8–10, 96–97, 100, 106, 119, 145

Index

fern 11, 25, 102, 113, 116, 118–124; *see also*
  Asplenium; bracken fern; hay-scented
  fern; interrupted fern; lady fern;
  Osmunda; *Pteridium*
Ficus (fig) 114; *see also* sycamore
The Figure a Poem Makes 75, 79, 140
fire 1, 8–9, 24–25, 28, 41, 45, 50, 54, 58,
  73, 90, 91, 94–95, 97, 101, 103, 110–111,
  119, 123, 130, 144
"Fireflies in the Garden" 90
firewood 3, 23, 28, 32, 67, 95, 105, 130,
  136, 137
fish 25, 60, 85, 88, 118, 123
"Fish-Leap Fall" 25
flock (birds) 71, 77, 84, 132
flood 37, 57–58
flower 2, 9, 14–16, 20–22, 25, 30, 33–37,
  42, 50, 53, 55, 61, 63–64, 69, 71–72, 74,
  78–79, 81–83, 85–92, 97–98, 100, 102,
  104–105, 109–112, 115, 121, 124, 126,
  128, 130–131, 143, 145; *see also* bloom
"Flower Guidance" 87
foliage 82, 128, 135
"For Once, Then, Something" 121
forest 4, 7–9, 17, 23–26, 31, 46, 48, 63, 79,
  81–82, 87, 91, 102–109, 111–113, 116–117,
  119, 121–122, 129, 132, 137, 141–143
"Forest Flowers" 87, 112
"A Fountain, a Bottle, a Donkey's Ears and
  Some Books" 97, 99, 105
Franconia (NH) 15, 18, 25, 52, 56, 65, 71, 91
Freud, Sigmund 46
frog 85, 115
"From Plane to Plane" 61
Frost, Carol (son) 52,
Frost, Elinor White (wife) 14–15, 55, 86,
  117
Frost, Irma (daughter) 52
Frost, Isabelle Moodie (mother) 13, 17
Frost, Jeanie Florence (sister) 13, 17, 75
Frost, Lesley (daughter) 16, 24, 51, 125
Frost, William Prescott, Jr. (father) 13, 17,
  40
fruit 2, 13, 25, 49–50, 52–55, 72, 91, 109–
  111, 118–119, 123–124
fungus 33

Gale River 56
Gallishaw, John (Jack) 42
garden 3, 15, 17, 20, 29, 38, 50, 52, 58, 63,
  68, 72, 86–90, 92, 94, 104, 108, 130, 135
Gardner, Delphis 15
"Gathering Leaves" 135
"Genealogical" 23–24, 141

generation 67, 90, 139, 141
"The Generations of Men" 56, 96, 100,
  104–105
gentian 16
George, Henry 17
German 41
germinate 33, 139
"Ghost House" 51, 55, 96, 100, 104–108,
  119, 141–142
Gibson, Wilfrid 14, 42
"The Gift Outright" 1
"A Girl's Garden" 50, 52
glacier, glaciation 81, 141
Glass, Everett 132
"Going for Water" 55–56, 92
"Gold Hesperidee" 52–53
goldenrod 2, 143
"Good-by and Keep Cold" 52–53, 72, 80,
  130
grape 4, 76, 91, 111, 113–114, 116–119, 123
grass 24–25, 34, 37, 61, 63, 66, 77, 92,
  104–105, 125, 132, 143
gravestone 100, 106, 142
grazing 2, 4, 7–8, 24, 48, 103–104, 109, 142
"Greece" 40
grindstone 13, 54, 55, 61
"The Grindstone" 54, 61
growth 4, 23–24, 31, 58, 68, 71, 83–85,
  105–106, 108, 111, 113, 117, 126–127,
  129–130, 135, 137, 141–142
The Guardeen 54, 76
"The Gum-Gatherer" 27–28, 30–32, 57–58
gunfire 132

Haines, John W. (Jack) 42, 122
"Happiness Makes Up in Height for What It
  Lacks in Length" 85
hardhack 116, 118
Harrison, Benjamin 6
harvest 23, 25, 28, 39, 44, 50, 52–55, 61,
  65, 79, 83, 91, 94, 114, 118–119, 128, 137
hay 4, 8–9, 13, 15, 23, 25, 34–35, 48–49,
  53, 58, 60–65, 68–69, 94, 96, 131–132,
  143, 145
hay fever 18, 24
hay-scented fern 120
heal-all 2, 16, 88–89, 115; *see also* *Prunella*
health 18, 26, 28
heart 9, 42, 45, 63–64, 73–74, 82, 85, 93,
  119, 126
hearth 9, 55
hedgerow 3
hemlock (*Tsuga canadensis*) 74, 103
herb 24, 102, 104

Index

hike 144
"The Hill Wife" 50, 121, 123
"A Hillside Thaw" 72, 76
homestead 24, 96, 100–101, 106
Hood, Thomas 24
house 2–3, 8–10, 22, 24–26, 43–44, 49, 51, 55–56, 59, 68, 70, 73–75, 87, 93–97, 99–101, 104–108, 113, 117–119, 124–125, 128, 132, 136, 139, 141–145
"The Housekeeper" 45, 51–52, 55, 62
How to Know the Ferns 20
How to Know the Wild Flowers 14
"A Hundred Collars" 68, 130, 141
Hyla 85, 115; *see also* peeper
"Hyla Brook" 58, 60, 81, 85, 115, 136, 143

"I Could Give All to Time" 39
ice 4, 56, 70, 74–77, 117, 141, 143
Ilex 123; *see also* black alder
"Immigrants" 149*n*1
"The Importance of Being Versed in New England Ways" 29
"In a Vale" 86, 133
"In Hardwood Groves" 30, 91, 135
In the Clearing 51, 66, 88
"In the Home Stretch" 8, 48–49, 52, 55, 118, 122
"In Time of Cloudburst" 38, 50, 58
"In White" 115
"In Winter in the Woods Alone" 79, 126, 130
Indian 24; *see also* Native American
interrupted fern 120
"Into My Own" 106
"The Investment" 44, 49
"Iris by Night" 43

juniper 102, 109

Kennedy, John Fitzgerald 1, 6
"Kitty Hawk" 51–52, 115

lady fern 120
lady's slipper 36–37
Lafayette (mountain) 18
Lake Willoughby (VT) 120
landscape 3–7, 11, 13–14, 17, 23–25, 27, 31, 45–46, 59, 64, 74, 85, 95, 98–99, 101–102, 106, 108–111, 119, 124, 126, 131, 138, 140–142, 144–145
lantern 45, 74–75
"The Last Mowing" 50, 98, 104–105, 111, 114, 141–142
"The Last Word of a Bluebird" 69, 77, 84

"A Late Walk" 64, 78, 92
Lawrence (MA) 13, 95
leaf 8, 10, 15, 30, 35, 44, 54, 69–70, 77–80, 82, 84, 91–94, 103, 111, 117, 121–122, 124, 126–130, 134–137, 143
"A Leaf Treader" 79, 135
"Leaves Compared with Flowers" 111
"The Lesson for Today" 45
"Let's Not Think" 81
lilac 8, 10, 59, 69, 96, 100–101, 113, 124–126
"The Line-Gang" 31
"A Line-Storm Song" 88, 121
"Lines Written in Dejection on the Eve of Great Success" 66
"The Literate Farmer and the Planet Venus" 45
lizard 72
"Locked Out" 87
"Lodged" 20
"Looking for a Sunset Bird in Winter" 77–78
Lowell, Amy 99, 125–126
"Lucretius Versus the Lake Poets" 115–116

Maianthemum 115
Maine 23–24, 103
"The Man in the Tree" 52
maple 15, 29, 68, 79, 91, 103, 105, 111, 113, 126–131, 136, 143; *see also* Acer
"Maple" 15, 29, 91, 127–130, 143
A Masque of Reason 122
Massachusetts 2, 4, 13, 16, 25, 37, 40, 95, 107
meadow 7–8, 16, 23, 34–35, 48–49, 55, 58, 60–61, 63–64, 68, 87, 96, 102, 104, 106, 143–144
meadowsweet 102, 104
melting 58, 70, 75–76, 139
"Mending Wall" 2, 52, 66, 106, 142
metaphor 6, 13, 15, 17, 19–22, 27, 38, 46, 55, 60, 69, 75–76, 80, 93, 116, 127, 129, 132, 138–140
microbe 46
"The Middletown Murder" 75
"Midsummer Birds" 86
milk 49, 54, 65–66
milkweed 15, 53, 85, 88
"The Milky Way Is a Cowpath" 67
"Misgiving" 93
"A Missive Missile" 20
mold 99
molder 137; *see also* decay
"Moon Compasses" 143–144
mosaic 108–109, 111; *see also* patchwork

moth 2, 4, 15, 78, 88–89
mountain 4, 18, 24, 27–29, 31, 38–39, 55, 57–58, 66, 74, 76, 81, 95, 99–100, 105, 109, 119, 140
"The Mountain" 37, 50, 58, 66, 72, 76, 99, 119, 122, 139, 143
Mountain Interval 29, 31, 55
mow 2, 7–9, 15, 24–25, 34, 37, 45, 48, 50, 60–65, 68, 96, 104–105, 111, 121, 131–132, 142, 145
"Mowing" 35, 37, 61, 63–64, 87
"My Butterfly" 77, 79, 143
"My November Guest" 92

name 8–9, 16, 24, 29, 34, 36, 40, 48, 51, 57, 60, 65–66, 91, 98, 114–117, 120, 122–123, 127–130
narrative 5, 11, 66, 73, 120, 138, 140–141, 143–145
Native American 9, 24, 39, 103; *see also* Indian
natural history 4, 14–15
naturalist 5, 8, 13–14, 21, 27, 90, 138, 144
nature 4, 7, 10, 14, 17, 19, 21–23, 27, 33, 44–46, 49–50, 59, 61, 79, 82, 89, 100–101, 106, 109–110, 113, 116, 131, 134, 141
nectar 15, 42, 88–90
"The Need for Being Versed in Country Things" 7, 8, 10, 13, 17, 19, 21, 23, 48, 64, 68–69, 95–97, 101–102, 108, 112–113, 124–126, 132, 134, 138, 142, 145
"Never Again Would Birds' Song Be the Same" 107–108
New Book of the Proprietors of New and Undivided Land in Shrewsbury 16
New Hampshire 13, 15, 17–18, 25, 37, 40, 48, 56, 65, 71, 91, 96, 99, 105, 120, 123
"New Hampshire" 33, 51–52, 54, 116–119
New Hampshire 93, 118–119
New York 107
night 2–3, 8–9, 16, 28, 41, 43, 51–52, 65, 72, 74–75, 80, 83, 86–90, 97, 107–108, 113, 131–134
nighthawk 107–108
"La Noche Triste" 40
nomenclature 115–116
North of Boston 67
"The Nose Ring" 50
"Not of School Age" 52
"Not to Keep" 42
"Nothing Gold Can Stay" 10, 21, 80
"November" 39, 43, 79, 94, 128, 135
"Now Close the Windows" 93
nursery rhyme 66

oak 78, 103, 117, 143
observation 14–17, 19–21, 25, 35, 51, 54, 74, 85, 88–90, 96, 99, 108–109, 116, 126, 129, 138–139
"October" 91, 135
odor 15, 29, 32, 86, 119; *see also* scent
"Of the Stones of the Place" 50
"The Old Barn at the Bottom of the Fogs" 26
"An Old Man's Winter Night" 74–75
"On a Bird Singing in Its Sleep" 139
"On a Tree Fallen Across the Road" 79, 126
"On Going Unnoticed" 35, 87
"On Looking Up by Chance at the Constellations" 90
"On Taking from the Top to Broaden the Base" 38
"On the Heart's Beginning to Cloud the Mind" 45
"Once by the Pacific" 17, 39
"One Favored Acorn" 88, 128
"One Guess" 114
"One Step Backward Taken" 58
"The Onset" 57, 69–70, 115, 117, 122, 130
orchard 8, 23, 43, 48–49, 51–55, 61, 72, 80, 83, 105–106, 127, 130, 143–144
orchid 11, 16, 31, 33–37, 45, 64, 87, 115, 143; *see also* Calypso; coralroot; *Cypripedium*; lady's slipper; pale orchis; *Platanthera*; *Pogonia*; ram's horn; rose pogonias
Osmunda 120; *see also* interrupted fern
"Our Hold on the Planet" 46
Our Place Among the Infinities 23, 44–45
"Our Singing Strength" 71, 84, 132
"'Out, Out—'" 28–29, 32
"The Oven Bird" 85, 97, 114

pale orchis 35, 37, 87
"Pan with Us" 109–110
Paradise-in-Bloom 79
"The Parlor Joke" 107
Pasteur, Louis 14, 138
pastoral 42
pasture 7–9, 23, 25, 48–49, 54, 56, 84, 102–104, 106, 109, 131
"The Pasture" 56, 65, 84–85, 136, 143
patchwork 49, 96, 107–109; *see also* mosaic
"Paul's Wife" 58
pea 30, 139
"Pea Brush" 26, 30–32, 81, 92, 115, 117
peace 41–42, 61
peach 48, 69, 80, 116
pear 116

Index

peeper 81, 115; *see also Hyla*
Pelham (MA) 25, 99
"Peril of Hope" 52, 72, 141
petal 8–9, 13, 22, 52, 83, 89–90, 111
Petra and Its Surroundings 96
pick, picking 2, 35, 45, 51, 53, 77, 87, 92, 111, 118, 132, 142–143
pine 2, 16, 25, 39, 48, 103, 106, 110, 124, 143
pioneer 103, 116
pistil 8–9, 13, 21–22, 145
pitch 28, 31–32
pitchfork 13
Platanthera 34, 37
Platanus 114; *see also* sycamore
plow 7, 24, 48–51, 63, 104, 142
"Plowmen" 49
plum 116
"Pod of the Milkweed" 15, 53, 85, 88
Pogonia 37
pollen 88–90, 104
pollination 36, 88–89
pool 4, 30, 60, 80–82, 91–92, 105, 130, 143
potato 20
prayer 34, 83, 133
"A Prayer in Spring" 80, 83, 88, 114
Proctor, Richard Anthony 23
Prunella 16, 115; *see also* heal-all
Pteridium 120; *see also* bracken fern
"Pussy-willow Time" 80, 83–84
"Putting in the Seed" 52, 67, 83–84, 139

quarry 20
"The Quest of the Orchis" 151*n*31
"The Quest of the Purple Fringed" 34, 83, 91, 123
question 4–5, 33, 45, 49, 154*n*30, 79, 88–89, 93, 97, 114, 116–117, 120, 125, 131
"Questioning Faces" 9

"The Rabbit-Hunter" 122
ragweed 24
rain 9, 20, 25, 28, 58, 62, 71, 74, 76, 81, 99–100, 111, 134–135, 139
rainbow 43
ram's horn orchid 36
"Range-Finding" 42, 88, 131
raspberry 102, 104
realism, reality 20–22, 49, 65–66, 70, 83, 86, 110, 139–140
religion 46
"Reluctance" 78–79, 83, 90, 93
reproduction 85, 90, 131, 135
resin 26–28, 32, 103

resurgence 7, 10, 85, 101, 107–109, 113, 124, 141
"The Return of the Pilgrims" 149*n*1
ring (tree) 4, 31
"The Road Not Taken" 1, 67, 128, 135
rock 16, 50–51, 76, 95, 100, 105, 119, 141–142; *see also* stone
A Romantic Chasm 122
root 24, 26, 30, 71–72, 81–82, 102, 104, 118, 122–124, 128–129
rose 87, 116, 125
"The Rose Family" 116
"Rose Pogonias" 34, 37, 64, 143
ruin 9–10, 52, 54, 62, 82, 87, 96, 100, 119, 141
"The Runaway" 96

"The Sachem of the Clouds" 136
sacrifice 33, 35, 44
salamander 3
San Francisco (CA) 13, 17, 51, 75, 96
"Sand Dunes" 38–39
sap 15, 26, 29–32, 130
sapling 3, 103, 105, 126
scent 27–29, 32, 51, 53–54, 78, 119–120
science 1, 4, 44, 46, 114, 116, 126, 131
Scientific American 5
scythe 13, 35, 55, 60–61, 63–64, 87, 104
sea 9, 38–39, 114
search 10, 21, 29, 31, 34, 36, 56, 77, 83, 128–129, 134
season 7–8, 10–11, 18, 28, 31, 48–49, 52–53, 55, 58, 61, 64–65, 67–74, 76, 78–79, 80, 83–86, 90–91, 93–94, 97, 105, 111, 117, 130, 132, 135–136, 138, 141
seed 15, 22, 30, 33–34, 56, 67, 71, 82–83, 87–88, 90, 102, 106, 121, 126, 128, 142
seedling 33, 83, 103, 105–106, 126–127, 129–131, 130–131, 139, 142–143
"The Self-Seeker" 35–37, 87, 115
"A Servant to Servants" 120
shrub 3, 7, 102–105, 111, 113, 116, 118, 122–124, 126, 130, 132, 141
Sierra Nevada 17
sleep 45, 51, 53, 74, 94, 128
smoke, smokeless 7, 25, 45, 91, 109, 130, 134, 136–138, 144, 145
snake 57, 64
snow 2, 9, 15, 28–29, 50, 54, 57–58, 61, 64–65, 69–79, 81, 93–94, 117, 135–136, 138–139
"Snow" 133
soil 10, 24, 34, 37–39, 48–50, 58, 72, 81–82, 92, 97, 102–104, 113–114, 122–124, 135–137, 139, 143

Index

soldier 40–44
"A Soldier" 43
"Something for Hope" 50, 98, 104, 110–111, 116, 130, 142–143
soot 111
sound 28, 56–57, 61, 67, 72, 115, 133
"The Sound of Trees" 126, 128
spark 90, 130
"Speaking of Metaphor" 20
Spiraea 102, 104, 111; *see also* hardhack; meadowsweet; steeplebush
"Spoils of the Dead" 86
spring ephemeral flowers 82, 92
"Spring Pools" 4, 30, 81–82, 91–92, 105, 130, 143
spring (season) 10, 30, 37, 50, 52–53, 57–58, 67–71, 74, 77, 80–87, 92–93, 103, 107, 115, 117, 130, 135, 143
spring (water) 24, 55–56, 58–59, 72, 76
sprout 30, 34, 105, 143
spruce 25, 27–28, 105, 111, 143
squash 94
"The Star-Splitter" 9, 44, 50, 95, 97, 99, 141–142
Steeple Bush 111
steeplebush 102, 104, 143; *see also Spiraea*
stone 2, 16, 19, 48, 50, 57, 142, 145; *see also* rock
stone foundation 7, 56, 96–97, 121, 124
stone wall 2, 7, 13, 52, 66, 106, 142, 145
"Stopping by Woods on a Snowy Evening" 1–2, 65
"Storm Fear" 73–74
stream 10, 25, 48, 55–60, 85, 92, 97–98, 101, 109, 119, 123, 135–136, 139, 143; *see also* brook
"The Strong Are Saying Nothing" 50, 63, 83, 88
"The Subverted Flower" 87
sugar 15, 30–31, 82–83, 135
sugar maple 127, 130, 143; *see also Acer*
sugarhouse 29, 83, 130
summer 2, 8–9, 14, 22, 25, 53–54, 58, 64, 68–70, 72, 75, 77–78, 80–82, 85–94, 96–97, 99, 136, 138, 143
"Summering" 85, 87
"A Summer's Garden" 86, 88–89, 130, 135
sweetfern 102, 116, 118
sycamore 114
"Sycamore" 114; *see also Ficus*
Syringa 124; *see also* lilac

telephone 73
"Ten Mills" 26, 114

thatch 134
"The Thatch" 108, 134
"There Are Roughly Zones" 69, 73–74, 80
This Is My Best 67
Thomas, Edward 42–44
Thoreau, Henry David 14, 96–97, 102, 125
thorn 58
thrush 16, 86, 107, 133–134, 144
timber 23–25, 32, 39, 95, 112
"Time Out" 115
"A Time to Talk" 62–63
"The Times Table" 7, 10, 58–59, 99, 101, 106, 110, 124–125
"To a Moth Seen in Winter" 15, 78
"To a Young Wretch" 28, 32, 80
"To Earthward" 119
"To E.T." 43
"To the Thawing Wind" 74, 76, 80
tomato 71
"Traces" 32
transformation 11, 23–24, 98, 101, 112–113, 128, 143
"Tree At My Window" 126
Trillium 30
trunk (tree) 16, 82, 117, 133, 138
"The Tuft of Flowers" 25, 55, 61, 63, 87, 88, 104, 114
"Two Look at Two" 15, 60, 143
"Two Tramps in Mud Time" 67, 71, 77, 80–81, 84, 92

underbush 23, 103, 107
"Unharvested" 44, 52, 54, 128
"An Unhistoric Spot" 161*n*54
The Unmade Word 139
unseasonable weather 52, 70–72, 78, 91
Untermeyer, Louis 50, 63, 85, 126
"U.S. 1946 King's X" 44

"The Vantage Point" 108
veery 107, 144
Vermont 18, 48, 95, 120, 123
versed 10, 19–20, 59, 101, 112, 142, 144
"The Vindictives" 24
vine 4, 91, 114, 116, 118–119, 123, 136
violet 89

"Waiting" 64, 197
walk 3, 5, 11, 14, 29, 57, 59, 63, 96, 107, 111, 116, 120, 137–138
"Wanton Waste" 88
war 40–45, 61, 66, 73, 94, 120–121
Warren, Robert Penn 95
waste 20, 23–25, 30–31, 33, 39, 43–47,

179

Index

53–54, 56, 62, 79, 88–89, 94, 97–98, 100, 104, 118, 128, 135, 137
"Waste or Cod Fish Eggs" 88
weed 3, 7, 24, 48, 57, 63–64, 78, 92, 98, 102–105, 116, 118, 121, 141
well (water) 48, 55, 96, 118, 121, 145
"West-Running Brook" 59–60, 97–98, 123, 139
West-Running Brook 93
Whicher, George 104
whisper 61, 63
white 1–2, 15–16, 50, 56–57, 65, 70, 76–77, 88–89, 111, 117, 121, 138, 143
White Mountains 18
white pine 39, 103, 143
Whitman, Walt 125
"Why Wait for Science" 44
"Wild Grapes" 4, 76, 111, 114, 116–118
"Willful Homing" 73
willow 58, 80, 83–84
"The Wind and the Rain" 57
"Wind and Window Flower" 74
winter 9–10, 15, 44, 51–54, 56, 61, 64, 67–82, 84, 89–90, 92–94, 102, 107, 117, 122–123, 130–131, 133–138, 143
"A Winter Eden" 52, 72, 77–78, 82, 114, 122
"Winter Has Beaten Summer in Fight" 91, 130
"Winter Ownership" 77–78
"Winter Winds" 74, 130
winterberry 123
"A Winter's Night" 75
witch hazel 78
A Witness Tree 94
wood, woods 2, 4, 7, 9, 14–15, 23–31, 37, 49, 55, 59, 61, 67, 77–79, 82, 84, 86–87, 94, 97, 99, 102–110, 117, 119–120, 123–124, 126–127, 130, 133, 136–138, 143–145
"The Wood-Pile" 7, 62, 77, 97, 130, 134, 136–138
woodchuck 53, 141
woodpecker 55, 105, 114

"A Young Birch" 25, 30, 111, 117, 126